Environmental Transformations

AFRICAN LITERATURE TODAY 38

Guest Editors: Cajetan Iheka
Stephanie Newell

JAMES CURREY

GUIDELINES FOR SUBMISSIONS

The Editor invites submission of articles on the announced themes of forthcoming issues. Submissions will be acknowledged promptly and decisions communicated within six months of the receipt of the paper. Your name and institutional affiliation (with full mailing address and email) should appear on a separate sheet, plus a brief biographical profile of not more than six lines. The editor cannot undertake to return materials submitted, and contributors are advised to keep a copy of any material sent. Articles should be submitted in the English Language.

Length: Articles should not exceed 5,000 words.
Format: Articles should be double-spaced, and should use the same type face and size throughout. Italics are preferred to underlines for titles of books. Articles are reviewed blindly, so do not insert your name, institutional affiliation and contact information on the article itself. Instead, provide such information on a separate page.

Style: UK or US spellings are acceptable, but must be used consistently. Direct quotations should retain the spellings used in the original source. Check the accuracy of citations and always give the author's surname and page number in the text, and a full reference in the Works Cited list at the end of the article. Italicize titles of books, plays and journals. Use single inverted commas throughout except for quotes within quotes which are double. Avoid subtitles or subsection headings within the text.

Citations: Limit your sources to the most recent, or the most important books and journals, in English. Cite works in foreign languages only when no English-language books are available. Cite websites only if they are relatively permanent and if they add important information unavailable elsewhere.

For in-text citations, the sequence in parentheses should be (Surname: page number). No year of publication should be reflected within the text. All details should be presented in the Works Cited list at the end of the article. Consistency is advised. Examples:

Githiora, Chege. *Sheng: Rise of a Kenyan Swahili Vernacular*. Woodbridge: James Currey, 2018.

Diabate, Naminate. 'African Queer, AfricanDigital: Reflections on Zanele Muholi's *Films4peace & other works*.' *ALT 37: Queer Theory in Film & Fiction*. Ed. Ernest N. Emenyonu. Guest Ed. John C Hawley. Woodbridge: James Currey, 2018.

Smith, Victoria Ellen, ed. *Voices of Ghana: Literary Contributions to the Ghana Broadcasting System, 1955-57* (Second Edition). Woodbridge: James Currey/ Accra: Sub-Saharan Publishers (Ghana & Nigeria), 2018.

Ensure that your Works Cited list is alphabetized on a word-by-word basis, whether citations begin with the author's name or with an anonymous work's title. Please, avoid footnotes or endnotes. Do not quote directly from the Internet without properly citing the source as you would when quoting from a book. Use substantive sources for obtaining your information and depend less on general references.

Copyright: It is the responsibility of contributors to clear permissions.

All articles should be sent to the editor, Ernest N. Emenyonu, as an e-mail attachment
(Word)Email: eernest@umich.edu
African Literature Today
Department of Africana Studies
University of Michigan-Flint
303 East Kearsley Street
Flint MI 48502 USA
Fax: 001-810-766-6719

Books for review to be sent to the Reviews Editor. Reviewers should provide full bibliographic details, including the extent, ISBN and price:
Obi Nwakanma, University of Central Florida, English Department, Colburn Hall, 12790 Aquarius Agora Drive, Orlando, FL 32816, USA
Obi.Nwakanma@ucf.edu

AFRICAN LITERATURE TODAY

ALT 1-14 BACK IN PRINT. See www.jamescurrey.com to order copies

ALT 1, 2, 3, and 4 Omnibus Edition
ALT 5 The Novel in Africa
ALT 6 Poetry in Africa
ALT 7 Focus on Criticism
ALT 8 Drama in Africa
ALT 9 Africa, America & the Caribbean
ALT 10 Retrospect & Prospect
ALT 11 Myth & History
ALT 12 New Writing, New Approaches
ALT 13 Recent Trends in the Novel
ALT 14 Insiders & Outsiders

Backlist titles available in the US and Canada from Africa World Press and in the rest of the world from James Currey, an imprint of Boydell & Brewer

ALT 15 Women in African Literature Today
ALT 16 Oral & Written Poetry in African Literature Today
ALT 17 The Question of Language in African Literature Today
ALT 18 Orature in African Literature Today
ALT 19 Critical Theory & African Literature Today
ALT 20 New Trends & Generations in African Literature
ALT 21 Childhood in African Literature
ALT 22 Exile & African Literature
ALT 23 South & Southern African Literature
ALT 24 New Women's Writing in African Literature
ALT 25 New Directions in African Literature

Recent and forthcoming titles*

Nigeria edition (ALT 24–33): HEBN Publishers Plc

African Literature Today continues to be published as an annual volume by James Currey (an imprint Boydell & Brewer since 2008).

North and South American distribution:
Boydell & Brewer Inc., 68 Mount Hope Avenue, Rochester, NY 14620-2731, US

UK and International distribution:
Boydell & Brewer Ltd., PO Box 9, Woodbridge IP12 3DF, GB.

ALT 26 War in African Literature Today
ALT 27 New Novels in African Literature Today
ALT 28 Film in African Literature Today
ALT 29 Teaching African Literature Today
ALT 30 Reflections & Retrospectives in African Literature Today
ALT 31 Writing Africa in the Short Story
ALT 32 Politics & Social Justice
ALT 33 Children's Literature & Story-telling
ALT 34 Diaspora & Returns in Fiction
ALT 35 Focus on Egypt
ALT 36 Queer Theory in Film & Fiction
ALT 37
ALT 38 Environmental Transformations*

Environmental Transformations

AFRICAN LITERATURE TODAY 38

James Currey
is an imprint of
Boydell & Brewer Ltd
PO Box 9, Woodbridge
Suffolk IP12 3DF (GB)
www.jamescurrey.com
and of
Boydell & Brewer Inc.
668 Mt Hope Avenue
Rochester, NY 14620–2731 (US)

www.boydellandbrewer.com

First published 2020

British Library Cataloguing in Publication Data
A catalogue record for this book is available from the British Library

ISBN 978-1-84701-228-9 (James Currey hardback)

This publication is printed on acid-free paper

Contents

REVIEWS

*** ALT 37 (2019)
Chapter 5: From Grace Ogot to Yvonne Owuor: Fifty Years of Depicting Kenyan Lands & Landscapes by Ng'ang'a Wahu-Muchiri
A version of this chapter was first published in Moradewun Adejunmobi and Carli Coetzee (eds), Routledge Handbook of African Literature (2019), as Chapter 17: Ng'ang'a Muchiri, 'Depiction of Kenyan Lands and Landscapes by Four Women Writers'; Reproduced with permission of The Licensor through PLSclear.

***STOP PRESS/TRIBUTE
Versatile and prolific novelist Chukwuemeka Ike died while we were going to press with this issue. We will carry a tribute to his legacy in the next issue, ALT 39.

Notes on Contributors

Guzal Akram is a resident of Lansing, Michigan, and is currently earning a masters in English language and literature from the University of Michigan-Flint. Before enrollment in the master's programme she graduated from Lansing Community College with associates in creative writing. She loves reading suspense and thrillers.

Psalms E. Chinaka (PhD) is a Senior Lecturer in the Department of English Studies, University of Port Harcourt, Nigeria. He is a prolific writer and critic with notable publications in *Tydskrif Virletterkunde*, *JALA* and other reputable international journals. He is also a poet – the author of *Apocalyptic Gong* (Kraft Books 2017) and *The Art of Poetry* (Pearl Publishers International 2017).

Michelle Louise Clarke is a PhD student at SOAS, London. Her work engages with ecocritical discourse within African speculative fictions. She is particularly interested in how speculative genres and imaginative scenarios can be used to produce very real outcomes for policy implementation and sustainable futures. Her thesis explores how colonial imaginings of wilderness, oceanic and outer space frontiers are deconstructed and reimagined within African literatures. Her recent publications include a book chapter entitled 'New Waves: African Environmental Ethics and Ocean Ecosystems' and an editorial on 'African Science Fiction' for *Vector.*

Juliana Daniels (PhD) is a female literary scholar with interests in gender and children's studies, environmental sustainability, and human rights in literature. She is also interested in all three genres of literature. Her first drama text is Muddles, a gender relations literary text published in 2019. She is a Senior Lecturer in Literature at the Department of English Education, University of Education, Winneba, Ghana.

Sule Emmanuel Egya is Professor of African Literature and Cultural Studies at Ibrahim Badamasi Babangida University, Lapai, Nigeria. He is also an award-winning poet and novelist who writes under the pen name E. E. Sule. His latest books are *Power and Resistance: Literature, Regime and the National Imaginary*, and *Makwala* (a novel).

Dokubo Melford Goodhead (PhD) is a Kalabari from the Niger Delta. A graduate of the University of Nigeria and the University of Washington, he taught at Spelman College and was Associate Director of the African Diaspora and the World Program.

Louise Green, author of *Fragments from the History of Loss: the Nature Industry and the Postcolony* (2020), is an Associate Professor in the English Department at Stellenbosch University. She is interested in critical theory, studies in modernity and globalization and tracing the elusive, mobile and diverse formations of value in late capitalist society. Her research proposes Africa as an important site for a philosophical engagement with the universalizing impulse that marks contemporary narratives of environmental crisis.

Katherine E. Hummel is a PhD candidate in English Language and Literature and a certificate student in the Science, Technology, and Society programme at the University of Michigan, Ann Arbor. Her dissertation project examines infrastructure as an object that links together the historical spatial logics of colonial regimes with contemporary environmental issues, and argues that critical attention to genre and form can help literary studies of infrastructure move beyond questions of representation. Her publications have appeared in *Studies in the Novel* and *Interdisciplinary Studies in Literature and Environment*.

Betty Ige, a writer, author and social entrepreneur, comes from a background that cuts across creative writing, media/journalism, academics and administration. She has published articles, short stories, and poems in journals, anthologies, newspapers, and magazines. Ige is the vice chairman of Association of Nigerian Authors (ANA), Kwara State chapter. She is currently a doctoral candidate at ECWA Theological Seminary, Igbaja (ETSI), Nigeria.

Cajetan Iheka is Associate Professor of English at Yale University, where he teaches courses in African literature, ecocriticism, and world literature. He is the author of *Naturalizing Africa: Ecological Violence, Agency, and Postcolonial Resistance in African Literature* (Cambridge University Press, 2018), winner of the 2019 Ecocriticism Book Award of the Association for the Study of Literature and Environment, and co-editor of *African Migration Narratives: Politics, Race, and Space* (University of Rochester Press, 2018). His articles have appeared in or are forthcoming in refereed venues such as *Interdisciplinary Studies in Literature and Environment*, *Environmental Ethics*, *Research in African Literatures*, and *The Cambridge Companion to the Environmental Humanities*

Jerome Masamaka is a Ghanaian creative writing doctoral candidate at Murdoch University, Australia. As a keen climate change apologist, his poetry reflects environmentalist apprehensions. His research interests include literature on the environment, ecocriticism, zoocriticism, literary utopia, pan-African imaginaries and postcolonial writing. His long-term research projects intersect indigenous and migrant environmental utopias. His first two poetry volumes, *Hatchlings in Rott(e)Nest: Poems in Nonhuman Accents* and *Chiming for the Clime: Poems for Our Time*, are scheduled to be published in 2021.

James McCorkle is a Visiting Assistant Professor of Africana Studies at Hobart and William Smith Colleges. He is currently the Headquarters Director of the African Literature Association. His primary interests are contemporary re-configurations of slave narratives, contemporary poetry and poetics, especially within the African diaspora, and eco-poetics. As a poet, his works include *Evidences* (2003), *The Subtle Bodies* (2014), and *In Time* (2020).

Syned Mthatiwa is an Associate Professor of English at Chancellor College, University of Malawi. He holds BA and MA degrees from the University of Malawi, and a PhD from the University of the Witwatersrand, South Africa. Mthatiwa's research interest is in ecocriticism or ecophilosophy more generally, postcolonial literary and cultural studies, oral literature, popular literature, poetry and the novel.

Stephanie Newell is Professor of English at Yale University and Professor Extraordinaire at the University of Stellenbosch. She is the author of many books and articles on West African print cultures, newspaper history, popular literature and West African media audiences, most recently *Histories of Dirt: Media and Urban Life in Colonial and Postcolonial Lagos.*

Kelvin Ngong Toh holds a PhD in African Literature. He has published two plays, Fointama (2013) and Symphonic Shades (2020). He has a collection of poems that is under review for publication. Toh is Associate Professor and teaches African Literatures and Cultures at the University of Bamenda and the University of Buea in Cameroon.

Eunice Ngongkum holds a PhD from the University of Yaoundé 1 where she is presently Professor of African Literature and Culture in the Department of African Literature and Civilizations. Her research interests are in the domain of postcolonial African literatures, cultural studies, the environmental humanities and literary theory. She has published widely on these subjects in international and national peer-reviewed journals. A Fellow of the Alexander von Humboldt Foundation, she is also a poet and a short story writer. She is author of *Anglophone Cameroon Poetry in the Environmental Matrix* (2017) and *Dennis Brutus' Poetics of Revolt* (2018).

Sandra C. Nwokocha earned a PhD in English Literature at the University of Birmingham, in the United Kingdom in 2017. Since then she has been a freelance consultant specializing in evaluation and research with an emphasis on feminist literary criticism. She has published works including 'Subversive responses to oppression in Chimamanda Ngozi Adichie's *Purple Hibiscus*', *Journal of Commonwealth Literature* 54.3 (2017): 367–83, 'Theorising feminisms: a reflection on the controversies surrounding the (ir)relevance of mainstream feminism to cultures other than the West' (2018), 'Rethinking female sexuality in Adichie's *Half of a Yellow Sun*' (2019), and 'Sefi Atta', *The Literary Encyclopedia* (2019).

Alexander Opicho is a poet, an essayist and a short story writer from Kenya. He lives and works in Lodwar and Nairobi. He writes to protect the rights of the humble.

Uchechukwu Umezurike is a PhD candidate and Vanier Scholar in the Department of English and Film Studies, University of Alberta, Canada. An alumnus of the International Writing Program (USA), he recently co-edited *Wreaths for a Wayfarer*, a poetry anthology.

Ng'ang'a Wahu-Muchiri is Assistant Professor at the University of Nebraska-Lincoln where he designs and teaches courses in African literature, short stories, eco-criticism, and Caribbean writers. His current scholarly monograph is titled *Writing Land, Righting Land: Literary Depictions of Contemporary African Landscapes*. This work mines the metaphorical labour that land performs in twentieth and twenty-first-century African literature to subvert narratives that justify theft of African lands by elites and that resist postcolonial dystopian regimes.

Introduction

Itineraries of African Ecocriticism and Environmental Transformations in African Literature

CAJETAN IHEKA WITH STEPHANIE NEWELL

The geography of African ecocriticism has shifted considerably since William Slaymaker published his 'Ecoing the Other(s)' in 2001 and Anthony Vital's 'Toward an African Ecocriticism' appeared in 2008. Published in *PMLA*, Slaymaker's piece explains the slow response of African literary critics to environmental concerns. In his words, 'there is no rush by African literary and cultural critics to adopt ecocriticism or the literature of the environment as they are promulgated from many of the world's metropolitan centers' (132). Appearing seven years later, the title of Vital's work on J. M. Coetzee's *Life & Times of Michael K* suggests the continuing relevance of Slaymaker's observation. Marking the yet to come, the 'toward' of Vital's title prepares for the arrival of an African ecocriticism, an arrival that the essay anticipates by proposing methodological principles for an ecocriticism with African inclinations. One such principle, according to Vital, is that 'ecocriticism, if it is to pose African questions and find African answers, will need to be rooted in local (regional, national) concern for social life and its natural environment' (88).

Writing this introduction in January 2020, we can report the arrival of an African ecocriticism that has heeded Vital's recommendation as well as the quick maturation of this subfield. To put it succinctly, the field is growing rapidly as there is now a rush to adopt ecocriticism in African literary and cultural studies. The fact that Slaymaker's position is now dated is testament to the growing body of works in African ecocriticism, many of them published in the world's metropolitan centers while others are developed and published within Africa. In fact, one such book won the 2019 Best Ecocriticism Book of the Association for the Study of Literature and Environment (Iheka 2018). Another African-themed monograph was a finalist in the 2015 edition of the prize (Caminero-Santangelo 2014).

These books and other studies in African ecocriticism recognize the interconnection of colonialism with resource extraction and ecological degradation, thereby validating Bonnie Roos and Alex Hunt's claim that 'any postcolonial critique must be thoroughly ecocritical at the same time' (2010: 3). Examples include Byron Caminero-Santangelo's pioneering *Different Shades of Green: African Literature, Environmental Justice, and Political Ecology* (2014), Cajetan Iheka's *Naturalizing Africa: Ecological Violence, Agency, and Postcolonial Resistance in African Literature* (2018), and the most recent, *Of Land, Bones, and Money: Toward a South African Ecopoetics* (2019), by Emily McGiffin. In addition to these monographs, there is a corpus of journal articles and chapters in edited volumes such as Caminero-Santangelo's and Garth Myers' *Environment at the Margins: Literary and Environmental Studies in Africa* (2011), Ogaga Okuyade's *Eco-Critical Literature: Regreening African Landscapes* (2013), and Fiona Moolla's *Natures of Africa: Ecocriticism and Animal Studies in Contemporary Cultural Forms* (2016).

These representative texts highlight the erosion of African cultural and environmental riches because of colonialism, critique the continuous vulnerabilities of African environments following independence and the extractive logic of late capitalism and globalisation, while orienting their readers to sustainable environmental practices, some of which are rooted in indigenous cosmologies in Africa. Specific concerns addressed in these studies, and raised again by the contributors to this special issue, include the ecologies of resource extraction in regions such as the Niger Delta of Nigeria, the colonial underpinning of conservation movements across Africa, the ecological implications of rural–urban migrations, the gendered dynamics of environmentalism, the relationship between development and ecology, the commodification of human and animal lives, and the broader dynamics of human-animal relationships, just to mention some examples.

Building on existing scholarship while pushing the field in new and exciting directions, the articles in this volume interrogate the ways in which African environmental(ist) writing engages with major shifts in twenty-first-century thinking such as the identification of the Anthropocene, and they ponder the appropriate literary forms for articulating environmental questions as well as the possibilities and problems of representation. In their engagement with the diverse genres, themes and frameworks through which contemporary African writers address topics including urbanization, cross-species communication, nature and climate change, they help to define African environmental writing. They look at the literary strategies adopted by creative writers to convey the impact of environmental transformation in narratives that are historically informed by a century of colonialism, nationalist political activism, urbanization and postcolonial migration, and ask: how does environmental literature intervene in these histories? Can creative writers, with their powerfully post-human and cross-species imaginations, carry out the ethical work demanded by contemporary climate science?

Whereas to date the emphasis in African ecocriticism has largely been on the novel, poetry is the privileged site of enunciation for many articles in this special issue. Moreover, while Nigeria and South Africa tend to dominate ecocritical discussions, this volume extends consideration to understudied locales such as Cameroon and Malawi, and to writers whose works hardly register in ecocriticism to date, including John Ngong Kum Ngong and Steve Chimombo (see Ngongkum, Mthatiwa, this issue). Contributors ask about the ways in which poetry and fiction engage with environmental consciousness, and how African literary criticism addresses the implications of global environmental transformations. Can the perspective of honeybees be captured in poetry (Masamaka)? How does feminist criticism figure in environmentalist critique (Nwokocha)? Can poets generate environmental resistance and change through their critiques of urbanization (Egya)? Does *any* text in which the environment features become available to environmentalist criticism and, if not, where should we draw the limits (Green)? From Helon Habila's attention to environmental decimation in the Niger Delta to Nnedi Okorafor's and Kofi Anyidoho's imaginative cross-species encounters, contributors ask how literature mediates the specificities of climate change in an era of global capitalism and technological transformation, and what the limits of creative writing and literary criticism are as tools for discussing environmental issues (see Hummel, Clarke, McCorkle, this issue).

Several essays are insightful for their interrogation of the 'coloniality of being.' As Sabelo J. Ndlovu-Gatsheni explains, 'coloniality of being is very important because it assists in investigating how African humanity was questioned' in colonial discourse to justify the objectification and commodification of African life (490). Many contributors complicate and reject the autonomous human figure of the Western Enlightenment. They turn to African writings to demonstrate another possibility for the human, one based not on self-sufficiency but on relations with Others – humans and nonhumans. The African writings and the critics gathered here recognize that the humility to embrace this ecological human-in-relation is not only necessary but critical for the survival of a continent marred by forms of ecological violence: the continuing environmental degradation caused by oil exploration in the Niger-Delta, the ecological aftermath of war in different parts of the continent, illegal fishing on the continent's shores, and indiscriminate animal poaching, among others.

The diverse perspectives in this volume demonstrate that there is no single method or approach that defines African ecocriticism. What can be said, however, is that African ecocritical inquiry falls within the category of postcolonial ecocriticism with its attentiveness to how nonwestern literary artefacts have 'contributed to an ecological imaginary and discourse of activism and sovereignty' (DeLoughrey and Handley 8). Like the works that Graham Huggan and Helen Tiffin categorize as postcolonial ecocriticism, existing ecocritical work on Africa and those debuted here dissect 'the colonial/imperial underpinnings of environmental practices' and propose 'how the real world might be transformed' (Huggan and Tiffin 3; 13). Nevertheless, the articles in this volume reject a universal discourse of colonialism and the postcolonial experience by being attentive to the locational factors shaping developments in various parts of the postcolony. The indirect rule experience in Nigeria differs significantly from the settler colony model practised in Kenya. Even among settler colonies, there is a sharp distinction between the Kenyan experience and the South African situation, where the Apartheid past continues to reverberate in the present. While we can delineate similarities across Africa and between the continent and other postcolonial locales, this special issue heeds Caminero-Santangelo's caution that the necessity of plotting connections across postcolonial sites should not result in 'suppressing difference' (15).

The currents of African ecocriticism can be subsumed within two categories: the environmental justice vein and the ecological variety. Caminero-Santangelo's scholarship is most representative of the former kind of African ecocriticism. As he puts it, 'African environmental writing tends to prioritize social justice; lived environments; livelihoods; and/or the relationship among environmental practice, representation of nature, power, and privilege' (7). The environmental justice approach prioritizes humans caught in the interplay of colonization and globalization, as suggested in this volume in the articles by Sule Egya and Eunice Ngongkum. Given Africa's disadvantage in the distribution of ecological risks such as the degradation of oil communities in the Niger Delta, the dispossession of human communities of their ancestral land for developmental projects across the continent, and the seeming preference for the welfare of charismatic megafauna over human lives in conservation conflicts in places such as Kenya and South Africa, it makes sense that the environmental justice framework would appeal to scholars of African ecocriticism. Since its American origins, environmental justice presupposes human rights to a liveable and healthy environment; as such, scholars have found its language suitable for critiquing the environmental imbalances in Africa, for exposing the toxic landscapes of industrialization and globalization, and for archiving the resistance of African communities, including the Ken Saro Wiwa-led Ogoni struggle in Nigeria against the degradation of their environment by Shell and government collaborators (see Hummel, this issue). While mindful of human connection to the larger ecosystem, scholars working within this first mode insist on the primacy of human flourishing for a people whose denigration in colonial discourse was matched with physical/material abuses in colonial times and ongoing slow and accelerated violence since independence.

If the environmental justice approach privileges humans, the ecological mode manifests in a critical attentiveness to human and nonhuman entanglement in Africa, what Iheka terms 'aesthetics of proximity' in his book (21–56). While recognizing the value of human flourishing, the ecological approach recognizes the intertwinement of human and nonhuman beings in African cosmologies as it demands an ecosystemic thinking in the conceptualization of eco-challenges. What Ursula Heise terms multispecies justice is crucial for the ecological approach, that is the validation of rights and responsibilities toward both humans as well as nonhumans (198). In this mode of seeing, a radical reimagining of ethics and rights becomes necessary so that ethical considerations are not limited to human beings. At the centre of an eco-approach to African literature is a redefinition of the prerequisites of the human to encapsulate obligation to humans and other beings alongside shared agency among humans, other life forms, and things. Jerome Masamaka's article in this volume exemplifies this strategy, with its zoocritical attention to the perspective of honeybees in Kofi Anyidoho's poetry. Masamaka's approach has been made possible by the nonhuman turn in the environmental humanities, including the work of new materialists and animal studies thinkers including Rosi Braidotti, Jane Bennett, and Cary Wolfe. Yet it would be a mistake to fully locate the source of this kind of interspecies work in metropolitan theorizations: African indigenous traditions join other indigenous cosmologies in articulating an ecological poetics and praxis that are respectful of more-than-human lives. Conferring sacred value to land, trees, animals, and other 'earth beings', to use language from Marisol de la Cadena's work among the Andes, African communities recognize these ecological components as significant participants in an ecological relationship. As McGiffin puts it in the South Africa Xhosa context, nonhuman beings are considered 'essential citizens in the continuum of human and natural systems' (2).

Although the assembled essays straddle both strands of African ecocriticism, there is an increasing emphasis on the ecological approach. Essays in the ecological mode foreground indigenous cosmologies underpinning their contexts of production. While materialist theories inform these essays, they are firmly grounded in the ecocosmologies of African communities. If earlier works in ecocriticism heavily rely on the discourse of postcolonial ecocriticism, ecocriticism, and the environmental humanities, more broadly, many of the essays here take seriously the decolonial impulse in recent theorizations of the global South. Centering African epistemologies and praxis, these scholars practise the 'epistemic disobedience' that Walter Mignolo locates as the crux of decolonial thought (1). Refusing to normalize the hierarchical positioning of western knowledge at the apex, with other knowledge systems subordinated to it, our contributors prioritize African ways of knowing even when these are inconsistent with dominant paradigms.

In her introduction to *Natures of Africa*, Moolla asserts that 'the natural world and animals have been active agents in African cultural forms for as long as these forms have existed' because of the primacy of these agents in the African cosmologies underpinning these texts (9). Jacob Mapara's contribution to Moolla's volume uses Shona indigenous practices to illustrate this eco-cultural phenomenon. According to Mapara:

> Shona indigenous religion is anchored in a belief in ancestral spirits, mashavi and other religious figures, such as mermaids and mermen. These spirits are associated with certain regions and sites, like trees, groves, wetlands and pools. Fig trees and groves that have fig trees are considered sacred because they are places of worship. Consequently, the fig tree is not supposed to be cut down. Local spirit mediums must be consulted before certain wetlands may be cultivated. People are not supposed to swim or bathe in pools believed to be the abode of merfolk. It is apparent that these religious practices were meant to sustain life for the benefit of both humanity and fauna. (84)

Mapara may be writing of the Shona but his conclusions are applicable to other parts of the continent characterized by interspecies collaboration and communication. African writers, such as Tanure Ojaide, draw upon their society's worldviews to attribute agency to nonhuman forms and to highlight how such practices can challenge the instrumental view of the environment undergirding the current globalization era. This is no advocacy for some return to an uncritical form of tradition but to highlight the way that such value systems can engender a more sustainable relationship between the human and nonhuman components of the ecosystem. In other words, attributing agentic abilities to these nonhuman forms moves them away from the category of mere objects to be exploited and discarded. This move recognizes the otherwise 'inert' objects as life forces worthy of consideration.

The work of the Niger Delta-born writer and scholar Tanure Ojaide provides a helpful illustration of the ecological disposition of African ecocriticism. Besides Saro-Wiwa, no Niger Delta writer has received as significant attention as Ojaide, whose extensive oeuvre includes a novel, *The Activist*, essays, and collections of poetry, including *Delta Blues and Home Songs* and *The Tale of the Harmattan*. Ojaide's work is marked by the 'aggressive vision, powered by a righteous rage, to reclaim their nation' that Sule E. Egya identifies in contemporary Nigerian poetry (50). Reflecting on the aesthetics of outrage, Caminero-Santangelo recognizes Ojaide's use of 'monstrous' imagery to represent the 'geography of uneven development' in Nigeria (173). Caminero-Santangelo builds on the work of other scholars who have attended to the environmental critique in Ojaide's poetry and the influence of the oral tradition on his oeuvre (see essays by Tsaaior, Jua, Nwagbara in Okuyade's volume).

The scope of Ojaide's poetry accommodates both humans and nonhuman beings identified as victims and agents in the Niger Delta. Ojaide's 'Lessons from Grandma's night-time school', featured in *The Tale of the Harmattan*, for instance, laments the disconnect between humans and more-than-human lives due to ecological transformations. The double temporality of the poem is registered in the first stanza, where the persona declares that 'I used to throw a copper coin for head/ or tail'. The speaker later states that 'it used to be easy to make up one's mind,/ as head or tail belonged to the same disk' (20). As the poem continues, it becomes clear that the easiness of the past has given way to a complicated present. The poem's diagnosis is that 'we have lost respect for basic things'. The choice of 'respect' is significant because it echoes the fundamental attitude toward nonhumans in indigenous cosmologies, including in the Delta. In fact, Ojaide's collection is suffused with sacred trees and aquatic spaces inhabited by Mami Wata. In lamenting the loss of respect for basic things such as trees that are indiscriminately cut down in the first poem in the collection, 'The goat song' (9–11), or 'the community of plants and animals' in 'Priests, converts, and gods' (12–13), or the rivers blackened by oil deposits throughout the volume, Ojaide's poem marks the difference between the past and present.

In this three-part poem, the first and second sections lament the present where 'confusion paralyses the mind's every move' and fishing, a mainstay of the Delta economy, has become difficult, requiring deeper exploration of the sea. It is significant that the third/final part counters the present situation with a nostalgic recollection of a past marked by ecological harmony. In this past, the seasons 'feted residents with abundance' and the 'residents' in turn 'reciprocated hospitality with offerings' (12). It is this ethical reciprocity between humans and their environment that is lacking in the poem's present when respect has been lost. Later in this final section, readers learn of 'humans and spirits' who 'married for love of life' and of a people who 'consorted with birds and animals,/ communed with plants on fresh draughts.' In the last line of the poem, there is 'no cause for anxiety in the commonwealth'. The poem's final part underscores a shared ecology where humans are part of an ecosystem, of a commonwealth comprising humans and nonhumans. In fact, the description of humans as 'residents' in this section can be construed as a humbling rhetoric. Unlike terms such as owner and citizen with their domineering tendency, 'residents' indicates temporality and tentativeness, which is consistent with the non-anthropocentric leaning of this final part. Overall the poem suggests that interspecies communion between human and other life forms and between humans and spirits premised on respect are felicitous conditions for ecological thriving (see also Green, this issue). Ojaide's poem invites a reading that is cognizant of the Delta as 'complex assemblages of humans, animals, plants, and spirits' (McGiffin 6).

Foregrounding the nonhuman in ecological criticism is not a recourse to deep ecology with its prioritization of nature for its intrinsic qualities, without regard for human concerns. Critics of the ecological approach would say that it is premature to consider nonhumans in the African context with millions of people mired in poverty amidst other social crises. One critic recently wrote that 'I couldn't bring myself to talk about the dignity of animals in post-apartheid South Africa while that of humans (blacks) is even more precarious' (Eze 350). The singular-focus orientation of this position runs against the tenet of the ecological perspective, which calls for attention to shared vulnerabilities across species and the cultivation of an ethics of flourishing for various life forms.

There is value in addressing the needs of humans across the continent, but this noble task should not preclude a concern for nonhuman survival. In an era of the Anthropocene, marked by increased global warming, sea level rise, and threat of extinction, our critical practices need to be oriented toward 'reading for the planet,' to use Jennifer Wenzel's term (1). The articles in this special issue clearly demonstrate that reading planetarily, entailing attentiveness to various life forms across geographical locales, is particularly poignant for African literature, often marked by nonhuman agents and entangled spatialities.

WORKS CITED

Bennett, Jane. *Vibrant Matter: A Political Ecology of Things*. Durham: Duke University Press, 2010.

Braidotti, Rosi. *The Posthuman*. Cambridge: Polity Press, 2013.

Caminero-Santangelo, Byron. *Different Shades of Green: African Literature, Environmental Justice, and Political Ecology*. Charlottesville: University of Virginia Press, 2014.

Caminero-Santangelo, Byron and Garth Myers. *Environment at the Margins: Literary and Environmental Studies in Africa*. Athens: Ohio University Press, 2011.

de La Cadena, Marisol. 'Indigenous Cosmopolitics in the Andes: Conceptual Reflection beyond 'Politics''. *Cultural Anthropology* 25.2 (2010): 334–70.

DeLoughrey, Elizabeth M., and George B. Handley, eds. *Postcolonial Ecologies: Literatures of the Environment*. New York: Oxford University Press, 2011.

Egya, Sule. 'Art and Outrage: A Critical Survey of Recent Nigerian Poetry in English'. *Research in African Literatures* 42.1 (2011): 49–67.

Eze, Chielozona. 'Author's Response to *Reviews of Race, Decolonization, and Global Citizenship in South Africa*'. *Journal of the African Literature Association* 13:3 (2019): 349–51.

Heise, Ursula. *Imagining Extinction: The Cultural Meanings of Endangered Species*. Chicago: University of Chicago Press, 2016.

Huggan, Graham, and Helen Tiffin. *Postcolonial Ecocriticism: Literature, Animals, Environment*. New York: Routledge, 2010.

Iheka, Cajetan. *Naturalizing Africa: Ecological Violence, Agency, and Postcolonial Resistance in African Literature*. Cambridge: Cambridge University Press, 2018.

Mapara, Jacob. 'The Environment as Significant Other: The Green Nature of Shona Indigenous Religion'. In *Natures of Africa: Ecocriticism and Animal Studies in Contemporary Cultural Forms*. Fiona Moolla, ed. Johannesburg: Wits University Press, 2016. 77–96.

McGiffin, Emily. *Of Land, Bones, and Money: Toward a South African Ecopoetics*. Charlottesville: University of Virginia Press, 2019.

Mignolo, Walter. 'Coloniality of Power and De-Colonial Thinking'. In *Globalization and the Decolonial Option*. Walter Mignolo and Arturo Escobar, eds. London: Routledge, 2010. 1–21.

Moolla, Fiona, ed. *Natures of Africa: Ecocriticism and Animal Studies in Contemporary Cultural Forms*. Johannesburg: Wits University Press, 2016.

Ndlovu-Gatsheni, Sabelo J. 'Decoloniality as the Future of Africa'. *History Compass* 13.10 (2015): 485–96.

Ojaide, Tanure . *Delta Blues and Home Songs*. Ibadan: Kraft Books, 1998.

———. *The Activist*. Lagos: Farafina Books, 2006.

———. *The Tale of the Harmattan*. Cape Town: Kwela Books, 2007.

Okuyade, Ogaga, ed. *Eco-Critical Literature: Regreening African Landscapes*. New York: African Heritage Press, 2013.

Roos, Bonnie and Alex Hunt. 'Introduction: Narrative of Survival, Sustainability, and Justice'. In *Postcolonial Green: Environmental Politics and World Narratives. Bonnie Roos and Alex Hunt, eds*. Charlottesville: University of Virginia Press, 2010. 1–13.

Slaymaker, William. 'Ecoing the Other(s): The Global Green and Black African Responses'. *PMLA* 116.1 (2001): 129–44.

Vital, Anthony. 'Toward an African Ecocriticism: Postcolonialism, Ecology and Life & Times of Michael K'. *Research in African Literatures* 39.1 (2008): 87–121.

Wenzel, Jennifer. *The Disposition of Nature: Environmental Crisis and World Literature*. New York: Fordham University Press, 2020.

Wolfe, Cary. *Before the Law: Humans and Other Animals in a Biopolitical Frame*. Chicago: University of Chicago Press, 2013.

Literary Totemism and its Relevance for Animal Advocacy:

A Zoocritical Engagement with Kofi Anyidoho's Literary Bees

JEROME MASAMAKA

The recent 'animal turn' (Ritvo 2007, 121) in literary criticism has made an immediate impact in African literature, with the works of Wendy Woodward (2008) and Huggan and Tiffin (2010) drawing attention to ethical and ecological dimensions of representing animals in African texts. The representation of animals, Woodward argues, influences 'the ways humans conceptualize and respond to "real"... animals' (Woodward 14). African literature is replete with literary animals that are represented in diverse ways. For Kofi Anyidoho, a member of the ethnic Ewe people of Ghana whose culture includes animal totemism, literary representation of animals extends beyond literary tropes. His use of the honeybee as his alter ego reflects Ewe totemic practices. In this article, I locate Anyidoho's artistic strategy of articulating through the viewpoint of the honeybee within the theoretical context of animal totemism. I draw on Timothy Insoll's concept of totemism (2011) and animal-focused critical concepts from Kate Soper (2005), Wendy Woodward (2008), Huggan and Tiffin (2010) and Cajetan Iheka (2018) to discuss literary totemism in selected poems of Kofi Anyidoho and the relevance of this literary strategy for animal advocacy. I refer to poems from three volumes of poetry: *A Harvest of Our Dreams* (1984), *Earthchild with Brain Surgery* (1985) and *Ancestral Logic and Carribbean Blues* (1993). These three volumes are respectively rendered simply as *Harvest*, *Earthchild* and *Blues* in this article.

Kofi Anyidoho (1947–) is a renowned Ghanaian poet and literary scholar from the South-eastern Anlo[1] Ewe town of Weta in Ghana. He is a cousin of another famous Ghanaian Ewe poet, Kofi Nyidevu Awoonor (1935– 2013). The Anlo Ewes boast a rich oral poetry history with many famous traditional poet cantors emerging from that region between the late nineteenth- and early twentieth-century colonial era (Awoonor 1974). Significantly, Kofi Anyidoho's mother – Abla Adidi – was a well-known traditional poet/singer whose art form evidently inspired her son (Awoonor 2002, 12). The transition of Ewe oral poetry into a modern literary form was championed by both Kofi Nyidevu Awoonor and Kofi Anyidoho.

According to Oyeniyi Okunoye (2005), the 'Ewe traditions of dirge and the Halo (song of abuse) are recognized ... Ewe poetic practices that shape Kofi Anyidoho's creative project' (91). In addition to Ewe dirge and Halo, Anyidoho incorporates Ewe animal totemism in his poetry. The Ewe society is subdivided into fifteen clans, or tribal units, with a rich repertoire of animal totems. Ewe clans include *Lafe* (domestic animals, with monitor lizard and sparrow as clan totems), *Klevi* (the antelopes, with antelope as totem) and *Tovi* (the buffalos, with buffalo as totem) (Green 1981, 451). In addition to clan totems, some families and individuals have their own totems. Family or personal names such as Anyidoho (a hive of bees) and Nyidevu (hippopotamus) derive from the animal with which a family or the individual bearer identifies.

It is common practice among traditional and modern Ewe poets to articulate through an animal alter ego. These alter egos are usually derived from a favoured family or personal animal. Anyidoho's mother, Abla Adidi, adopted her family totem, the ant, as her artistic alter ego in her traditional dirge performances. Kofi Nyidevu Awoonor (2014) articulates through the perspective of *nyidevu* (hippopotamus) in some of his poems.[2] Performing poetry through a family or a personal totem is one of the literary legacies Anyidoho has inherited from his Ewe poetic tradition. Hence, the explicit and implicit representation of the honeybee as the speaking voice across Anyidoho's poetry corpus is influenced by Ewe totemic practices. Anyidoho uses a wide range of animals in his poetry. However, this article focuses on his use of the honeybee as this provides the best instance of literary totemism in his works.

As the human relationship with animals varies, so do the artistic strategies writers adopt in representing this relationship. Commenting on this, Kate Soper identifies 'the "naturalistic", the "allegorical" and the "compassionate"' animal 'registers' as some of 'the more notable' (303) animal representation strategies. While Soper's animal 'registers' are useful in reading the general repertoire of literary animals in Anyidoho's poetry, his use of the honeybee invites a broader critical consideration. Cajetan Iheka's 'aesthetics of proximity' (23) inspires us to pay critical attention to 'the spatial sense of nearness as well as a form of proximity brought about by similarities and shared characteristics' (22) in the human/nonhuman relationship in the African text. Human/animal proximity in the African context is well demonstrated in the Ewe cultural practice of animal totemism. Anyidoho's poetic appropriation of this cultural practice stretches Soper's registers and invites us to reflect on the 'sense of nearness' that motivates humans to avow affinity for favoured animals.

Timothy Insoll's etymological insight on totemism and his notion of the term's conceptual elasticity are relevant to this discussion. According to Insoll, 'the Ojibwa expression, *ototeman*, means, approximately, "He(she) is a relative of mine"' (1007). He proceeds to suggest a 'broad definition of totemism that … refers to the use of plants or animals by social groups as guardians or emblems that are ritually celebrated' (ibid.). I favour Insoll's broader notion of totemism that includes secular emblematic association with animals. Insoll suggests that totemism does not necessarily involve '"doctrinal systems" but [includes] "orientations that are deeply embedded in everyday practices"' (1004). The 'everyday practices' of totemism in some African societies, especially in the past, might derive from cosmological accounts and manifest as both spiritual and cultural rituals. Totemic practices still linger in some modern cultures and manifest mostly as secular demonstration of animal intimacy. Noting this, Christopher Manes (1996) remarks that 'cars and sports teams [being] named after animals (as if to capture sympathetically their power)' (18) is a manifestation of modern-day totemism.[3] Here, totemism implies an avowed human affiliation with a nonhuman species to which a group or an individual feels emotionally bonded. This secular form of totemic affiliation is more prevalent in the present era.

Symbolic allegiance to a favoured animal in our contemporary time manifests, in some instances, as national and corporate totemism (Neal 1985). Most nation-states parade their favoured animals on their coats of arm and sports teams. Some business and sporting companies display animal logos and catchphrases to exhibit the qualities of the animal with which they desire to be identified. In many African societies, local chiefs still parade paraphernalia festooned with totem symbols. Totemic appellations such as 'Desert Foxes', 'Indomitable Lions' and 'Super Eagles' are some of the common names that identify the favoured animals of some African national sports teams. This present-day fascination with animal affinity relives the totemic orientations often associated with indigenous societies. The prevalence of modern secular 'totemic symbols reflect the human propensity to … [speak] through … animals' (22), according to Neal. This propensity reveals human appreciation for nonhuman agency and acknowledges the human/

animal 'proximity' (Iheka 22) that brings us to reflect on the status of animals and our own nature. Totemic allegiance therefore expresses 'hopes, aspirations and ideals' (Neal 18) inspired by animals in human devotees. Anyidoho's poetry manifests artistic devotion to the insect from which his family derives inspiration.

Totemic association is demonstrated in diverse ways including through animal images and catchphrases. Among the Ewes, totemic displays involve adopting totem names and reciting, usually in moments of adversity, poetic statements of appellation or proverbial chants inspired by traits of the totem animal.[4] Anyidoho's poetry presents, in one significant instance, his apian totem chant in a way that illuminates the totemic significance of his artistic dependence on the insect. In 'Ancestral Roll-Call', Anyidoho (2011, 9) declares 'It is I *Kofi Anyidoho menya tatam o*.' He explains this line in the footnote: 'Anyidoho belongs to a class of Ewe names that constitute the core of longer poetic statements. Anyidoho means "a hive of honeybees". The full appellation – *Anyidoho menya tatam o* – may be interpreted as follows: it is not easy to bypass the bees to harvest their honey' (ibid.). We learn here that the natural trait of bees, to defend their hive, is the inspiration behind the Anyidoho family name. Anyidoho is not just identifying himself in this poem. His is avowing kinship with the bee as integral to his identity. This totemic association is invoked and dramatized in various ways in the poems I discuss.

In each of the three volumes considered here, the poet articulates through his apian alter ego in at least one poem and sustains that with implicit allusions in other poems. In *Harvest*, the eponymous 'Harvests of our Dreams' (6) and 'Our Fortune's Dance' (47) are articulated through extended apian perspectives. The most elegant instance of Anyidoho's artistic devotion to the honeybee is 'HONEYCOMB FOR BEECHILDREN' (6) from *Earthchild*. In *Blues*, 'DesertStorm' (63) provides the reader another extended perspective of a beehive. These core poems elaborately represent the honeybee as the alter ego through whose perspectives Anyidoho presents some of his ecological and political concerns.

I now offer a reading of some of Anyidoho's poems to show his strategies of explicitly staging literary totemism. I begin with 'HONEYCOMB FOR BEECHILDREN':

> For every dirge Adidi sang
> I now must weave a song of new birth-cords
> I must put a hand on funeral drums (1–3)

We spoke with voice of cuckoo birds
We drank moonbeams from lips of sunflowers

BeeChildren with ecstasies in our eyes
we dance fortune in cross-rhythms
we hum our joy to Mother-Queen at dawn (17–21)

We swarm around our HoneyComb
We watch rebirth of BeeQueendom. (25–6)
(*Earthchild* 6–7)

The first stanza of the poem establishes a close artistic and filial relationship between the persona and 'Adidi' (1). Adidi is a direct reference to the poet's mother. Although Abla Adidi performed her dirges through the ant alter ego in real life, she is represented here – and in other poems – as the queen bee ('Mother-Queen' 21) in Anyidoho's literary beehive. The persona wants to usher in a dispensation of peace to appease the dirges of 'Adidi' by singing[5] 'a song of new birth-cords' (2) that will stop the 'funeral drums' (3) and 'send chief mourners away' (4). The speaking voice belongs to a colony of ecstatic 'Beechildren' (19) dancing in 'cross-rhythms' (20) and humming 'joy to Mother-Queen' (21). In line with the 'poetic statements' (Anyidoho 2011, 9) on the honeybee, this poem represents the honeybee recognisable as the poet's alter ego.

In a dramatic rendition of the Anyidoho totem appellation, this poem presents the bee imperially controlling *his* hive. From the first stanza through to the end, the bee exudes power and agency. The bee is the subject of several active declarative statements. Lines such as 'I now must weave' (2), 'I could blow' (7), 'we dance' (20), 'we hum' (21), 'We swarm' (25) and 'We watch' (26) represent the bees' agentic vigour. Unlike the 'crab children' that must obey the 'mermaid's call' (6), the bees could 'ride the storm' (8), meet 'with stars' (15), act like 'cuckoo birds' (17) (pollination implied here) with the choicest flowers and do the waggle dance in 'cross rhythm'.[6] Armed with the 'gown of velvet flames' (12), the bee is well resourced to protect *his* hive and play vital roles in productive 'rebirth' (26). The detailed imagery of some of the traits we associate with bees is a tribute to the insect with which the poet has a long-standing family bond.

There is, of course, an allegorical subtext of a glorious precolonial African civilization 'long before the reign of thunderclouds' (10) blessed with limitless resources at the disposal of ecstatic

'BeeChildren' (19). The poem presents this previous contentment and security through the ecologically stable spectacle of a swarm of bees turning their back on 'thunderclaps' (23), taking refuge with '*baobab*' (22) and homing in their 'HoneyComb' (25). The poet's deployment of nonhuman symbiosis to create this stable condition encourages a reading that is attentive to 'multispecies presence' (Iheka 30). For texts such as this, Iheka suggests an alternative biocentric reading that is 'attentive to the … enmeshment of human and nonhuman lives and the implications of said enmeshment for ecological justice' (23). African landscapes in general are alive with multispecies presence as humans and nonhumans live in proximity. This proximity allows for human intimacy with animals. Critical attention to how Anyidoho's poetry depicts this human/animal affinity brings us closer to appreciating fully the nature of his artistic relationship with the honeybee. We can therefore appreciate the deep sense of human/nonhuman kinship conveyed in this elaborate rendition of the Anyidoho totem appellation.

Granted, this poem can be read as an anthropomorphic commentary on the poet's artistic relationship with his mother. Huggan and Tiffin have noted that 'anthropomorphism is … important' in providing the 'leap required to read observed animal behaviour and imagine animal being' (153–4). This leap, they remark, 'can best be harnessed by the literary imagination' (ibid.). Though the imagined bee in the first stanza is clothed in human attributes, the third stanza has blurred the human/nonhuman line so that the detailed imagery of apian habits undercuts focus on the human subject. Iheka calls this 'strategic anthropomorphism' which 'brings about ecological awareness' (14) of the value of nonhuman species. In that sense, the human/nonhuman ecological link in the fourth stanza is blurred so that we do not find it easy to tell whether the speaking voice is a bee speaking as if human or vice versa. Totemism allows us to presume on this interspecies transfer of traits which Woodward recognizes as a 'shared world' of 'collaborative subjectivity' (16). Certainly, the bees we encounter in this poem leap from Anyidoho's artistic imagination. Evidently, though, this imagination draws on both his empirical observation of real bees and the Ewe totemic world view of animals to represent the apian persona in 'collaborative subjectivity' with the implied human speaker.

In 'A Harvest of our Dreams' the imagery of a stable beehive is reversed. In a strategy that conflates Soper's animal registers, Anyidoho presents a gloomy reversal of fortune for his favourite insect:

The honey bee had plans in store
for his Mother-Queen: he went across the world
gathering fragrance from dreamy waterlilies
from lonely desert blooms
Some other gatherer came with plans
all for his own desires
Our hive went up in flames. I was away.
We will hum a dirge for a burden of these winds

Memories of our honeycomb floating through
seedtime within the soul beyond the reach of Song
Rowdy echoes burst upon our soul's siesta

And harvests go ungathered in our time.

(*Harvest* 6, 6–17)

Reading in line with Soper, we can see an allegorical angle to this poem if we take the beehive as illustrating colonial plundering of African resources. Also, the poem presents the industry of bees (6–9) in a 'straightforward' naturalistic manner we can attribute to the poet's 'empirical observation' (Soper 304) of the insect. Soper's 'compassionate' register '[brings] us to think about our treatment of animals' (307). This poem certainly induces pathos for honeybees and incites us to reflect on human violence to beehives. However, if we look beyond these literary registers we see that this poem is in dialogue—in a rather ironic way—with the inspired honeybee appellation. The much-vaunted natural defence in a beehive which looters cannot 'bypass ... to harvest their honey'[7] gives way to vulnerability as pillagers set the hive on fire while the apian speaker 'was away' (12). Anyidoho is here drawing our attention to a taboo violation that causes the 'we' (suggestively a merger of totem and devotee) to 'hum a dirge' (13) in lament of the violence. The taboo violation is tragic as beehives are naturally endowed to ward off threats. This violation, with fire, has a human footprint. This poem encourages reflection on human violence to bees and awareness of their ecological importance.

Totemic devotion involves the imposition of taboos that prohibit harm to totem animals. Among the Ewes, totemic animals are protected and respected by prohibitions on harming or eating them and performing ceremonial burials for them when they die a natural death. Violation of totem taboos often provoke spirited protest from other devotees. Devotion to animal totems therefore involves valorising animal traits as well as protesting or prohibiting violence to animals.[8] These twofold acts of totemic allegiance are evident in Anyidoho's artistic compassion for the honeybee in this poem.

'A Harvest of our Dreams' was written between February and April 1979,[9] a period of acute economic and political crises in Ghana. The resulting civil strife led to one failed military coup attempt in March 1979 and a successful one in June 1979. The civil upheaval in Ghana may have weighed on Anyidoho's mind when composing this poem. Nonetheless, as the poet consistently articulates through an apian alter ego, he creates this analogy between a plundered beehive and the economic crisis that plagued his country. Bees were gaining popularity in Ghana in the 1970s (Adjare 1981) as Ghanaians saw wild bee looting as a viable source of income at a time of economic crises. The crude and unprofessional approach of looters seriously endangered bees (Antwi-Dadzie 2002). For Anyidoho, to whom the insect is a family and artistic totem, concerns for a starving nation and that for his favoured insect merge into one. The tone of protest in this poem comes through the imagery of ecological injustice in the third stanza and that of a lost harvest in the last line. Anyidoho's economically distressed country is imagined here in analogy with a plundered beehive.

Anyidoho's literary protest for honeybees is worth considering in the context of current global interest in the welfare of bees. Greenpeace International is currently (since it produced a technical report on bees in 2013) running the 'Save the Bees' campaign to draw attention to the urgent ecological need to safeguard the welfare of bees in Europe. The Greenpeace US branch reports that 'Honey bees … perform 80 percent of all pollination worldwide' and that 'Seventy out of the top 100 human food crops – which supply about 90 percent of the world's nutrition – are pollinated by bees' (Greenpeace USA). Despite this staggering ecological value of bees, Greenpeace warns that human activities – such as the use of pesticides and destruction of bee habitats – are causing bee populations worldwide to dwindle. The shortfall of bees in some countries has led to the boom in the live bee export trade, which recorded a high of US$48.1 million in 2018 (World's Top Exports). A healthy bee population is not only beneficial for bumper harvests. An ecologically sound apiculture provides benefits such as wax and honey. The natural honey industry alone is reportedly worth over two billion dollars a year with 2018 recording US$2.246 billion (World's Top Exports). Due to the massive ecological and economic value of bees and the urgent need to reverse their dwindling population worldwide, the United Nations has set aside 20 May for an annual celebration of bees with 2018 marking the first World Bee Day.

Interest in bees is also gaining attention in Africa in the wake of the drought and locust invasion (since 2019) which is causing famine in some East African countries (Deutsche Welle 2020). In May 2019, the BBC reported on how constructive apiculture in Africa can help restore ecosystems, protect wildlife, increase crop yields and generate income for farmers. The value of bees to Africa's economy and general ecological balance is so immense that the welfare of bees should be a matter of critical concern for all Africans and not just a few environmental enthusiasts. In view of the worldwide advocacy for the welfare of bees, Kofi Anyidoho's artistic commitment to the 'golden insect'[10] offers us a relevant literary conversation on the importance of honeybees, and other nonhuman species, in the African environment. Of course, literary animal protest has a limited political force (Huggan and Tiffin 13–14). However, we can appreciate that Anyidoho's literary devotion to the honeybee serves as an 'interventionist or even activist enterprise' (ibid.) in encouraging biocentric sentiments for bees.

Beyond the possibility of Anyidoho's literary compassion for bees to shape 'a desired [conservationist] outcome' (Huggan and Tiffin 14) for the welfare of the insect, 'DesertStorm' reveals the personal inspiration humans can draw from their favoured animals. The poem is a lyrical reflection on the strain of family separation as well as a sarcastic commentary on the Gulf War of the early 1990s. In a meditative and sombre mood, the persona is 'flying away to' (11) London at the precarious time of war. Yet,

> no matter how far afield
> the HoneyBee may fly
> he must swim the FireFloods
> back to his MotherHive
> where they say the honey
> flows in slow dribblets,
> the QueenBee's labours
> forever lost to wayward
> dreams of Moonchildren. (18–26)
>
> --
>
> And out there in the Gulf
> A widowed mother's only son
> Bleeds to Death in DesertStorms. (51–3)
>
> (*Blues* 63–5)

These lines depict the potential starvation of hardworking bees who are losing their precious honey to 'wayward' (25) looters. The reader of 'A Harvest of our Dreams' and 'Desert Storm' is again confronted with the violation of a beehive where the honey 'flows in slow dribblets' (23). Anyidoho's enduring empathy for bees is triggered, in this instance, by the Gulf War. The poet's empathy for the mortal separation of an 'only son' from his 'widowed mother' (52) in the crossfires of the war reminds him of his own separation from his 'MotherHive' (21). In a manner reminiscent of an Ewe totem devotee who recites totem appellations in the face of difficulty, the poet draws personal inspiration from the homing prowess of his favoured insect. The honeybee must waggle back to *his* hive regardless of 'FireFloods' and 'how far afield' *he* flies. The young casualty of the Gulf War cannot return to his mother. The poet eulogizes bees who fight stormy weather and predatory dangers in the hive to fly back to their queen bee. Here is another tribute to the golden insect whose persistence through peril comforts the poet as he 'was flying away into new snowstorms' (11) at a perilous time. This poem provides an instance of Anyidoho's reflection on life explicitly conveyed through the perspective of the honeybee from whom he draws inspiration.

It is important to add that some poems in Anyidoho's corpus only refer to the honeybee in refrain. The lines 'how soon again in our hive/ shall we swarm around our honeycomb?' (34–5) establishes the apian perspective in 'Hero and Thief' (*Earthchild* 14) and 'Our Fortune's Dance' (*Harvest* 47, 10–11). In 'The Homing Call of Earth' (*Earthchild* 43–4), the apian persona is identified in the single line: 'So I must reject the honeyed call of distant dreams' (29). In 'Kingmaker' (*Earthchild* 13–14), these three lines – 'Go crawl naked.../ into splendour halls of QueenMother's naked dreams/ (7–8)... Give him honeycombs and spiced cornmeals' (14) – remind the reader of the central role the honeybee plays in Anyidoho's poetry. Even though the honeybee is mentioned in fewer lines in these poems, we see an intertextual link to the poems in which the insect totem plays a more dominant role.

Most poems in Anyidoho's corpus do not make a direct reference to the honeybee. In many of those poems, however, language is constructed so the reader can recognize imagery or the viewpoint of the bee. In 'HONEYCOMB FOR BEECHILDREN', words such as 'whirlwind' (7), 'storm' (8), 'ride' (8), 'rainbow [preferred colours of bees]' (11), 'flames' (12), 'thunder' (17), 'sunflowers' (17), and 'hum' (21) describe the natural environment and habits of bees.

This imagery is part of a recurring intertextual diction – we may compose with 'harvest', 'field', 'fruit', 'thorn', 'earth', 'sky', 'fly' and 'cloud' – which resonates in several poems across Anyidoho's corpus. The physical features conveyed in these words help the reader to see the world from a human perspective and the vantage point of bees. Discussing literary totemism in Anyidoho's poetry is, therefore, not a suggestion that all his poems explicitly represent his artistic totem. That would be superfluous and trivial. Ultimately, a mix of explicit and implicit demonstrations of his association with the honeybee reveals an artistic commitment to the nonhuman species that inspires his family and his art.

Undoubtedly, literary animal representation has consequences and relevance for the way society relates to the real animal (Woodward 14). Anyidoho's literary devotion to the honeybee invites us to pay homage to the insect whose ecological activities put food on our tables. Literary animals, as the poet demonstrates, could be an extension of an established cultural connection with animals. By refashioning this cultural affinity for animals in his poetry, Anyidoho is nodding at the human desire to '[speak] through' (Neal 22) animals and thereby acknowledging the 'common attributes' (Iheka 23) they share with humans. Certainly, the enmeshment of human and nonhuman lives in the African environment is a remarkable phenomenon of symbiotic interdependence that demands ecologically sensitive human behaviour. By articulating his poetic vision through a nonhuman totem, Anyidoho adds to 'the diversity and complexity' (Soper 303) of literary animals in African literature and also inspires us to reflect on the close ecological bond that humans share with animals in the African environment.

NOTES

1 Anlo is the dominant traditional state of the Ewe people.

2 'To Those Gone Before' and 'A Dirge', from Awoonor 2014, 222–4.

3 Manes uses animism here. Totemism and animism are sometimes used in similar context as they are sometimes implied in the practice of each other. See Neil (1985).

4 The Ewe proverbial statement translated as 'one hand cannot catch a buffalo' is a common chant for the *Tovi* clan whose totem is the buffalo (Agbemenu 2010, 14).

5 Anyidoho is also an oral poet/cantor who performs his poems before live

audience. Some of his audio poems feature his mother, Adidi (Awoonor 2002).

6 The waggle dance of bees still baffles many ethologists in its coded complexity.

7 See Anyidoho 2011, 9.

8 Protesting violence to a sacred animal, which is common in India, belongs to the religious significance of animals which falls outside the scope of this article.

9 Indicated under the poem (*Harvest* 8).

10 The honeybee is regarded as golden insect in the honey industry. See Adjare 1981.

WORKS CITED

Primary Sources

Anyidoho, Kofi. 1984. *A Harvest of Our Dreams*. London: Heinemann.

_______. 1985. *Earthchild with Brain Surgery*. Accra: Woeli Publication Services.

_______. 1993. *AncestralLogic and CaribbeanBlues*. Trenton: Africa World Press.

_______. *The Place we Call Home*. 2011. Oxfordshire: Ayebia Clarke Publishing Limited.

Secondary sources

Adjare, Stephen O. 1981. *The golden insect: a handbook on beekeeping for beginners*. Warwickshire: Intermediate Technology Publications. https://www.cabdirect.org/cabdirect/abstract/19830213767, accessed 24 January 2020.

Agbemenu, Cephas Yao. November 2010. *Collection of Ewe Proverbs*. https://afriprov.org/images/afriprov/books/ewe100proverbs.pdf, accessed 24 January 2020.

Antwi-Dadzie, Yaw. 2002. 'Economic Analysis of Beekeeping in the Jasikan District of the Volta Region'. Unpublished MPhil Thesis, University of Ghana.

Awoonor, Kofi. 1974. *Guardians of the Sacred Word: Ewe Poetry*. New York: NOK Publishers.

_______. 2002. Foreword. In *PraiseSong for TheLand*. Kofi Anyidoho. Accra: Sub-Saharan Publishers.

_______. 2014. *The Promise of Hope*. Dakar: Amalion Publishing.

BBC News. 2019. 'The untapped potential of Africa's honeybees'. https://www.bbc.com/future/article/20190507-honey-bees-africas-untapped-resource, accessed 26 October 2020.

Deutsche Welle. 24 January 2020. DW News coverage on locust invasion in East Africa.https://www.dw.com/en/billions-of-locusts-swarm-over-east-africa/a-52138582, accessed 25 January 2020.

Glotfelty, Cheryll and Harold Fromm, eds. 1996. *The Ecocritical Reader: Landmarks in Literary Ecology*. Athens: University of Georgia Press.

Green, E. Sandra. 1981. 'Land, Lineage and Clan in Early Anlo'. *Africa: Journal of the International African Institute* 51.1: 451–464.

Greenpeace International 'Save the Bees' Campaign: http://sos-bees.org, accessed 25 January 2020.

Greenpeace USA. https://www.greenpeace.org/usa/sustainable-agriculture/save-the-bees/, accessed 25 January 2020.

Huggan, Graham and Helen Tiffin. 2010. *Postcolonial Ecocriticism: Literature, Animal, Environment*. New York: Routledge.

Iheka, Cajetan. 2018. *Naturalising Africa: Ecological Violence, Agency, and Postcolonial Resistance in African Literature*. Cambridge: Cambridge University Press.

Insoll, Timothy. 2011. 'Animism and totemism'. In *Oxford Handbook of the Archaeology of Ritual and Religion*. New York: Oxford University Press. 1004–16.

Manes, Christopher. 1996. 'Nature and Silence'. In *The Ecocriticism Reader: Landmarks in Literary Ecology*. Cheryll Glotfelty and Harold Fromm, eds. Athens. University of Georgia Press. 15–29.

Neal, Arthur G. 1985. 'Animism and Totemism in Popular Culture'. *Journal of Popular Culture*. 19.2: 15–23.

Okunoye, Oyeniyi. 2005. '"We too Sing": Kofi Anyidoho and Ewe Poetic Traditions in Elegy For the Revolution'. *Journal of Commonwealth Literature*. 40.1: 91–111.

Ritvo, Harriet. 2007. 'On the animal turn'. *Daedalus*. 136.4: 118–122.

Soper, Kate. 2005. 'The Beast in Literature: Some Initial Thoughts'. *Comparative Critical Studies*. 2.3: 303–9.

Woodward, Wendy. 2008. *The Animal Gaze: Animal Subjectivities in Southern African Narratives*. Johannesburg: Wits University Press,.

World's Top Exports. 30 December 2019. http://www.worldstopexports.com/natural-honey-exporters/, accessed 21 September 2019.

Reading for Background:

SUYI DAVIES OKUNGBOWA'S *DAVID MOGO, GODHUNTER* AND 'THE END OF THE WORLD AS WE KNOW IT'[1]

LOUISE GREEN

> Some speculative fiction may be unconcerned with realism, but mine sure as heck is deeply concerned with it. (Okorafor 2015, 25)

> Afrofuturism, then, is concerned with the possibilities within the dimension of the predictive, the projected, the proleptic, the envisioned, the virtual, the anticipatory and the future conditional. (Eshun 2003, 293)

Nnedi Okorafor makes the comment quoted above in her keynote address to the 35th International Conference on the Fantastic in the Arts in 2014. In the address, 'Writing Rage, Truth and Consequence', she describes the curious concatenation of events that resulted in her receiving word that she had won the World Fantasy Award for Best Novel for *Who Fears Death* while visiting a student in prison. Or rather not receiving word since during the actual visit no mobile phones were permitted. Her despair at seeing the prison filled with young black men, her sadness for her student, her elation at receiving acknowledgement of her work, her 'residual claustrophobia' (Okorafor 2015, 23) become examples of the contradictory forces acting on her as a writer by virtue of her unavoidable location in a specific time and place, within the USA in the second decade of the twenty-first century. She uses this detail to emphasize the fact that for her writing fantasy is not about escaping from the real. Rather, any form of imagining the future is always a response to the world as it is at the moment of writing. Fantasy permits contradictory and diverse elements from the present to be organized into a 'proleptic' realism, one which anticipates not simply future events but also the surface density of imagined future everyday experiences. In the era of the Anthropocene, the future has become the focus of a diffuse but pervasive global anxiety. As the unpredictable and damaging side effects of modernity proliferate and environmental transformation becomes more and more evident, the future becomes not only radically volatile but also a contested site in global world politics. In this context, fiction becomes an important form for exploring the implications of the present from the perspective of the future not in the abstract as a set of predicted 'scenarios' but rather through intimate attention to detail.

African literature's contribution to this exploration of the implications of environmental transformation is, however, often overlooked. In his book, *Different Shades of Green* (2014), Byron Caminero-Santangelo suggests that understanding African literature's response to environmental crisis requires thinking beyond the limitations of Western conceptions of the environment. His selection of texts and his careful readings of them in relation to environmental activist movements are designed to show the imbrication of the environment in particular social and political histories. He explores the various powerful counternarratives offered by literary fiction to dominant assumptions about Africa and African environments. Similarly, Cajetan Iheka reveals that within a substantial body of African literary works, the environment does not appear as a static 'backdrop' (Iheka 2019, 22). Instead, as his nuanced readings reveal, the environment and nonhuman and supernatural entities appear to demand recognition of the unavoidable interconnectivity between protagonists and setting. In this paper, I, too, suggest that it is important to dwell on what is often overlooked. I suggest that responses to environmental transformation can be found not only in direct references to environmental damage, destructive industrial processes and climate change but also in more indirect ways through a focus on this 'backdrop' – the environment that often forms part of the overlooked conditions of possibility of the action of the novel.

This paper proposes a method of reading fiction that focuses not on plot and characters but rather on the backdrop or background. Through the work of description, the piling up of what Roland Barthes call 'insignificant notation', a 'reality effect' is constituted that can itself be read as a critical reflection on environmental transformation. Suyi Davies Okungbowa's debut novel, *David Mogo, Godhunter* (2019), is a work of speculative fiction set in Lagos. African speculative fiction emerges in the twenty-first century as a distinct and recognizable category with the work of novelists and filmmakers such as Nnedi Okorafor, Lauren Beukes, Dilman Dila and Wanuri Kahiu. As Jane Bryce notes, texts by these authors draw on a long tradition within Africa of 'speculative storytelling' that is oriented towards the future (Bryce 2019, 3). Like many of these writers and film makers before him, Okungbowa draws on speculative narrative strategies to represent a postcrisis world. Yet the crisis the novel describes is not the result of nuclear fallout or the effects of climate change. Instead the source of the disaster is more enigmatic – a group of gods displaced by internal conflict who have fallen to earth. While the plot of the novel focuses on the battle of the protagonist, David Mogo, with the pantheons of fallen gods who have laid the city to waste, it is the description of background that intrigues me, Okungbowa's careful inventory of what has been lost in the crisis.[2] Across the three sections into which the novel is divided, 'Godhunter', 'Firebringer' and 'Warmonger', the scale of the destruction escalates. While the foreground of this novel is itself intriguing, my intention in this paper is to read its background and to read it allegorically as a critical reflection on current anxieties about 'the end of the world as we know it' (Okungbowa 2019, 249).

This mode of approaching texts by reading the background was provoked both by the urgent claims of climate change which threatens to effect major environmental transformation, but also by certain popular responses to climate change which make universalist claims about the importance of transforming humanity's relations with the natural world.[3] Confronted by the scale of the problem of climate change, which appears to exceed all previous human scales, such writers turn a historical reality into a philosophical or existential problem. And it is a philosophical problem of a particular kind, one which invites a turn to introspection. Instead of these large and by now somewhat repetitive gestures I want to suggest the importance of the minute detail and the particular work of description.

For Amitav Ghosh, the novel as a form is ill-suited to registering the instability and unpredictability that is introduced by climate change precisely because of its investment in a particular kind of descriptive detail. The narrative conventions associated with realism emerged during the nineteenth century, which was, he asserts, 'a time when it was assumed, in both fiction and geology, that Nature was moderate and orderly: this was the distinctive mark of the new "modern" worldview' (Ghosh 2016, 22).[4] A period of unusually stable climactic conditions, the nineteenth century, thus provided the necessary conditions to support the illusion of nature as a stable background for human drama. Geological theories that claimed the pace of change in natural systems was slow and cumulative appeared more 'rational' and modern than those proposing change as the result of sudden, catastrophic events.

Usually the background in a novel is established through description of many insignificant but recognizable details of the real world. In the essay 'The Reality Effect' published in 1968, Barthes discusses the particular function of description in the nineteenth-century realist novel. After drawing attention to the puzzling inclusion in such novels of many insignificant details which are not in any way relevant to the plot, he concludes that their function is to produce a 'reality effect', to demonstrate that the action takes place in the real world. This work of description, Barthes proposes, is constrained both by the actual dimensions of reality itself but also by aesthetic considerations, by previous genres of description. Part of the pleasure of reading a novel is that we recognize the world that is being represented to us either from our own experience or from previous descriptions in realist genres which now might include not only fiction but also television, film, the news and the various new genres finding publication on the internet such as blogs and social media entries. When a writer describes a landscape, a street, a house, a shop, a highway, a mall, a house, a cell phone, a laptop, we are already familiar with these things. They confirm that whatever takes place in the novel is taking place in a world which is commensurable with that of the reader, even if it does not directly resemble it.

Description gives weight to the narrative through anchoring it in the material world. In his discussion of the emergence and disappearance of the figure of the bourgeois, Franco Moretti suggests that detailed description in the nineteenth-century realist novel functions to reassure the reader about the stability and order of the world. These descriptions, which he calls 'fillers' because they do not make a significant contribution to the plot, '*rationalize the novelistic universe*, turning it into a world of few surprises, fewer adventures, and no miracles at all' (Moretti 2014, 82). This is not simply because these novels document an orderly and rational world, but also because 'the logic of rationalization pervades *the very rhythm of the novel*' (82). The pleasure of reading lies in the way the small details of the everyday are narrativized. He draws a parallel between the practice of double entry bookkeeping and the realist novel, suggesting that both operate as forms of accounting which impose a rational control on the potentially disorderly world of things.

In the early twenty-first century, Ghosh suggests, 'there is no place where the orderly expectations of bourgeois life hold unchallenged sway' and the kinds of climactic events that mark the current moment 'are not easily accommodated in the deliberately prosaic world of serious prose fiction' (26). In fact, such dramatic events represented in serious fiction tend to be seen as implausible, evidence of questionable authorial intervention which belongs more properly in the fantastic world of science fiction. In this paper I turn to a work of speculative fiction, yet it is one which continues to invest considerable energy in realist description.

As a genre characterized by encounters with difference, speculative fiction frequently makes use of a form of realism to document the unfamiliar world that the narrative constructs. In the interests of building a credible and plausible world, it deploys the register of scientific objectivity. The ambitious task of mapping an alternative world requires an anthropological realism that can offer an authoritative account encompassing description but also explanation and elucidation. Yet the world described, because it is not anchored in mimetic realism, remains radically open to transformation. In speculative fiction, details about the world are often both familiar and strange, referencing a recognizable reality while at the same time describing an environment fundamentally transformed often by catastrophic events. Although *David Mogo, Godhunter*, is a work of speculative fiction, I would argue that the conventions of realism it draws upon are closer to those of nineteenth-century fiction. Okungbowa deliberately generates a 'reality effect' through the accumulation of small details of the everyday. Yet in this case realist detail is deployed not as a form of reassurance but rather as a painstaking documentation of imagined future decay and dissolution. In doing this, the novel effectively gives shape to the inchoate anxiety about what might emerge after 'the end of the world as we know it'. A form of predictive realism, it extrapolates from elements in the present, to give material weight to a radically uncertain future reality.

As a strategy, reading for background suggests an alternative way of approaching description, not as indicating reality in the abstract but as indicating a particular kind of reality. Instead of seeing these many details that generate the reality effect as simply 'fillers', I suggest it might be possible to engage in an allegorical reading of them following the logic of synecdoche. Synecdoche is the term for figures of speech which register the movement between the part and the whole, the specific and the general, the material and the thing itself. Synecdoche offers a figure for describing the immensely complex feedback loops that link concrete instantiations to abstract systems and individual actions to generalized effects. It invites us to consider how the absence of one part from the whole might create not simply a partial lack but rather a disorganization of all the remaining parts in which a new state might be generated that would have been impossible to foresee in the old. The many material things that find their way into the novel by way of detailed description can thus be read as themselves parts which gesture beyond themselves and act as linkages between specific actions and particular kinds of wholes.[5]

Despite the fact that Okungbowa's *David Mogo, Godhunter* is clearly not making a claim to realism, description plays an important part in the narrative. The unreality of the novel, already indicated in the title, is underlined in the third sentence of the novel, which signals with the introduction of an unfamiliar yet intelligible word that the world the character inhabits does not precisely resemble the current one. The word is 'godessence' and it refers to something David Mogo, a demigod or *orisha'daji*, is able to sense when he approaches a god or wizard, as an 'icy heat' on his collarbone. Yet while the world of fallen gods and godhunters doing battle situates the novel clearly within the genre of speculative fiction, Okungbowa pays significant attention to generating a 'reality effect' through the use of detailed realist description. The following extract takes place near the start of the novel on David Mogo's visit to a client wishing to employ his services:

> Let's start with how my new client remains the Baálè of the long-abandoned Agbado community, retaining the palace right past the slum's railway crossing. From the outside looking in, you'd never picture such a sophisticated interior. I am seated in a soft couch under ceiling lights. Ceiling lights oh, not hanging bulbs. D'you know when last anyone was able to get ordinary power in Lagos? Papa Udi and I haven't seen a blink of power in our house since The Falling over a decade ago. We run a 650VA Yamaha generator for three hours every day; just enough to charge our phones and watch the evening news. (7)

Throughout the novel Okungbowa names the specific areas of Lagos in which the action is taking place – 'Agbado', Ìsàlẹ̀ Èkó, the Oshodi Interchange – mapping the imagined city onto the real city through the use of proper names. These proper names give the weight of material location to the narrative's more fantastical elements – anchoring the action by attaching it to a set of verifiable co-ordinates in Lagos. These topographic details offer the city as a concrete extratextual reality, not only in which the action takes place but also on which the destruction of the catastrophic event can be enacted. Okungbowa's version of Lagos is both familiar and unfamiliar: itself and a ghostly, destroyed remnant of itself.

The conversational tone of the first-person narrator generates an intimate relationship with the reader, inviting them to confirm the experience of a shared reality – one in which access to electricity in Lagos is uncertain and inhabitants have to make do with portable generators to charge their electronic devices. In the future reality of the novel, this precarious attachment to the energy that is the invisible prerequisite for modern electronic commodities and the lifestyle associated with them has become more extreme, no longer available at all except to the very rich. This descriptive detail, irrelevant to the plot of the novel, subtly reminds the reader not only of the irony of the fact that 'a petrostate like Nigeria is often plagued by fuel shortages' (Wenzel 2017, 7) but also that 'even in this era of hydrocarbon modernity, too many people have too little access to energy, and the exorbitant consumption of a relative few will shape the future for millennia to come' (7). Jennifer Wenzel (and others) use the terms 'hydrocarbon modernity' or 'petromodernity' to draw attention to the fact that modernity as a mode of living emerges as the result of the energy released by the rapid consumption of stored fossil fuels. Britain's industrialization was made possible by the replacement of wood as an energy source with coal, which allowed it to run as if it had eight more islands of equivalent size to exploit. With the transition to oil, this 'harvesting of compressed time' (8) became even more extreme. Wenzel includes Timothy Mitchell's remarkable ratio that 'a single litre of petrol used today needed about twenty-five metric tons of ancient marine life as a precursor material' (Mitchell quoted in Wenzel, 7). Okungbowa's novel does not make any overt reference to the environmental impact of 'hydrocarbon modernity' or 'petromodernity' and the consequences of burning fossil fuels to power unsustainable lifestyles in countries far away from the points of extraction. Instead he describes the absence of energy and the practices of everyday life that emerge after the end of a national power grid. Such a catastrophic future – 'the end of the world as we know it' as petromodern subjects – already exists albeit intermittently, the novel seems to be suggesting, in the Lagos of the present.[6]

The novel offers a detailed description of a Lagos marked by the ghostly traces of a destroyed consumer culture – empty malls, abandoned businesses, broken signs, peeling advertisements: 'A Pep shop is half-secured by a mucky chain, as if the owners decided last-minute their goods weren't worth it. A chubby sewage rat perches on the chain and doesn't move, even when I pass by, too busy munching on its own business' (Okungbowa 2019, 29–30).

The novel registers an ambivalent attitude towards modernity manifested as a set of global practices associated with consumption. Okungbowa's description of an abandoned 'Pep shop', can be read allegorically to refer beyond this particular shop to the chain, Pep

Stores, one of the retail outlets of the South African retail company Pepkor. Pepkor was started in South Africa in 1965 but has since expanded into twelve African countries including Nigeria. A purveyor of relatively cheap clothing, furniture, cell phones and financial loans, Pepkor forms part of the international organization of the world around particular forms of consumption. In its 2018 Integrated Report, Pepkor makes explicit the way in which consumption is conceptualized not simply as a financial transaction but as a social mission. The report includes the claim that 'Pepkor's values and culture are centred on the unwavering goal of improving the lives of our customers, who mostly find themselves in very challenging circumstances. We strive to make their lives easier and better' (Pepkor 2018, 4). Although this appears to be a laudable aim, the underlying assumption of the report is that a better life is one surrounded by the goods and services Pep can provide. In describing the company's operations in African countries, the report explains that 'The business continues to make it possible for its customers and their families, with a very limited budget, to live with dignity and pride' (Pepkor 2018, 36). Despite challenging circumstances (Pepkor is partly owned by Steinhoff, a company whose executives were found in 2017, to have committed a massive accounting fraud that took the form of an entirely fictional form of double entry bookkeeping) the Integrated Report is able to present profits and expansion alongside social mission and social responsibility to produce an upbeat account of its year.

The Pep shop has no particular relevance to the plot of the novel but through a practice of reading for background, it is released from its role as insignificant detail to act as a fragment from the narrative of development. The Pep shop can be read allegorically, then, as referring not only to Pepkor and its operations but also more generally to the processes of globalization which allow companies to define the parameters of a life 'lived with dignity and pride'. Drawing on a narrative of 'needs', Pepkor constitutes its customers in terms of lack.[7] The company can then enfold its own pursuit of profit within a benevolent commitment to fulfilling this lack. Through acquiring manufactured commodities, Pepkor's customers can become worthwhile individuals, integrated into modern modes of living. In the novel, Okungbowa encodes within his description a particular orientation towards the shop and all that it stands for. The Pep shop is only 'half secured' as if 'the owners decided last minute their goods weren't worth it'. The narrator's detached gaze registers the shop's irrelevance in the context of the postcrisis condition, in which modern consumer society has been swept aside along with the strange values that made consumer goods necessary to pride and dignity. He does this not directly through making a social judgement but indirectly through reading the details in the landscape – seeing in the half-secured chain evidence of doubt as the regime of value sustaining the goods' worth crumbles away. The confident and satisfied rat perched on the chain adds an additional mocking judgement on the aspiration of the commodity to transform the consumer into someone valuable. In the realist novels of the nineteenth century, the material objects described gave the narrative a sense of stability. But the commodity which emerges in the second half of the twentieth century in the era of mass production and accelerated consumption is a much more ephemeral object. While commodities often are material objects, their place in everyday life is much more fleeting. Goods change from commodities to waste, only briefly entering a phase of use in between. If the real cause of climate change is not primarily the result of our relations with the natural world but rather our relationship with those strange objects of modernity – commodities whose production, distribution, and ultimate disposal are accelerating the disruption of earth's systems – the novel's description of the failed, destroyed landscape of consumption draws attention not to the effects of climate change but rather to its disavowed cause. Through a radical estrangement of these familiar spaces, the habitual actions and modes of assigning value are undercut not only by the actual destruction (which might, after all, be repaired) but also by the novel's constant reminder of the precariousness of the future.

The use of a first person present tense narration is itself indictive of precariousness, as if the current moment, the moment of narration which is also the moment of the action, is all that remains. Nothing is safely in the past; there is no time for retrospection. But there is also no faith in the future as a position from which the present might be narrated. This breathless immediacy is appropriate for describing the condition which I have described elsewhere as 'living in the subjunctive'. The subjunctive is a grammatical form which codes hesitation and uncertainty. Although in the twenty-first century there is widespread recognition of the damaging effects of human activities on the environment in broad terms, what remains difficult to conceptualize is how everyday life might be altered to avoid specifically damaging actions. As a result, the future remains radically contingent on crucial but undefined actions in the present.[8] Those actions that might be effective, such as stopping international air travel and preventing the shipping of inessential commodities around the world, appear too radical to contemplate. Yet this is precisely the world that the novel depicts as if it has taken place, not as a rational response to out of control carbon emissions, but as a side effect of the ineluctable violence of displaced gods.

Reading speculative fiction allegorically is not a new approach.[9] The often-mythic register of such novels invites speculation about a deeper secondary meaning which might be mapped onto the action of events. Often however, these allegorical readings focus on the foreground. What I am proposing here though is a different sort of allegorical reading, one which focuses on the background. As I hope to have shown, such readings find in the insignificant details of the setting crucial responses to environmental transformation. The allegory of the background does not offer a coherent narrative, but rather presents fragments which link the novel to a specific history. The end of the world as we know it in the novel is not the spectacular devastation of nuclear fallout or total environmental collapse. Instead it is these eerie haunted empty spaces of consumption once humans are no longer there to animate these spaces and commodities with their narratives of desire. The narrator does not celebrate this destruction. Instead he faces it with a certain mostly dispassionate level-headedness. Only towards the end of the novel, as the destruction mounts, does he acknowledges the pain of loss associated with the devastation of the city: 'For the first time in years, I almost shed tears once I step out of the airport and see the bare, charred wasteland of Lagos' (Okungbowa 2019, 273). Yet while the protagonist mourns the loss of the city, the background continues to draw attention to the absurdity of the particular habits of living of the consumer present and the differential and unequal ways in which different people inhabit those spaces.

The last section of *David Mogo, Godhunter*, 'Warmonger', begins with the narrator describing his attachment to the overhead baggage compartment of an airplane. Driven out of the Oshodi Interchange market, David Mogo and a group of others resisting the gods have found temporary refuge at the abandoned airport. Avoiding facing up to his own role in what is to come, David Mogo retreats to the comfortably dark space of the baggage compartment. 'It is,' he notes, 'a big one, a massive international carrier. It's my first time in a plane, which is sad, considering it's abandoned, left to rust in the Murtala Muhammed International airport in Ikeja, Lagos. I found it parked in one of the abandoned hangars in the abandoned airport in the technically abandoned Lagos' (Okungbowa 2019, 241–2). I want to end with this curious image of David Mogo taking up a space previously devoted to the baggage of international travellers. Although the crisis appears to be localized, the novel avoids any mention of the world beyond Lagos. In this postcrisis world, the rest of the world recedes from the narrative and there appears to be nothing outside this destroyed consumer landscape. The airplanes are reduced from being iconic fragments of globalization to being no more than material detritus, rusting metal objects. Yet by occupying this space in a way that it is not supposed to be occupied, the narrator seems to be suggesting with a sort of dark humour the possibility of finding innovative ways of inhabiting the destruction left behind by modernity. Reading for background makes it possible to read speculative fiction as deploying realism in an allegorical register, in a way that disaggregates the everyday into fragments which can be picked up, turned over and examined. Dislodged from their familiar place as 'insignificant details', these realist fragments become parts that can be recombined to imagine new and potentially less destructive futures.

NOTES

1 The phrase 'the end of the world as we know it' is quoted here from *David Mogo, Godhunter* (Okungbowa 2019, 249).

2 There are a number of ways in which the novel can be read in terms of Cajetan Iheka's 'aesthetics of proximity'. Most obviously is the way in which 'nonhuman life-forms – material and supernatural' enter the narrative in the form of wizards, gods and in the case of the main protagonist, a half-god (Iheka 2019, 25). Although at the start of the novel David Mogo is a god hunter, as the narrative progresses the clear distinction between categories become blurred as humans and gods from different pantheons form alliances in the battles to take possession of Lagos. In this paper, however, I resist the intriguing plot of the novel to focus instead on the way it describes the setting.

3 Environmentalist Bill McKibben is one of the earliest to make this call in his book *The End of Nature* (1990) but it remains an important part of at least some strands of ecocriticism. Timothy Clark, in the introduction to *The Cambridge Introduction to Literature and the Environment,* notes that: 'The moral impetus behind ecocriticism … necessarily commits it to take some kind of stance, however implicit, on the huge issue of what relationship human beings should have to the natural world' (Clark 2011, 5).

4 Ghosh (2016, 20–2) describes the success of the theory of gradualism over the alternative theory of catastrophism as a method for understanding geological time as part of this investment of a conception of nature as 'moderate and orderly' (22).

5 'Following the logic of the synecdochic figure allows movement back and forth between the part and the whole, the specific and the general and the material and the thing itself. Through this operation of substitution, which works both ways, the form permits the most abstract ideas to be anchored in historical particularity' (Green 2020, 6–7).

6 Rem Koolhaas had made a similar claim about Lagos twenty years earlier, although for different reasons, seeing it as a model urban form of the future. Esthie Hugo notes that it was Lagos' chaotic, provisional, innovative quality 'that first drew Koolhaas' attention, leading him to famously declare that "Lagos is not catching up with us [the global north]. Rather we may be catching up with Lagos" (2001, 652). This African urban centre is compelling to think with, then, because of the particular temporal vision that it performs by way of its futuristic present' (Hugo 2017, 47).

7 See Ivan Illich's discussion of the emergence of 'needs' in the discourse of development, which constituted anyone not living according to the standards set by consumer society as living in a state of lack **(Illich 1992).**

8 '"Mood" as a grammatical form indicates the orientation of the speaker towards the subject. The subjunctive is the mood indicated in conditions of uncertainty. Within the form of the verb it codes hesitation, doubt, vagueness, insecurity and indecision' (Green 2020, 54).

9 See, for instance, the many readings of Okorafor's *Lagoon* which, although they do not define themselves overtly as allegorical readings, explore the potential of the mythical/alien creatures in the narrative to signify beyond themselves, whether to capture the uncanny of the Anthropocene itself (Hugo) or as figures through which to imagine 'new forms of postcolonial, feminist science' (Jue 2017, 184).

10 Kirk Sides' article on Wanuri Kahiu's short film *Pumzi* also offers an allegorical reading of the foreground, suggesting that it proposes a new form of storytelling, and offers an example of the way in which indigenous cultural forms might interrupt the 'hero' narrative so popular in Western culture. Although his analysis includes some reference to the setting, this setting only becomes meaningful in relation to developments in the narrative trajectory of the film (Sides 2019).

WORKS CITED

Barthes, Roland. 1986. 'The Reality Effect.' In *The Rustle of Language*. Roland Barthes. Oxford: Blackwell Press.

Bryce, Jane. 2019. 'African Futurism: Speculative Fictions and "Rewriting the Great Book"'. *Research in African Literatures* 50 (1–19) doi: 10.2979/reseafrilite.50.1.01.

Caminero-Santangelo, Byron. 2014. *Different Shades of Green: African Literature, Environmental Justice, and Political Ecology.* Charlottesville: Univerisity of Virginia Press.

Clark, Timothy. 2011. *The Cambridge Introduction to Literature and the Environment.* Cambridge: Cambridge Univeristy Press.

Eshun, Kodwo. 2003. 'Further Considerations on Afrofuturism'. *CR: The New Centennial Review* 3. 2: 287–302.

Ghosh, Amitav. 2016. *The Great Derangement.* Chicago: Chicago University Press.

Green, Louise. 2020. *Fragments from the History of Loss: The Nature Industry and the Postcolony.* State College: Pennsylvannia State University Press.

Hugo, Esthie. 2017. 'Looking Forward, Looking Back: Animating Magic, Modernity and the African City-Future in Nnedi Okorafor's *Lagoon*'. *Social Dynamics* 43.1: 46–58.

Iheka, Cajetan. 2019. *Naturalizing Africa: Ecological Violence, Agency, and Postcolonial Resistance in African Literature.* Cambridge: Cambridge University Press.

Illich, Ivan. 1992. 'Needs'. In *The Development Dictionary*. Wolfgang Sachs. London: Zed, 88–101.

Jue, Melanie. 2017. 'Intimate Objectivity: On Nnedi Okorafor's Oceanic Afrofuturism'. *Woman Studies Quarterly* 45.1&2: 171–88.

McKibben, Bill. 1990. *The End of Nature*. New York: Anchor Books/Doubleday.

Moretti, Franco. 2014. *The Bourgeois: Between History and Literature*. London: Verso.

Okorafor, Nnedi. 2015. 'Writing Rage, Truth and Consequence'. *Journal of the Fantastic in the Arts* 26.1: 21–6.

Okungbowa, Suyi Davies. 2019. *David Mogo, Godhunter.* Oxford: Abaddon Books.

Pepkor. 2018. 'Integrated Report 2018'. *Pepkor Holdings Limited.* https://www.pepkor.co.za/wp-content/uploads/2019/05/Pepkor-integrated-report-2018.pdf, accessed 28 October 2019.

Sides, Kirk. 2019. 'Seed Bags and Storytelling: Modes of Living and Writing After the End in Wanuri Kahiu's *Pumzi*'. *Critical Philosophy of Race* 7.1: 107–23. https://doi.org/10.5325/critphilrace.7.1.0107

Wenzel, Jennifer. 2017. 'Introduction'. In *Fuelling Cultures: 101 Words for Energy and Environment*. Imre Szeman, Jennifer Wenzel and Patricia Yaeger. New York: Fordham Univeristy Press, 1–16.

Poetics of Landscape:

REPRESENTATION OF LAGOS AS A 'MODERNIZING' CITY IN NIGERIAN POETRY

SULE EMMANUEL EGYA

INTRODUCTION

Lagos, as a modern city, has remained significant in the real and in the imaginary. It is perhaps the most commercially and culturally strategic city in Nigeria. It is home to the headquarters of many industries, the largest international airport in Nigeria, many electronic and print media houses, and, above all, Nigeria's biggest coastal gateway for importation and exportation. Until the early 1990s, when the seat of federal government moved to Abuja, it was Nigeria's political capital city. Besides housing the National Theatre complex, the city is known for its literary and book festivals, literary and cultural organizations and events, and indigenous publishers. In the imaginary, Lagos is the most thematised city in the Nigerian literary imagination, its character framed in diverse tenors as a city of life, of chaos, of survival, one that best exemplifies Nigerian modern life. In this essay, I am interested in how Lagos as a modern city is framed in Nigerian poetry. How do poets, one might ask, in their formation of literary alterity, contemplate the many attributes of Lagos, some of which are its disorderliness, environmental pollution, and displacement? My question is ecocritical, as my emphasis is on how the city, its landscape, and modern pressures on its environment influence the habits of its inhabitants, and how it is, in turn, influenced by their habits. Modern pressures refer to negative fallouts of urban development after colonialism. In its drive to be modern in the European sense, the city becomes vulnerable to urban political realities that shape its landscape. Nigerian poets have been keen in representing these realities – and most of the poets are anthologized in *Lagos of the Poets*, edited by Odia Ofeimun, a poet known for his passion for the city of Lagos. Ofeimun brings together previously published poems from collections, his main aim being to present Lagos as imagined by poets across Nigeria. The diversity of the poems is such that the anthology, in the words of the editor, 'seeks to provide a broad mirror of the city' (xlv). With a theoretical framework based on ideas from postcolonial ecocriticism and urban political ecology, this study reads selected poems from the anthology. I focus on the poems that foreground the city's environmental problems, and their consequences for Nigeria as a postcolony, my main objective being to foreground the ecological force of Nigerian poetry, namely the imaginative creation of alterity as a way of redeeming the city's ecological crisis.

LAGOS AS A POSTCOLONIAL CITY AND THE POETICS OF ECOLOGY

The smallest in terms of land mass in Nigeria, Lagos is the most populous city. It has 'a total land area of 3577.28 km2, of which 22% or 787 km2 consists of lagoon and creeks' (Olanrewaju et al. 2). With about twenty million inhabitants, the city is by all standards overpopulated. This is the result of rural–urban and urban–urban migration, as people from different parts of Nigeria consider Lagos the most urban city, which can offer them the most modern facilities. The general thinking is that going to live in Lagos is one way of becoming modern. But Lagos is also one of the most disorganized cities in Africa, its entropic energies harnessed by many Nigerian writers to comment on the ambivalence of Nigerian modernity – ambivalence marked by the presence of modern facilities and the absence of the orderliness that such facilities should enable (Dunton 68–78). Whether modernization implies orderliness or not, the best way to understand this ambivalence is to approach the city as a postcolonial centre. Since colonial time, the city has struggled under the pressures of colonial and neocolonial forces. It has been turned into a port for carting away human and material sources, for bringing in foreign materials and civilizations. It has laboured under heavy commercialism. The presence of heavy industrial machineries, the movement of heavy trucks, and the constant inflow of people to satisfy the labour demand of these (mostly foreign) industries, among others, are not matched with commensurate infrastructure, a situation that brings about entropy, the type that Nigerian poets have thematized in relation to their aestheticization of the city. The city, like most postcolonial spaces, is exploited by forces of capitalism, left to suffer local and global environmental problems. Byron Caminero-Santangelo and Garth A. Myers explain this phenomenon by saying

> Global environmental problems [...] have already deeply affected many Africans. Yet most Africans are not the primary sources of these problems, nor do many Africans generally benefit from the resource exploitation that engenders them. More localized problems too are often shaped by global factors that are difficult for many Africans to address, in particular

> the shaping of local political, cultural, and economic conditions by the legacies of colonialism and (neo)imperial capital. (9)

The city's drive to maintain its colonial legacies, to remain the capital of commerce, has put it under undue pressures, with environmental consequences that are, to say the least, devastating. For instance, the city experiences floods, some of them fatal, every year. They are mainly flash floods that are caused by lack of proper drainage, by lack of town planning that ought to clear buildings and structures out of waterways. Floods and other similar environmental hazards are also caused by the drive to be modern in line with the dictates of colonial authorities. The city's desire to expand, in the sense of a megacity, has resulted in 'unapproved development of marginal land, massive reclamation of swampy areas (for industrial operational bases and high class residential developments without adequate provision of drainage)' (Oyinloye et al. 58).

In spite of its failings as a modern city, Lagos has sustained what one might see as an imaginary of Western modernization, one that attracts those who have not visited it, and produces, at best, mixed feelings in those who have visited it, as we will see in the poems. Ofeimun, in his lengthy preface to *Lagos of the Poets*, harps on this imaginary, intimating how in his own case he 'was literally overcome and arrested by our city [Lagos] by the lagoon' (xix). He elaborates on it:

> You may be Edo, Ijebu, Kanuri, Igbo, Efik, Fulani or ara oke Yoruba. After Lagos has taken you over, you are genuinely different from other Edo, Ijebu, Kanuri, Igbo, Efik, Fulani or ara oke Yoruba. [...] Lagos broadens your sympathies. Quintessentially urban, she provides just that modicum of anonymity to enable every stranger [*sic*] function as indigene and every indigene labour as stranger. [...] Lagos is voluptuous in asserting a sense of being a centre, not so much of excellence, as the city-logo posits, but a drive, a never failing capacity to absorb and to remake whatever it takes into her own. (xxiii)

Ofeimun writes of the city as one that is not innocent, overwhelmed as it is under the pressures to be an excellent example of a modern city (its logo is 'centre of excellence'). Fascination with the city is born of the ambivalence earlier mentioned. On the one hand, Lagos, as Ofeimun says, has the 'capacity to absorb and remake' its inhabitants, indigene or settlers, through its gestures of modernity. On the other, it is '[b]ig, boisterous, chaotic, with busy-body propensities in full play' (xxii), a quality that undercuts its capacity to modernize its inhabitants, if we think of modernization 'as a global imposition of specifically Western social, economic, and political forms' (Cooper 113).

Poets are extremely concerned about the idea of place. Writing about this, M. Nourbese Philip (169–82) suggests an organic relation between poet, language, and place. A poet, she opines, has a primary relation with the word, the language of her art. But what is important to the poet in constructing her language is the place in which she is rooted, the place with which she is organically (read: that enables her poetic birthing) linked. For most of these poets, writing about Lagos (in which they live, or which they have constantly visited) is a way of fashioning their poetic subjectivity. With regard to the environment, the poems discussed in this work are testaments to the idea that '[an] understanding of local surroundings permits many people to gain awareness of the ecosystem services upon which their lives depend' (Paul and Anne Ehrlich 325).

Lagos of the Poets demonstrates that Anglophone Nigerian poetry has been keen about the character of postcolonial urbanization, even though there has been no matching critical attention in this regard. There is a sense in which, as Nik Heynen et al. point out, 'most of environmental theory has unjustifiably largely ignored the urbanization process as both one of the driving forces behind many environmental issues and as the place where socio-environmental problems are experienced most acutely' (2). The urbanization process these poems are concerned with is undergirded by power relations in which the ordinary people, the main inhabitants of the city, are implicated. For these poets, therefore, the way to write about Lagos is to foreground the plight of the victims of capitalism. They even go further to cast Lagos as itself the real victim, in that its inhabitants' desire for economic and industrial expansion, and the attendant population increase, is the very locus of its environmental shortcomings, some of which are severe shortages of facilities, overpopulation, different forms of pollution, flooding, etc.

Given this premise, urban political ecology becomes crucial for scaffolding an ecocritical reading of the poems. Urban political ecology, as Garth Myers points out, emphasizes 'the agency of the marginalized poor' (23). Heynen et al. give a detailed explanation of the political force of urban political ecology:

> The central message that emerges from urban political ecology is a decidedly political one. To the extent that cities are produced through socio-ecological processes, attention has to be paid to the political processes through which particular socio-environmental urban conditions are made and remade. From a progressive or emancipatory position, then, urban political ecology asks questions about who produces what kind of socio-ecological configurations for whom. (2)

Unveiling the power relations at the base of the urbanization process in Lagos, with its negative consequences for the environment, is what the poetry under study has done. In other words, it is attentive to the 'socio-ecological processes' not as processes in themselves but as the results of the imperialist and capitalist ideologies at the heart of the (pseudo)modernity of Lagos.

With postcolonial ecocriticism, a greater attention is paid to the fate of the human and nonhuman in the face of the environmental crisis resulting from insufficient urban planning. Beyond such a focus, there is also the need to contextualize the intentionality of the poets within the frame of environmental justice. As Graham Huggan and Helen Tiffin (11–16) point out, the marriage of postcolonialism and ecocriticism strengthens the notion of advocacy and activism. I read the poems selected here with the aim of projecting what Hubert Zapf calls ecological force, which is the result of the activism injected into the aesthetics of imagining the city of Lagos. In Zapf's words,

> To describe [a] cultural work in terms of an ecological *force* is meant to imply that it is conceived as a dynamic, transformative aspect of discourse, which is not fully accounted for in merely conceptual or rhetorical terms but involves a form of energy, a vital movement of acting and reacting between signifiers, bodies, minds, selves, environments, chronotopes and, pervading them all, the fundamental interaction between culture and nature. (28)

My argument is that these poems, mainly artistic descriptions of what the city is, its failings and chaos, have in them an ecological force that imagines a Lagos that overcomes its environmental infirmities, because that is what a poem, as an artistic rendition, is capable of creating in our minds. In other words, even if they describe the environmental crises of the city, they have a transformative force, since poetizing the environment amounts to transforming it from the present state of crises to that of imaginary transcendence. This is possible because of the latitude poetry offers for alterity. This is what Roman Bartosch, following Derek Attridge, means when he argues that poetics, especially as regards environmental conditions, 'requires that we leave behind old ways of talking about nature and opt for the unknown and uncertain instead' (12); that is, the unlimited possibilities alterity offers.

THE CITY IN THE POEM

Each poet, it is important to reiterate, appears to have a personal feeling for Lagos. The poet is concerned with Lagos to the extent that the city as an imaginary offers her a poetic access point. From this point, the poet understands and assesses the city, especially with regard to its pretensions to Western modernization. The result is that the poet becomes critical of the city, of the powers that underline its urbanization process. And yet the poet, through poetic alterity, makes us imagine a city that eventually transcends its environmental conditions. This is possible because in negotiating its alterity the poem develops an ecological force by thematizing and historizing the city's clear ecological problems, on the one hand; and, on the other, by aesthetically signposting environmental redemption, beyond the depiction of the problems.

Ahmed Maiwada develops the metaphor of a woman in the poem 'Lagos Welcomes You'. But the woman – an 'Ex-sweetheart' (2) to the poet-persona, indicating his return to a loved city – is increasingly growing unkempt, coarse and neglected. The female-figured city waves her 'sweaty palms,/ Swarming you with salty smiles/ Of unwashed teeth' (2–4). The female body becomes the figurative context through which the poem delineates the city's environmental problems, its inattentiveness to waterways and proper waste disposals. The clogged arteries of the city is therefore captured by the constipation of the overfed, slovenly woman:

> Unsleeping, she will yawn,
> Unlocking the tons of un-chewed
> Garbage in her mouth, as her
> Constipated colons
> Rumble with stolen hopes. (10–14)

The woman does not have healthy habits, as she does not sleep, does not eat well, and as such is condemned to constipation. This metaphor, extended throughout the poem, points to the urbanization process of Lagos. One of the environmental problems the city continues to grapple with is the lack of adequate drainage and waste control, especially in the context of its astronomical population. The city therefore lacks an urban metabolism. The notion of urban metabolism and circulation has been developed by urban ecologists, as Erik Swyngedouw says, from the 'mid-nineteenth century [...] deeply connected with projects, visions, and practices of modernization, and with the associated "modern" transformation of the city' (22). It was imperative, as human society expanded at the onset of Western modernity, to develop concepts and practices that would enhance the healthy flow of matters. The human body, as viewed by medical epistemology, offered the metaphor for developing these concepts and practices. 'The health of the body,'

Swyngedouw writes, 'became the comparison against which the greatness of cities and states was to be measured. The "veins" and "arteries" of the new urban design were to be freed from all possible sources of blockage' (32). Maiwada's metaphorization of Lagos as a woman (even if problematic from a feminist perspective) plays into the urban ecology idea of metabolism: the city as a constipated woman is a reference to the city as being inadequate. Beyond the poem's depiction of a city condemned to blockage, it, on the one hand, indicts the city officials for being wilfully inattentive to a major environmental problem; and, on the other, creates in the reader's mind the environmental benefits of getting rid of 'un-chewed/Garbage' found even in the most crucial parts of the city, as the 'mouth' metaphor indicates.

Afam Akeh's poem 'Bodies' stretches the notion of urban metabolism to the point of considering the teeming human bodies as matters that clog the arteries of the city. A lengthy descriptive poem in five parts, the poem touches almost all aspects of lived-life in Lagos: social, economic, political, cultural, and religious. With engaging images, 'Bodies' stresses the anonymity that Lagos offers to people, the lure of commercialism, and the resilience of the masses to endure all indignities of life just to live in the city. The overwhelming flows of human bodies, their negative consequences on the city, is a critical point emphasized in the poem. The opening stanza is apt:

> In the morning, in the busy streets of Lagos,
> You can push through thickets of bodies
> And meet no one: only money speaks
> In its many muscled tongues. (1–4)

The city's force of modernity is captured above. The metaphors range from the materiality of the city ('thickets of bodies') to its financialization ('only money speaks'), all of which have ecological effects. The word 'muscle' is used in different metaphorical expressions to suggest the violence underscoring competitions and conflicts in human relations in a city whose greatest problem is overpopulation. The point is more poignantly made in this stanza:

> I see them in the streets, in all places
> They would rather not be,
> Doing what everyone else is doing
> And hating themselves, wondering
> Why the world is full of God
> And muscled lives trample smaller lives
> And the small lives dream always of muscles, muscles. (48–54)

Life in the city becomes the survival of the fittest. Driven by rapacity, or the desire to acquire the material things of modern life, the people compete with one another for jobs, for businesses, both legitimate and illegitimate.

Human bodies as pollution is also represented in Austyn Njoku's 'Flood Lagos'. Here flood is deployed metaphorically to describe the ceaseless flows of human beings, especially in the slum areas of the city. Evening in Oshodi is a time of 'fleshy flood flow' (2). Afternoon in Idumota is a time of 'Human rivulets roaming/ Through all the creeks/ In Lagos Island' (8–10). With humans flowing ceaselessly like inundating water in the city, the poem concludes that:

> These dark floods of heads
> Pouring through Orile, CMS
> Neglecting not Mile Two
> Mile Twelve, Ketu, Ojota
> Ikeja, Mushin, Oyingbo,
> These human flux flooding Lagos
> Leave a mystery yet unraveled. (16–22)

Depicting overpopulation in the form of flood, as this poem does, is aimed at emphasizing the deep implication this has for the environment. On the one hand, the poem sees the overflowing of humans as a natural disaster, the way a flood is perceived; on the other, the humans, just like floods, leave in their wake the consequences of their actitivities that are injurious to the environment. The ecological force of this poem, therefore, could be seen in the ways in which it ironically draws attention to the need for an appropriately populated urban space, such that human beings do not overcrowd the city, to the detriment of the nonhuman. The absence of the nonhumans in the above poems is problematic, and illustrates the growing concern that 'The rubric of environmental justice, under which most African ecocritical studies are conducted, tends to deemphasize the nonhuman implications of environmental tragedies' (Iheka 2).

The masses, their travails and aspirations form the core of Akeh's and Njoku's poems. The city is structured in such a way that some neighbourhoods, especially those mentioned in the stanza of Njoku's poem above, are ideologically designed to be overpopulated. However, to fully understand the plight of the masses in the city, one needs to unravel the power relations captured in J. P. Clark-Bekederemo's 'Victoria Island,' which highlights the class consciousness of the modernizing city. The poem intimates the existence of the powerful people who 'In the interest of the public/ [...] took over land/ a family owned before the country began' (1–3). This power to take possession of lands belonging to locals is a colonial practice whereby powerful people seize lands from the weak ones, especially as Victoria Island in Lagos is where the rich and powerful have settled since the colonial period. They are even economically powerful enough to reclaim the land 'from swamp and sea' (5), one of the practices that informs the gentrification of Lagos. Class conscious, and flaunting their riches, like the 'muscled lives' of Akeh's poem above, they 'parcelled out the land/ Among themselves, their mistresses, liars/ And sycophants' (7–9). Victoria Island is therefore turned into a luxury neighbourhood, unreachable by the masses, including the real owners of the land. This practice of making some places exclusive to the powerful few is largely a colonial legacy. Myers stresses this in his reading of African cities, saying that '[w]hile the colonial separation between ostentatious, ornamental, exotic white elite landscapes and the hard-scrabble urban agriculture of the poor African majority has lost much of its racial dimensions, class and cultural inequalities and fractures are easily read in the city's landscape architecture' (21). Writers have been keen to declaim the inequalities suffered by ordinary people in Lagos, especially issues of dispossession and displacement, which is the thematic thrust of Clark-Bekederemo's poem. The poem's ecological force is located in its politics of contrast – the juxtaposition of the rich and the poor – that seeks to create a new way of thinking about the opulence of Victoria Island, one that reveals the dispossession and displacement behind its modern structures.

Dispossession and displacement are also central to Nnimmo Bassey's 'Maroko', a poem that captures the real event of demolition in a slum called Maroko. Colonel Raji Rasaki, while a military administrator of Lagos State, ordered the destruction of the slum in 1991 to clear space for urban gentrification. Many Nigerian writers, across genres, have historicized this event (see Maik Nwosu's *Invisible Chapters* and Ofeimun's 'Demolition Day'). The poem refers to the slum as 'Rustic city of many smiles' (2), where the poor eke out a living, commute to upscale areas such as Victoria Island for drudgery, and yet find happiness in being in Lagos. The poem's use of 'city' for the slum is deliberate, since the slum people also have a sense of living in the most urban city in Nigeria. But their happiness is constantly short-lived, assailed as it is by threats of displacement. The demolition day eventually arrives:

> Your scream is nothing
> In the face of his excellency's fart
> Nothing:
> To the jarring clang of his iron teeth. (3–6)

The cruelty of the military administrator (notice 'his excellency' without the initial capitals) is seen through the bulldozer's iron teeth of destruction. The people are helpless. The structures that replace the slum are, in the framing of the poem, made up of 'Corruption's sand' (11). Like most poems on the incident, this one is concerned with the power relations underlining incidents of dispossession and displacement, the poet taking side with the 'Rustic city, home of the dispossessed' (19). The poem's strategy of taking this side emphasizes its aesthetic alterity in which the masses' fortitude is foregrounded. It is also the earth's fortitude, in that the constructions of 'Corruption's sand' is the modern way of turning the natural into the urban through anti-environmental gentrification.

In other words, the gentrification of Lagos has dire consequences for the environment, and invariably for the humans whose activities engender ecological catastrophe. In most cases, the poor suffer most, but there is no human that is not affected. This point is central to Clark-Bedekeremo's second poem on Victoria Island entitled 'Victoria Island Re-visited'. The poem reads:

> They say the sea is raging at the Bar
> Beach of Lagos, knocking at the doors
> Of homes built by contract finance
> On public land for a few to collect
> Millions. How has it harboured
> For so long this structure with a bottom
> So patently false and rotten
> It cannot but founder one day?
>
> Next they will be drawing upon
> The public purse to salvage the hulk.

A sequel to the earlier poem, this poem is an ironic way of pointing out the ecological consequences of erecting modern structures that everyone, including the rich and powerful living in Victoria Island, have to face. The poet-persona adopts a cynical manner of referring to the powerful ones with the pronoun 'they' – the Nigerian elite who find a niche in Victoria Island, but one that is ironically built on falsehood and rottenness (read: public corruption). Even as the upscale area is threatened by the rise in sea level, the rich and powerful (since most of them are past and present top government officials) use public money to take care of the situation. In other words, there is always money and modern technological infrastructure to deal with ecological crisis in upscale areas because of the people who live in such places. The sharp contrast to that is presented in Ogaga Ifowodo's 'Driftwood' as the poem centres on the effects of flooding on neighbourhoods inhabited by poor people, as well as on nonhumans. In this poem, the incident of flooding leaves humans and nonhumans afloat on the inundated water, dead, belly-up, so that 'corpses like driftwood,/ like slain dog on highway, live with us/ to mark the rotting of living flesh' (39–40). In Clark-Bekederemo's poem and that of Ifowodo, the real message is that humans, rich or poor, cannot escape the consequences of their anti-environmental actions – actions mostly undertaken by the powerful ones. Ifowodo's poem is sensitive to the nonhumans, projecting the suffering of 'Driftwood, dead hyacinth/or the emptied pack/of Benson & Hedges' (1–3), among others, in the wake of flooding. If Lagos is a modern city, this poem seems to argue, then it is one that does not take into cognisance the nonhuman component of the environment, such as modern drainages for the free passage of waters and other matters.

CONCLUSION

The poems in *Lagos of the Poets* demystify Lagos as a modernizing force, paying close attention to the ecological problems the city faces in its urbanization process. Through the poetic prism, it is clear that the city does not after all provide the fulfilments of modern facilities, and it is riddled with urban inadequacies. The city's ecological inadequacies are telling, and yet it remains perhaps the most urban city in Nigeria, the implication of which is that other cities in the country may even suffer from worse environmental shortcomings. My argument has been that the representation of these shortcomings in the studied poems is a form of critique, a transformative one that reflects the socio-ecological realities of the city and at the same time creates an alterity through which we can imagine an ecologically better Lagos. Most of the poems, therefore, adopt a strategy of depiction in which the city's environmental problems are laid bare, as well as their effects on the poor, and the power relations informing the neglect of some areas and the gentrification of others are revealed. Beyond that, the poems pursue an urban political ecology that privileges the plight of the mass inhabitants of the city, but more importantly the nonhumans, such as elements of the natural world, who must be taken into account in the urban process of modernizing Lagos. In other words, the ecological force of the poems, embedded in their power of alterity, presents the city as one that urgently needs environmental and urban political rehabilitation.

ACKNOWLEDGEMENTS

This research is supported by TETFUND's National Research Fund, Nigeria.

WORKS CITED

Akeh, Afam. 'Bodies'. In *Lagos of the Poets*. Odia Ofeimun, ed. Lagos: Hornbill House, 2010. 82–7.

Bartosch, Roman. *EnvironMentality—Ecocriticism and the Event of Postcolonial Fiction*. Amsterdam and New York: Rodopi, 2012.

Bassey, Nnimmo. 'Maroko'. In *Lagos of the Poets*. Odia Ofeimun, ed. Lagos: Hornbill House, 2010. 294.

Caminero-Santangelo, Byron and Garth Myers. 'Introduction'. In *Environment at the Margins: Literary and Environmental Studies in Africa*. Byron Caminero-Santangelo and Garth Myers, eds. Ohio: Ohio University Press, 2011. 1–21.

Clark-Bekederemo, J. P. 'Victoria Island'. In *Lagos of the Poets*. Odia Ofeimun, ed. Lagos: Hornbill House, 2010. 80.

———. 'Victoria Island Re-visited'. In *Lagos of the Poets*. Odia Ofeimun, ed. Lagos: Hornbill House, 2010. 81

Cooper, Frederick. *Colonialism in Question: Theory, Knowledge, History*. Berkeley: University Press of California, 2005.

Dunton, Chris. 'Entropy and Energy: Lagos as City of Words'. *Research in African Literatures*. 32.1 (2008): 68–78.

Ehrlich, Paul and Anne Ehrlich. *One with Nineveh: Politics, Consumption and the Human Future*. Washington, D.C.: Island Press, 2004.

Heynen, Nik, Maria Kaika and Erik Swyngedouw. 'Urban Political Ecology: Politicizing the Production of Urban Natures'. In *In the Nature of Cities: Urban Political Ecology and the Politics of Urban Metabolism*, Nik Heynen, Maria Kaika and Erik Swyngedouw, eds. London: Routledge, 2006. 1–20.

Huggan, Graham and Helen Tiffin. *Postcolonial Ecocriticism: Literature, Animals, Environment*. London: Routledge, 2010.

Ifowodo, Ogaga. 'Driftwood'. In *Lagos of the Poets*. Odia Ofeimun, ed. Lagos: Hornbill House, 2010. 44–45.

Iheka, Cajetan. *Naturalizing Africa: Ecological Violence, Agency, and Postcolonial Resistance in African Literature*. Cambridge: Cambridge University Press, 2018.

Maiwada, Ahmed. 'Lagos Welcomes You'. In *Lagos of the Poets*. Odia Ofeimun, ed. Lagos: Hornbill House, 2010. 111.

Myers, Garth. *Urban Environments in Africa: a Critical Analysis of Environmental Politics*. Bristol: Policy Press, 2016.
Njoku, Austyn. 'Flood Lagos'. In *Lagos of the Poets*. Odia Ofeimun, ed. Lagos: Hornbill House, 2010. 68.
Nwosu, Maik. *Invisible Chapters*. Lagos: House of Malaika and Hybun, 2001.
Ofeimun, Odia. 'Demolition Day'. In *Lagos of the Poets*. Odia Ofeimun, ed. Lagos: Hornbill House, 2010. 181–2.
———. 'Preface to *Lagos of the Poets*'. In *Lagos of the Poets*. Odia Ofeimun, ed. Lagos: Hornbill House, 2010. xix–xlvi.
Olanrewaju, Caroline C., Munyaradzi Chitakira, Oludolapo A. Olanrewaju and Elretha Louw. 'Impacts of Flood Disasters in Nigeria: A Critical Evaluation of Health Implications and Management'. *Jamba: Journal of Disaster Risk Studies*. 11.1 (2019): 1–9.
Oyinloye, Michael, Isaac Olamiju and Ogundiran Adekemi. 'Environmental Impact of Flood on Kosofe Local Government Area of Lagos State, Nigeria: a GIS Perspective'. *Journal of Environment and Earth Science*. 5.3 (2013): 57–66.
Philip, M. Nourbese. 'Earth and Sound: The Place of Poetry'. *The Word Behind the Bars and the Paradox of Exile*. Kofi Anyidoho, ed. Illinois: Northwestern University Press, 1997. 169–182.
Swyngedouw, Erik. 'Metabolic Urbanization: the Making of Cyborg Cities'. *In the Nature of Cities: Urban Political Ecology and the Politics of Urban Metabolism*. Nik Heynen, Maria Kaika and Erik Swyngedouw, eds. London: Routledge, 2006. 21–40.
Zapf, Hubert. *Literature as Cultural Ecology*. London: Bloomsbury, 2016.

Poetic Style and Anthropogenic Ecological Adversity in Steve Chimombo's Poems

SYNED MTHATIWA

Steve Chimombo (1945–2015) is regarded as Malawi's most versatile and prolific writer. As a novelist, short-story writer, poet, playwright, and academic, he published a number of works in his lifetime. In his writings he tackles a range of social, economic, political, cultural and environmental issues in his country and beyond. Bright Molande (2011) characterizes him as a writer with a tragic vision as in his works he mostly depicts the tragedies of colonialism, postcolonialism, neocolonialism and post-independence in Africa. Chimombo fits Ngũgĩ's description of a writer as someone who 'responds, with his total personality, to a social environment which changes all the time', one who acting like 'a kind of sensitive needle, [...] registers, with varying degrees of accuracy and success, the conflicts and tensions in his changing society' (Ngũgĩ 1972, 47). One of the changes that Chimombo registers concerns the environment, the focus of this article. In focusing on the environmental issues in Chimombo's poetry this article departs from the popular approach to his poetry by critics, who have mostly read Chimombo's poetry from social, cultural and political perspectives (see Nazombe 1983; Roscoe and Msiska 1992; Msiska 1995; and Molande).

Chimombo's interest in environmental issues and landscapes is evident in his earliest published poetry, which exploited the mythical phenomenon of Napolo as an aesthetic and mythological framework to explain various tragic and cataclysmic events in the world of politics and nature; in the case of the latter those associated with water and wind (Molande 32–3). In Malawian myth and cosmology Napolo is believed to be a giant subterranean serpent spirit that causes 'heavy rains, landslides, hurricanes, earthquakes and floods every time it erupts from its subterranean lair' (Molande 32) to embark on a river or air voyage to the lake or sea. In most cases the invocation of the mythic Napolo in Malawi follows disastrous events of huge proportions that become incomprehensible to the human psyche. In Chimombo's poetry Napolo assumes many guises and these include functioning as a metaphor for Malawi's first president – Dr Hastings Kamuzu Banda – and his oppressive regime (Msiska 74), an oracular voice and godhead, beside the literal representation as a mythic subterranean serpent spirit. It is when Napolo is represented literally that Chimombo's interest in nature and landscapes is exposed. In such instances Chimombo paradoxically credits Napolo with destructive and creative powers – that is to say Napolo does not only destroy but also brings about renewal to the face of the earth.

In a poem titled 'III Napolo: In the Beginning' (9–11), for example, Napolo comes along with rains that people prayed for during a drought and wreaks havoc while also creating new physical features such as rivers. Anthony Nazombe correctly observes that the creative power of Napolo 'suggests the re-creation of the earth in an atmosphere reminiscent of the scene immediately after the biblical Flood.' He goes on to observe that Napolo emerges 'from this and the other poems as an inscrutable being, capricious in the extreme, and as capable of creating as he is of destroying' (105). In poems that he wrote later in his career Chimombo's interest in the environment and its welfare is more explicit.

In this article my interest focuses on four poems by Chimombo which deal with environmental matters from his collection titled *Napolo and Other Poems* (2009). The poems bear the titles 'Mlauli's Musings,' 'The Cry at Birth,' 'Zomba Mountain' and 'Usayelekele Mine'. While these poems are also amenable to social, cultural and political readings, it is not my intention to focus on these aspects here. The selected poems reveal Chimombo's environmental consciousness and his displeasure with the current anthropogenic ecological adversity. In the poems Chimombo laments human despoliation of the environment through activities associated with capitalist development and progress. Another interesting aspect in these poems is that in each one of them Chimombo adopts a different poetic technique to communicate his message. I consider Chimombo a writer who uses poetry as a medium to address questions of the environment in the age of the Anthropocene and I suggest that the change in technique in the four poems constitutes the poet's search for a proper style, voice and language that would communicate his discontent with the ways in which we relate with and treat ecological others.

In my analysis of the poems I draw from Cajetan Iheka's use of the concept of proximity and Rob Nixon's notion of slow violence. In his book *Naturalizing Africa* (2018) Iheka emphasizes the need to recognize the proximity of nonhumans to humans in terms of space and 'shared biological characteristics' (5). He rightly notes that nonhumans are 'companions in a precarious world' who share with humans 'vulnerabilities such as suffering and death as well as [...] victimhood' (5). In emphasizing proximity Iheka signals the need for the development of a relational selfhood for humans with respect to the ways in which we interact with nonhumans. He envisions the construction of an ecological self that is not hyper-individuated or hyper-separated from other entities in nature, but one that is entangled with these entities, one that is in a symbiotic web with other existents. In the book Iheka also suggests that 'narrow anthropocentric conceptualizations of the environment are now insufficient' (5) and, instead, there is need to adopt 'strategic anthropomorphism [which] occurs when the lines between humans and nonhumans are blurred to undercut notions of superiority and to bring about ecological awareness and/or restoration' (14). My reading of this is that he recommends an attitude of humility on the part of humans. In doing so he does not only evoke the question of interdependence in nature but also a transpersonal ecology, that is, a cosmological and psychological outlook that holds a view of the world/cosmos that acknowledges the connectedness of all entities on the planet as 'leaves on the tree of life' (Fox 1995, 161) and encourages 'a psychological identification with all phenomena' (Eckersley 1992, 62). This outlook seeks to cultivate a sense or experience of self that extends beyond one's egoistic, biographical, or personal sense of self to include all beings. As I will illustrate in my discussion below, Chimombo's poetry reveals what Iheka calls an 'aesthetics of proximity' in reference to 'the processes by which African literary artefacts depict the interconnectedness of human lives with Others in the environment' (Iheka 23). In the poetry Chimombo also exposes an attitude of a self in relationship or in proximity with other aspects of nature.

Rob Nixon's concept of slow violence in the book *Slow Violence and the Environmentalism of the Poor* (2011) is also relevant in my discussion of Chimombo's poems. Nixon defines slow violence as 'a violence that occurs gradually and out of sight, a violence of delayed destruction that is dispersed across time and space, an attritional violence that is typically not viewed as violence at all' (2). For Nixon, violence is generally associated with immediacy, spectacularity, explosiveness and 'instant sensational visibility' (2). Unlike ordinary violence then, slow violence 'is neither spectacular nor instantaneous' and it takes time for its full impact to be felt (Nixon 2). In some of the poems discussed in this article Chimombo gestures towards slow violence when he engages with issues of radiation and pollution from chemical fertilizers, uranium mining, nuclear weapons and unhygienic waste disposal practices. He also shows awareness that the victims of slow violence are often the poor, people whose 'unseen poverty is compounded by the invisibility of the slow violence that permeates so many of their lives' (Nixon 4). For Chimombo the rich and powerful, both local and foreign, unleash slow violence on poor communities in their quest for power, wealth and influence.

A reading of the poem titled 'Mlauli's Musings' (91–3) reveals both Chimombo's displeasure with the state of affairs in the world and his country with regard to immorality and poverty and his acknowledgement of humanity's 'unique capacity to significantly alter the ecosystem, for better or worse' in our age (Iheka 5). In the poem Chimombo presents moral degeneration, corruption, bad governance, unemployment, high population growth and environmental degradation in his country as events that were foreseen by Mlauli, a legendary prophet and rainmaker among the Mang'anja, Chewa and Nyanja people at Kaphirintiwa in Malawi. The use of prophecy as a stylistic device to depict social and environmental problems imbues the message with a sense of solemnity and seriousness as a warning to humans about moral degeneration and ecological adversity occasioned by their non-ecological practices. In the poem Chimombo highlights the plight of humans and nonhumans as a result of environmental exploitation in our era when he writes:

> Mlauli said he had foreseen
> all these happenings before;
> and indeed his predictions
> came to be, in our life time.
>
> The fields will no longer be ravaged
> by locusts because they're radioactive.
> Instead the army worm will invade
> and eat away the hearts of the stalks.
> Fake fertilizers will be fed to the soil
> making fools wonder why there's famine. (91)

The fact that the fields are radioactive shows that they are hazardous not only to human but also nonhuman lives. The reference to fake fertilizers that lead to famine reminds one of the Farm Input Subsidy Programme (FISP) in Malawi through which the government gives free inputs to poor subsistence farmers who cannot afford them in the rural areas to boost food production. The programme was introduced in the 2005/6 growing season and soon after there were associations of the programme with fake fertilizers that never dissolved when applied in the field and never had any noticeable impact on the crops they were meant to improve. It is these fertilizers that inspired Chimombo's poetic lines above. The recipients of the fertilizers were never warned about the negative effects of fertilizers, fake or not, to the environment. Chemical fertilizers are said to contaminate groundwater, to contribute to global warming and to make top soil acidic leading to low crop yields. Since the 'damage caused by [these] fertilizers is often long-term and cumulative' (Buckler 2017, np), the fertilizers can be considered agents of slow violence. Research has also shown that long-term use of chemical fertilizers can lead to 'an accumulation of radioactivity in soils that can be harmful to [...] farmers and consumers of the products' (Rajačić np).

The idea of army worms invading fields and eating 'away the heart of stalks' is aimed at emphasizing the destructive nature of the pests that supposedly took over from locusts. Army worms generally eat leaves and not stalks, let alone hearts of stalks. Although locusts are pests, they are also beneficial to people as food, and here one recalls scenes from Chinua Achebe's *Things Fall Apart* where locusts emerge as a delicacy for the people of Umuofia. However, the radioactive nature of the soil that has been soured by fertilizers leaves people with pests that do not benefit them in any way. While in the above extract environmental adversity mainly impacts human lives, in the third stanza we encounter Mlauli's pronunciations on the plight of other creatures. We read:

> Rivers and lakes will be exhausted
> or emptied because of over-fishing
> Jungles will be silent because of poaching;
> forests will be bare because of burning.
> The air will become foul for breath,
> the water poisonous because of pollution. (91)

It is clear to see that the future Mlauli was talking about is the age of the Anthropecene, when several animal species have gone extinct while others are on the brink of extinction. Hunting and overfishing, both in Africa and elsewhere, have left some fish and animal species greatly endangered. Chimombo through Mlauli also underlines anthropogenic ecological adversity when he talks about 'forests [that are] bare because of burning,' of air that is 'foul for breath' and water that is 'poisonous because of pollution'. Polluted air and water do not only affect humans but other animals as well. In this poem Chimombo shows environmental awareness and understanding of humanity's role in environmental spoliation. The poet's word choice here helps to create images and vivify environmental ruin. In using words such as 'empty', 'silent', 'bare' and 'foul', Chimombo appeals to our senses to enable us see, hear and taste the effects of environmental damage. Although not explicitly stated there is an implied censure to humanity in the poem for its destruction of the environment.

'The Cry at Birth' (121–2) is another poem where Chimombo shows his environmental awareness and subtly critiques humans for bringing alterations to the environment that threaten humanity's very survival. In this poem Chimombo relies on rhetorical questions to paint a bleak, dreary and hopeless picture of the world full of moral squalor, diseases, suffering and environmental adversity. Using rhetorical questions as a device enables Chimombo to highlight the problems in the world today. The rhetorical questions also enable him not only to 'express strong feelings of outrage [and] vehement indignation', but also to 'jolt readers [...] out of a state of complacency/ stupor' (Abioye 2009, 3). In the poet-persona's view our world with its environmental and moral problems would not appeal to a newborn baby which is why babies cry on entry into the world at birth. The choice of children as potential victims of anthropogenic ecological problems is intended to highlight the innocence of some of those who suffer the impact of environmental damage. A tragic vision permeates the poem giving the impression that life is almost impossible in the world today. This hyperbolic rendering of the situation is aimed at shocking the reader and bringing the challenges in the world sharply before his/ her eyes. Writing about environmental challenges unleashed by humans in the world, Chimombo says:

> What baby at birth wouldn't choke
> The second it started breathing the air
> Ready to explode with global warming?
> Ordained to drink from the city sewers
> Chock-full with piss, shit and condoms
> Or fetuses that didn't survive as he did? (121–2)

Global warming is one of the major environmental problems of our age which threatens our very existence and that of countless other species in the world. Climate change and global warming are aspects of slow violence (Nixon) whose effects are felt more by poor people in developing countries. In the lines above Chimombo imagines a newborn baby choking upon breathing the air that is '[r]eady to explode with global warming'. Here Chimombo creates the impression that rising temperatures heat the air to the point where it is ready to explode with the intention of making the phenomenon vivid and imaginable to the reader while also drawing attention to the seriousness of the problem. In the extract Chimombo also highlights the problem of water pollution, especially in urban areas, as a result of improper waste disposal practices. He uses scatological imagery not only to shock readers into acknowledging the problem but also to show the ugliness of the situation propelled by poor hygiene and moral decrepitude. The word 'ordained' underlines the impossibility of escape from the bleak situation awaiting the child.

In the fifth stanza Chimombo highlights the problem of deforestation and pollution of water bodies such as lakes when he asks:

> What baby at birth wouldn't retch,
> Predestined to see the myth-infested forests
> Burnt down by man on the rampage?
> Or lakes poisoned, gardens invaded by army worms?
> Destined to dine on mad-cow diseased beef
> Or migratory birds infected with avian flu? (122)

The image of 'man on the rampage' underscores the carelessness and irresponsibility of humans in dealing with other aspects of nature. The expression 'myth-infested forests' is evocative of an animist worldview which sees forests as enchanted and deserving respect. However, instead of according respect to the forests and showing a transpersonal ecological view, rampaging humans go on to burn and destroy. But while recognizing human culpability on environmental despoilment Chimombo also recognizes the caprices of nature which, for instance, lead to death through diseases such as mad-cow and avian flu.

Chimombo's poetic style in handling environmental issues changes in 'Zomba Mountain' (94–6), the third poem of interest for me in this article. Among other aspects of style, the poem relies on alliteration for its effect. Zomba Mountain is in a district of the same name in southern Malawi. In this poem Chimombo reveals his awareness of proximity between humans and nonhumans, in this case landscapes. The poem is autobiographical as it exposes the ways in which the poet and his people interacted with the mountain of the title and records the changes that have taken place over time as a result of capitalist development. In documenting these changes the poet seeks to contrast traditional ways of relating with nature, which acknowledged proximity, with modern capitalist ways. In the poem Chimombo uses apostrophe and a conversational tone to show propinquity and familiarity with the mountain and to underscore affection and kinship with the landscape. Chimombo begins the poem by looking back to when he and his people found themselves on the slopes of Zomba Mountain. He tells us:

> Great grandfather, founder of the clan,
> baskets of spirits under each arm
> claimed your slopes for our village.
> We spread between the green banks
> of two rivers: Naisi and Naming'azi,
> planted and reaped in the fields,
> played and prayed in the forests,
> hurted and hunted, lived and loved
> under the giant gaze of your granite face. (94)

Chimombo grew up in a village that is located at the foot of Zomba Mountain and between the two rivers of Naming'azi and Naisi as in the extract above. The mountain was a familiar and imposing presence in his life, for even as an adult he lived in Zomba and taught at the University of Malawi's Chancellor College situated at the eastern foot of the mountain. Like a familiar and benevolent friend, the mountain watched as life unfolded in Chimombo's village, as we note from the expression 'under the giant gaze of your granite face'. The reference to 'green banks' evokes a period when nature was vibrant, a time before the ravages by humans, while the parallelism in the lines 'planted and reaped in the fields,/ played and prayed in the forests,' emphasizes the harmonious relationship that existed between the people of the village and their mountain neighbour.

In the poem Chimombo goes on to highlight the ecologically friendly manner in which he, personally, related with the mountain, in ways that reveal his inscription onto the mountainscape:

> I read your visage like verse:
> savored your similes,
> mined your metaphors
> wrapped in the roaring rivers
> or buried in the bowels of boulders;
> deciphered symbols of import
> in crag, cranny, or crevice;
> scanned cliffs clad in clouds
> or rain-laden for fresh inspiration. (94)

Here we have an image of a writer who went in search of inspiration from the mountain, inscribing himself onto the landscape as he 'savored similes', 'mined [...] metaphors', 'deciphered symbols' and 'scanned cliffs.' The mountain was beneficent to the poet whose dealings with it were harmless and appreciative rather than exploitative.

Later in the poem Chimombo introduces a sharp contrast in the ways of relating with the mountain when capitalist development comes into the picture. The respect and reverence that informed the poet and his people's interaction with the mountain are replaced by a more violent and disrespectful interaction by capitalists. We read:

> Now, great grandfather resurrected
> would not recognize your visage.
> They blasted your boulders down,
> smashing myths to smithereens.
> They graded your undergrowth,
> mashing water-maids under wheels.
> They pulverized the wood spirits,
> flattening out their sighs and songs. (95)

The choice of words here is evocative of violence and ruthlessness and exposes the 'pain' endured by the mountain. Violence-related words such as 'blast', 'smash', 'grade', 'mash', 'pulverize' and 'flatten' vividly show the ruthlessness of the developers who do not care about the mountain but about economic gain. Thus the respectful, animist and relational attitude of Chimombo and his people is today replaced by a mechanistic and exploitative one. The use of apostrophe and a conversational style where the mountain is addressed directly invites us to sympathise with the landscape that is being brutalized. The result of this brutalization is the destabilization of a people's culture and belief systems as well as ecological balance as Chimombo laments:

> Napolo no longer bursts the banks
> of Naming'azi, Satemwa, or Naisi;
> no myths meander down Mulunguzi;
> no lore slithers down the Likangala
> past paw steps of lion, leopard, or lizard.
> They all vanished into the valley below.
>
> Now the crows fight ants over leftovers
> of crumbs of cake from the cottages,
> or canned beef, beans, or bottled water
> from the backpackers on the camping site.

Concrete, steel pipes, plastic, and bricks
sprout in banks, boulders, and pathways. (95)

The absence of Napolo and the repetition of the word 'no' in the initial position in the first stanza quoted above emphasizes the subversion of ecological harmony on the mountain. The sense of loss of aspects of cultural and religious value, such as myths, for Chimombo and his people, is emphasized by the predominance of the liquid 'l' and nasal 'm' and 'n' sounds – which help create a sad tone – in the alliterative words in the first stanza above and by the slow rhythm occasioned by the words. Chimombo also underscores the dislocation of ecological harmony on the mountain through the hard to imagine but disturbing image of crows fighting ants over leftovers from cottages and camping sites one finds on the mountain captured in the second stanza above. The environmental despoliation and ecological dislocation are also underlined by alliteration through the harsh 'k', 'p', and 'b' sounds which draw our attention to the world of nightmare created by capitalist development. The reference to '[c]oncrete, steel pipes, plastic, and bricks/ [that] sprout in banks, boulders, and pathways' emphasizes the mountain's ultimate humiliation as capitalist development/ progress marches on without regard to its impact on nonhuman nature.

The final poem for my purpose here is 'Usayelekele Mine' (133–4), which deals with the deleterious effects of uranium mining on the environment. The poem is a thinly veiled reference to Kayelekera open-cast uranium mine in Malawi's northern district of Karonga owned by Paladin (Africa) Limited, a subsidiary of Paladin Energy from Australia. Kayelekera mine was commissioned in 2008 and in 2014 it was put into care and maintenance due to low prices on the uranium market. Recent media reports indicate that Paladin will sell the mine to Lotus Resources (Etter-Phoya 2019). In the poem Chimombo highlights the environmental impact of Usayelekele (read Kayelekera) mine and depicts as greedy and deceptive the mining company and those who authorized the uranium mining at the expense of the people and other aspects of the environment that will be affected by radiation. He also accuses nongovernmental organizations and chiefs of selling their consciences by endorsing the mine instead of championing environmental justice by insisting on a proper environmental impact assessment (EIA) before the mine started operations.

In terms of style Chimombo uses multiple voices in the poem to expose the motivations of the various parties interested in the mine. Three voices are discernible and these belong to a politician or government official who authorized mining at Kayelekera, a commentator, and the mine owner. What these say highlights greed and hunger for power, duplicity and insensitivity to the plight and suffering of others, both human and nonhuman.

When the poem opens we hear the prevaricating voice of someone who may be a politician or a government official:

> Usayelekele Mine is not mine,
> But you can buy me,
> And of course the mine,
> At the affordable price
> Of deforming my children,
> And, if any, my grandchildren,
> With radioactive waste. (133)

The idea of offering him/herself for sale along with the mine shows how lowly the speaker values him/herself and his preparedness to sell his soul and natural resources for money. The evocation of deformity of children and grandchildren with radioactive waste points to the danger associated with the product of the mine. Although the product is not mentioned in the poem, there is an allusion to uranium at Kayelekera. In the second stanza of the poem we hear the voice of a commentator who mentions that a president who sought financial resources as he wished to remain in power and to be remembered after his death is the one who orchestrated the sale of the mine. Here Chimombo points a finger of blame at the Democratic Progressive Party (DDP) and its president, Bingu wa Mutharika, who granted the mining licence to Paladin in 2007. He also accuses the politicians and Paladin of lying to the nation on the question of waste disposal when he writes: 'It is no big deal, to tell the truth,/ Where they dump the waste' (133). When read as a poem about Kayelekera, these lines ring chillingly true.

Wilfred Masebo mentions that the Malawi government's 'decision to grant a mining licence to Paladin based on the company's draft EIA was criticized by civil society groups in the country' (Masebo 2013, 3). The report 'emphasized potential economic benefits of the project [...] while downplaying negative environmental impacts. It also lacked environmental and radiological baseline data, figures and maps to present the project, and long-term tailings management/ site rehabilitation plans' (Masebo 4). Unsurprisingly, an independent report by Bruno Chareyron (2015) on the environmental impact of the Kayelekera uranium mine mentions discovery of radiation 'hot spots in the environment of the mine and a high uranium concentration in the water flowing from a stream located below the open pit and entering the SERE river' (1). The report also documents a shocking discovery of 'million tonnes of radioactive and chemically polluting wastes [...] disposed of on a plateau with very negative geological and hydrogeological characteristics' (1). We are reminded here of the words of Iheka, who accuses oil companies and other multinational corporations of disregarding and disrespecting 'the environment in the communities where they operate' in Africa. Iheka goes on to say '[b]y disregarding "best practices" adopted in their home countries and in other Western countries, the companies continue to treat these African environments as devoid of people or constituted by disposable people' (13). Jim Green (2018) echoes these words with reference to Paladin's Kayelekera when he says '[s]tandards at Kayelekera fall a long way short of Australian standards – and efforts to force Australian mining companies to meet Australian standards when operating abroad have been strongly resisted'. He further mentions that '[t]he Kayelekera project would not be approved in Australia due to major flaws in the assessment and design proposals' (np). Here we note a clear evocation of Rob Nixon's conception of slow violence which goes hand in hand with 'human disposability' (Nixon 4), especially of the poor from the global South. Jason Moore's notion of capitalism as the Capitalocene, through which the specific humans (white, male and bourgeois) responsible for 'planetary crisis today' are identified (Moore 2019, 53), comes to mind here, as does Françoise Vergès' concept of racial Capitalocene, which brings environmentalism into dialogue with questions of 'capital, imperialism, gender, class, and race' (Vergès 2017, 83). However, in the poem, Chimombo does not apportion blame only to capitalists, but also to greedy indigenes such as chiefs, leaders of NGOs, and the president.

In the poem 'Usayelekele Mine' Chimombo also evokes Nixon's slow violence when he allows us to hear the voice of the mine owner who gloatingly says:

> The radiation is a slow time bomb.
> You don't feel it in your lifetime
> My conscience was auctioned off
> Like the NGO's, chief's, or minister's
> Mismolded by international self-interests (133)

Blame here is apportioned to people and groups who should have stood up for environmental justice but were compromised. Later, boasting of skills in duplicity the miner says:

> Usayelekele Mine is my latest challenge,
> I bring to it my vast vacuous experience,
> Activated intellectual bankruptcy,
> Blinkered myopia and double dealings.
> Currently I'm majoring in obfuscation,
> Sustainable disinformation, and moneymaking.
> My thesis: to make this an explosive package. (134)

The above boasts prove true in as far as Kayelekera is concerned. Paladin was accused of being secretive on matters relating to environmental impact assessment before commencing mining activities, even refusing 'to provide information to local communities prior to the performance of a substantive EIA' (Masebo 3). The EIA process was also questionable on the grounds of independence and objectivity. Paladin subcontracted Knight Piesold (KP) 'to investigate various aspects of the EIA' rendering 'the objectivity of the outcomes [dubious] on grounds that a business-client relationship existed between KP and Paladin' (Masebo 3). Further, in his report on Kayelekera, Chareyron accuses Paladin of failing to produce and make public a detailed report 'about the degree of radiological and chemical pollution of the stream and rivers' around Kayelekera following spills of contaminated 'water from the Run-of-Mine stockpile area and waste rock dumps' in March 2013 and January 2015 (14, 65). All this is evidence of 'double dealings', 'obfuscation' and 'disinformation' geared towards 'moneymaking' that will lead to a very 'explosive package' for Malawians.

In the poems discussed above Chimombo emerges as a poet who is environmentally conscious and one who is displeased with human exploitation and abuse of the environment in our age of global capitalism. He is, by and large, a poet whose views are in line with current environmental orthodoxy. In style, he experiments with a new approach in each of the poems discussed as a way of searching for a proper voice, attitude, tone or language with which to communicate his ecological message. The use of prophecy, though problematic as it evokes inescapability, also helps to give the environmental message in 'Mlauli's Musings' an aura of solemnity and importance. The rhetorical questions in 'The Cry at Birth' invite us to reflect on the various challenges – including environmental ones – in the world today, while apostrophe in 'Zomba Mountain' signals proximity and a relational selfhood that calls for an ecocentric attitude in life. Further, multiple voices in 'Usayelekele Mine' allow us to appreciate the motivations and attitudes of the different speakers towards uranium mining in Malawi and its impact on the environment, impact that is best captured by Rob Nixon's notion of slow violence. In adopting various stylistic approaches to communicate messages on the environment Chimombo could also be telling us that in dealing with such an important subject of our time a writer should constantly adopt various strategies to ensure that the intended audience gets the message. He seems to suggest that the question of the environment today, to borrow with modifications an expression from the Igbo people of Nigeria, can be compared to a dancing masquerade, and if one wants to grapple with it, one cannot stand in one place.

WORKS CITED

Abioye, Taiwo O. 'Typology of Rhetorical Questions as a Stylistic Device in Writing'. *The International Journal of Language Society and Culture* 29 (2009): 1–8.

Buckler, Laura. 'The Hidden Dangers of Chemical Fertilizers'. Environmental Protection. 2017. https://eponline.com/Articles/2017/12/07/The-Hidden-Dangers-of-Chemical-Fertilizers.aspx?p=1, accessed 8 February 2020.

Chareyron, Bruno. 'Impact of the Kayelekera Uranium Mine, Malawi'. EJOLT Report No. 21. 2015. http://www.ejolt.org/wordpress/wp-content/uploads/2015/02/150222_Report-21.pdf, accessed 8 February 2020.

Chimombo, Steve. *Napolo and Other Poems*. Zomba: WASI Publications, 2009.

Eckersley, Robyn. *Environmentalism and Political Theory: Toward an Ecocentric Approach*. London: UCL Press, 1992.

Etter-Phoya, Rachel. 'Paladin Selling Its Stake in Malawi's Kayelekera Uranium Mine'. Mining in Malawi: News, Research and Initiatives in Malawi's Extractive Industries. 24 June 2019. https://mininginmalawi.com/2019/06/24/paladin-selling-its-stake-in-malawis-kayelekera-uranium-mine/, accessed 8 February 2020.

Fox, Warwick. *Towards a Transpersonal Ecology: Developing New Foundations for Environmentalism*. New York: State University of New York Press, 1995.

Green, Jim. 'Who Cleans Up the Mess When an Australian Uranium Mining Company Leaves Africa?' *The Ecologist: The Journal for the Post-Industrial Age*. 18 June 2018. https://theecologist.org/2018/jun/18/who-cleans-mess-when-australian-uranium-mining-company-leaves-africa, accessed 8 February 2020.

Iheka, Cajetan. *Naturalizing Africa: Ecological Violence, Agency, and Postcolonial Resistance in African Literature*. Cambridge: Cambridge University Press, 2018.

Masebo, Wilfred. 'The Kayelekera Uranium Mine and Economic Development in Malawi'. *Backgrounder* 53 (2013). https://www.researchgate.net/publication/327690130, accessed 8 February 2020.

Molande, Bright. 'Postcolonial Tragic Vision in Steve Chimombo's Writing'. PhD thesis, University of Essex, October 2011.

Moore, Jason W. 'The Capitalocene and Planetary Justice'. *Maize* 6 (2019): 49–54.

Msiska, Mpalive-Hangson. 'Geopoetics: Subterraneanity and Subversion in Malawian Poetry'. In *Essays on African Writing 2: Contemporary Literature*. Abdulrazak Gurnah ed. Oxford: Heinemann, 1995.

Nazombe, Anthony. 'Malawian Poetry in English from 1970 to the Present Day: A Study of Myth and Social Political Change in the Work of Steve Chimombo, Jack Mapanje, Frank Chipasula and Felix Mnthali'. PhD Thesis, Sheffield University, 1983.

Ngugi wa Thiong'o. 'The Writer in a Changing Society'. *Homecoming: Essays on African and Caribbean Literature, Culture and Politics*. London: Heinemann, 1972 repr. 1981. 47–50.

Nixon, Rob. *Slow Violence and the Environmentalism of the Poor*. Cambridge: Harvard University Press, 2011.

Rajačić, Milica M., et al. 'Radio Activity in Chemical Fertilizers'. Institute for Nuclear Sciences "Vinča", University of Belgrade, Belgrade. https://inis.iaea.org/collection/NCLCollectionStore/_Public/44/128/44128586.pdf, accessed 8 February 2020.

Roscoe, Adrian and Mpalive-Hangson Msiska. *The Quiet Chameleon: Modern Poetry from Central Africa*. London: Hans Zell, 1992.

Vergès, Françoise, 'Racial Capitalocene'. In *Futures of Black Radicalism*. Gaye Theresa Johnson and Alex Lubin eds. London and New York: Verso, 2017. 78–87.

Female Autonomy in Kaine Agary's Yellow-Yellow

SANDRA C. NWOKOCHA

The feminist notion of autonomy, a self-governing ability, has been almost absent from moral philosophy until recently. The absence suggests that the ethical concerns of men, such as universality and neutrality, maintain a dominant position in shaping traditional ethics, resulting in the allegorical idea of an atomistic individual who is distanced from the social associations in which real agents are entrenched. From Immanuel Kant's notion of a rational being who possesses the moral power of 'being a law unto itself' (Kant 1785, 108) to John Rawl's perception of persons with the capacity to formulate principles of justice in the 'original position […] behind the veil of ignorance' (1971, 12), autonomy is underpinned with the implicit masculine ideal of the 'self-made man' who is metaphorically isolated. This unilateral stance is limiting in comprehending other dimensions of moral reasoning, particularly feminine notions of caring and issues of private life (Mackenzie and Stoljar 2000) that acknowledge independence and interdependence by valuing the agent who opts for social relationships. This uncritical moral perception has contributed considerably in influencing the ways contemporary Nigerian (and by extension African) women's texts are read, interpreted and understood, as critics, eager to explore postcoloniality with its associated moral and environmental decadence, undermine the intricacies surrounding the independence of the fictional figures in such works. Concentrating on Kaine Agary's *Yellow-Yellow* (2006), this essay challenges such reactionary readings by highlighting female autonomy as a recurrent motif that runs throughout the novel. Structured around self-asserting and self-originating agents, it argues that the heroines' quest for autonomy, not necessarily environmental degradation, is responsible for their distinctive preferences for single parenthood and abortion. By authorizing both options as valid, Agary is read as an avant-garde Nigerian feminist writer who advances a feminist worldview that permits new ways of thinking about family – a line of thought that, I believe, is yet to receive attention from her critics.

Critical reviews of Agary's *Yellow-Yellow* have fixated on environmental degradation with its resultant moral pollution. Critics have described *Yellow-Yellow* as a novel that depicts the Niger Delta milieu, an '[e]cologically devastated world bedevilled by youthful restiveness, militancy, criminality, and varying degrees of ecocide pointing in the direction of Armageddon' (Awhefeada 2013, 96). Necessitated by this region's ills, Agary problematizes the 'abandonment of ecological stewardship [...] by oil-prospecting bureaucracies and the Government of Nigeria' (Ohagwam 2018, 12), the 'displaced male-image' (Chukwumah 2013, 47), and the 'psychological effects of single parenthood [to foreground] the crime rate and moral decadence in the soçiety' (Nwangwu and Iboroma 2018, 22, 32). This type of reading, while foregrounding the ecological effects of the activities of the multinational oil companies, often overshadows the feminist undercurrent of the text. Conversely, I argue that although the environment is notably an issue in the text, Agary's focus is, however, on the autonomous choices of the female characters. In my analysis, I examine the degree of such independence and the effects of these choices in empowering, and possibly disempowering, Agary's women.

Yellow-Yellow relates the story of Zilayefa, a teenage biracial girl of Greek and Nigerian parentage who is raised by her single mother, Binaebi. Through the recommendation of Ikechukwu, her local church pastor, Zilayefa migrates from the countryside to the metropolis of Port Harcourt, where she is placed in the custody of Sisi, an influential old woman, and her young acquaintance, Lolo. She encounters many challenges in Port Harcourt: she struggles to accept the bias against her racial identity and the vacuum left by not knowing her father. She fills this gap when she maintains a friendship with 60-year-old Kenneth Alaowei Amalayefa, a retired admiral, and Sergio, a white expatriate who is in his late forties. Her sexuality blossoms in the course of these associations; she eventually becomes pregnant and consequently aborts the foetus through self-induced abortion. Zilayefa, through the experience, advances to a higher level of knowledge and understanding that enables her to assert her agency by personally charting her future.

With an emphasis on self-asserting agents, *Yellow-Yellow* mostly relates the stories of women who play an active determining role in the choices and actions they undertake. From the point of view of the narrator, Zilayefa, the reader learns about her mother Binaebi, an orphan and secondary school graduate, who migrated to the city of Port Harcourt in search of a job opportunity. This decisive move by 18-year-old Binaebi typifies her as an autonomous agent who possesses the capacity through migration to influence the course of her own life.

Autonomy as a self-governing ability has dominated feminist discussions, with scholars variously contending autonomy to be value-laden because autonomous agents' preferences are mostly influenced by normative restraints, or value-neutral, as the agents' self-right prevails over right-rules. Positioning confrontation of domination as the hallmark of an effective feminist model for autonomy, Natalie Stoljar advances a strongly substantive, value-laden account, noting that 'only a strong substantive theory, namely, one that places restrictions on the contents of agents' preferences, explains the feminist intuition [as] preferences influenced by oppressive norms of femininity cannot be autonomous' (2000, 95). Stoljar's value-laden model of autonomy is prescriptive in its action-guiding principles that mandate agents to repudiate and fulfil specific values before their autonomy can be authorized. Agary upholds a similar view through the character of Zilayefa, who renounces maternal guidance, opting instead for self-rule. However, construing a woman as nonautonomous based on her preferences for subordinating feminine norms might be controversial, precisely as it views her as a socially isolated personality who places reasoning before any social commitment. What Agary describes instead are social entities who feel the impact of society on a daily basis and, through such experiences, carve out their distinctiveness.

Conversely, value-neutral feminists take a circumventing posture by placing no restrictions on the values that agents might independently elect to live by. Focusing on respect for values and the agency of women, Marilyn Friedman's value-neutral autonomy pronounces that the moment 'an agent chooses or acts in accord with wants or desires that she has self-reflectively endorsed, then she is autonomous [as it] does not matter whether someone's concern is itself the product of her socialisation' (2000, 5). Diana Meyers takes the discussion further, stressing that autonomy comes in degrees, since an agent's aptitude for critical reflection may function at various intensities of sophistication, contingent on her socialization and learning (1987). Meyers' and Friedman's models are informative in recognizing feminist efforts to respect the dissimilarities and diversity of agents. Their conceptions consider autonomy to be relational, noting social and familial influence in hindering or aiding an agent's aptitude for critical reflection, and the fact that autonomy functions in degrees. In *Yellow-Yellow*, notions of autonomy are explored as Agary, less keen on depicting male dominance, focuses mainly on the daily life choices of her female characters. By authorizing Binaebi's decisive urban migration, Agary contributes to the ongoing feminist discussions on autonomy.

The journey to the city transforms Binaebi's life as she maintains a relationship with a Greek sailor, Plato Papadopoulos: for the 'few weeks that [Plato] was in Port Harcourt, [Binaebi] was in heaven. She believed that she had found her life partner and that this man would take care of her [but] he left Port Harcourt without saying good-bye leaving behind his planted seed in [her] *belle*' (YY 7). This momentary relationship is indeed notable, one that objectifies Binaebi's body as a sexual commodity meant to be consumed and dumped at will. Charles Feghabo, in a postcolonialist reading of the text, contends that Binaebi's supposed 'otherness [as a] mulatto [is responsible for Plato's] devaluation of her humanity and her "womanity" [since such reduction is entrenched in a racist ideology of] the colonized being inferior [to the colonizer]' (2014, 315–32). Binaebi's experience is, for Feghabo, 'quintessential [to most] young Delta girls [who] have had their dignity ravaged [by] expatriates [who are] mostly males without their spouses' (2014, 322).

Much more than highlighting a gendered undertone that is entrenched in age-old ethnic differences, Agary describes instead social conventions in which female sexual autonomy is contained through sexual objectification. Plato's philandering demeanour that leads to the objectification of Binaebi's body is, I will demonstrate, similar to that of Admiral, whose liking for young Ijaw girls precipitates his ultimate relationship with Zilayefa, whom he views primarily as a sexual object. However, as emotionally wounding as Binaebi's experience might be, a careful reader will realize that it is condensed in the background as a flashback, with Agary intending not to trivialise this experience but to focus attention on Binaebi's eventual response: '[she] went back to her village [having] chosen to give [Zilayefa] life over the pursuit of her dreams' (YY 173). Agary through such representation centres attention on Binaebi's future rather than her past and thereby transforms the tempo of the text from androcentric to womancentric.

Binaebi's homecoming is, for Agary, an audacious act that validates the womancentric perception of the text. Through Binaebi's resolution, attention is centred on women's issues thus transforming the trend of the plot from androcentric to womancentric as the emphasis shifts from 'what happened' to 'how' Binaebi chose to live her life from then onwards. Significantly, Binaebi's preference for single parenting ensures that she, and by extension her daughter, dominates the plot, while issues regarding their male acquaintances are incorporated as an appendage. Through her actions, she authenticates her dynamic self, a distinctive lifestyle which she knowingly elects to live according to her own dictates. The absence of male dominance, rather than detracting from it, enhances the feminist temper of the text, as its womancentric approach makes it a more compelling feminist work (Nwokocha 2017). By sanctioning such subjectivity, Agary frees her female characters from subsidiary roles as objects and victims, transforming them into sovereign entities who possess the ability to decide their own fates.

Binaebi's preference for single parenthood authenticates her feminist intuition for she dares to be different by heading the family in a society where dual parenting patently headed by men is the model and standard against which other families are compared. Discussing single parenting, Azuka-Obieke Uchenna observes that until 'recently, single parenting is alien to Nigerian family culture. Where they exist at all, they are ignored as [an] exceptional phenomenon' (2013, 112). Expounding further on this, Liv Haram observes that for 'a woman to live on her own without male protection and control is not only an alien idea [...], but it even rebels against prime gender notions' (2004, 222–3). Both scholars' works highlight the foreignness of single parenting and the repressive social attitudes to it in the exceptional cases where it seems to exist. To some extent, I share both scholars' view concerning oppressive social attitudes toward single parenting but am not convinced of its foreignness. I argue instead that single parenting is native to Nigerian society, although a part of the culture that is relegated to the background. Emphasizing the existence of a flexible gender system among Nnobi society, Ifi Amadiume articulates that women could usurp masculine roles and consequently wield significant influence in society by means of 'Igba ohu', where women who are considered male daughters bear children in their own names (1987, 40–2). Agary's female characters, much as Amadiume's women, take sole responsibility for their sexual autonomy through their choice of procreating without male partners. However, unlike Amadiume's women, whose freedom is intermittently interrupted by their paternal figure under whose influence they live, Agary's women are independently accountable to no man.

Agary, through Binaebi's maternal headship, calls for a reconsideration of the conventional notion of the two-parent family as ideal for a child's development. Binaebi, the reader is informed, exerts maternal influence over her daughter, whom she pushes and models towards the route of enlightenment, '[i]n her dream, [Zilayefa] would go to university and study a subject that would get her a good job with enough money to take care of [herself]. If [Zilayefa] could take care of [herself], then [she] could take care of [Binaebi]' (YY 10). It has been argued that children from households where both parents are present will be emotionally stable and adequately nurtured. Underlining the psychological effect of *Yellow-Yellow*, Julie Nwangwu and Ibiene Iboroma opine that since the family is endowed with the responsibility to impart 'ethics, morals and decorum [its break-up will result in] the child often los[ing a] sense of values, morals and standard etiquettes' (2018, 22). Uchenna agrees, stating that, 'Empirical evidence has equally shown that children from intact homes will be well taken care of [unlike] children from single parents [who] generally have less time to devote to each child. This can have a negative impact on their schoolwork and their social development' (2013, 113–14). Complementary roles in the upbringing of the child might be helpful for the psychological, social and emotional well-being of the child; however, Agary denounces the predilection to hold it up as a benchmark for evaluating a child's progress. Zilayefa exhibits an intense awareness that she lacks, and wants, a paternal figure, an emotional state that leads to her eventual relationships with older men whom she uses to gratify her paternal craving, but this never affects her academic performance, for, '[u]nlike other parents who kept their children busy, my mother would not allow me to do too much chores [as a result] I did well in school. Compared to my classmates, I was above average' (YY 9).

Where Binaebi asserts agency in her capacity to plan both for herself and for her daughter, what the reader soon sees in the character of Zilayefa is a self-originating personality who repudiates such influence, opting instead for independence through her escape plan to the city with the final destruction of her mother's farmland through the oil spillage. Narrating the incident, Zilayefa expresses, '[d] uring my second to last year in secondary school, one of the crude oil pipes that ran through my village broke and spilled oil over several hectares of land, my mother's farm included' (YY 3). The spillage is so devastating that the 'tick liquid spread out, spreading more land and drowning small animals in its path [with] the smell [...] so strong it made [Zilayefa's] head hurt and turned [her] stomach' (YY 4). As such, Binaebi 'in a single day [...] lost her main source of sustenance. However, [for Zilayefa] she had lost that land a long time ago, because each season yielded less than the season before [due] to oil spills, acid rain [and] gas flares' (YY 4). This experience, for Feghabo, is illustrative of the ecological imperialism that results in the disempowerment of the Niger Delta women through the 'ecoterrorism carried out by the oil companies in the region [that] robs women of the economic independence enjoyed in the past' (2014, 326–7).

The environment is certainly an issue; however, what Agary describes is a social structure in which women are systematically dispossessed of their inheritance. The dispossession is a devastating state in which Binaebi feels incapacitated to pursue her dream of sponsoring her daughter's university education. Nevertheless, much as the activities of these oil companies interrupt Binaebi's line of inheritance by disrupting her intention to sponsor Zilayefa's post-secondary education, the Ijaw men also reinforce such dispossession, mainly by demanding a 'healthy meal when they were hungry, disregarding the fact that the women had to walk extra kilometres to get firewood or cultivate and harvest the food now fertilized by their sweat and blood' (YY 40). Because these Ijaw men 'did not succeed at home [as breadwinners], they drew the line at women participating in communal meetings on serious town issues', an act that contributes to their sharing among themselves the monetary compensation sent by the oil companies: 'Amananaowei [the village chief] and his elders [...] shared it amongst themselves' (YY 40). Binaebi's standard of living is noticeably hampered the moment she loses her farmland to the oil spillage, a situation that is further aggravated by her exclusion from the communal gatherings where the monetary compensation that would have given her an alternative source of living is shared. Agary, in this context, narrates a systemic oppression of women that facilitates their social and economic disempowerment.

Arguably, the ecological destruction of the land is responsible for the massive migration into the urban area by rural dwellers. Binaebi's inability to pay for her daughter's final secondary school examination due to the oil spillage could be read as being responsible for Zilayefa's later migration into the city. I argue instead that Zilayefa's quest for autonomy, her burning desire to be free from restrictive maternal care, rather than the oil spillage, is accountable for her mission to escape to the city, as she detests Binaebi's obsessive longing for a 'coveted university degree [which made her] insist on being at the drawing table with [God]' to ensure that her life plan for her daughter is reflected (YY 43). This fixation on schooling, although admirable, is worrisome to Zilayefa since it involuntarily suppresses her sexual autonomy, and this is key to her city passion. Zilayefa is bent on leaving the village at all costs, as she configures such a move as helpful for her individuality: 'My head was crammed with thoughts of how I would make it to the city – Port Harcourt, Lagos, anywhere! I went about my daily business with robotic precision' (2003, 34). Her incomparable quest for self-rule is responsible for this desperation for the city, and had the oil spill not happened, she would still have migrated, as her mother has always nursed the intention for her to go to university. In fact, the oil spill threatens instead of expediting Zilayefa's city move. Being indigent means that Binaebi is unable to sponsor her child's higher education, and her fascination with maternal care demands that she refuses to permit her daughter's migration quest to an environment where she has no acquaintance to whom she can entrust the safety and welfare of her child.

It takes Zilayefa's subsequent uprising for her mother to, at last, concede to her escape plan. She devises a master escape plan by deciding to 'find someone to take me away [during] celebrations where many people came in from the city: [for] I figured it would be easy to slip away from my mother's watchful eyes and meet that special someone who would save me from certain death in my claustrophobic village' (YY 17). To be autonomous, as Stoljar asserts, agents must consider themselves as 'self-originating sources of claim [with a] sense of worthiness to act [and] being competent to answer for one's conduct' (2000, 107). Zilayefa similarly authenticates her distinctiveness in her capacity to invent a life plan that suits her disposition. She backs up her plan with action for before long: 'after I had made this decision, Mama Ebiye took me on a trip to Port Harcourt. We went to a bend-down boutique where I bought second-hand dresses in which I intended to execute my plan of action' (YY 17). Exclusively committed to self, Zilayefa's individualistic bearing and teenage uprising embody her feminist perception, for Binaebi reluctantly approves of Zilayefa's migration plan and informs her that 'Pastor Ikechukwu [their local church pastor] was going to help me find a place to stay in Port Harcourt' (YY 44). Armed with the recommendation note from Pastor Ikechukwu, she finally secures sponsorship from Sisi, a tall, plump, biracial wealthy single-parent woman in her mid-70s who 'offered to pay my exam fees, and anything related to my education' (YY 68).

Zilayefa ultimately consents to her mother's plans, intending to go to the university, but not until she has experienced life on her own terms, rather than declining it based only on her mother's cautionary tales. For Stoljar, agents should refute influences that quench their ability to achieve autonomy. Zilayefa is also distinct in the manner she, while getting input from all sides, positions herself in a kind of liminal space, sorting out what she wants to do and how she can do it on her own terms. Encouraged by Sisi, and Lolo (Sisi's 25-year-old acquaintance) to remain focused and never to be 'carried away by city life' (YY 68–9), Zilayefa validates her normative competence in the manner in which she assembles this advice, and sorts and evaluates it by reflectively endorsing some statements and repudiating others. For instance, Zilayefa sanctions Lolo's self-confidence but repudiates her restrictive relationship by nurturing a liaison with Admiral. Curious about the sort of relationship Admiral wants, Zilayefa enquires of a friend Emem, who is similar to her with regard to age and interests: 'How will I talk to him? He is a fine man, but he is old enough to be my father'. Emem retorts, '[w]hen he is rubbing your body, do you think he will be thinking about how old you are? [She laughingly adds] make sure he uses his raincoat o, [for the] last thing you want is to get pregnant with Grandpapa' (YY 133). It then dawns on Zilayefa what the sort of relationship that Admiral demands is, and, 'although it was early enough to change my mind and opt out [...] I was not sure I wanted to' (YY 132–3).

Choosing to retain her relationship with Admiral, Zilayefa demonstrates her strong sense of authority in asserting her individuality by deliberately using Admiral to fill her need for a paternal figure: 'I had never lacked female affection from my mother, and now Lolo, but I had never experienced attentive, male affection, except my brief experience with Sergio. I felt as though I was about to experience that, and I was pleased with the prospect' (YY 140). It could be argued that this prospect endangers Zilayefa's autonomy, as the relationship empowers Admiral to exploit her sexually. A particular incident that gives credence to this happens in the text during the actual sexual intercourse: 'I got up and went to give him a kiss on the cheek [...] but before I could plant the kiss, he took me by surprise and pulled me into his chest and planted his lips on mine [...] then he lifted me up and placed me gently on his king-sized bed' (YY 144). The expression 'to give him a kiss' is the only active role carried out by Zilayefa in this context; she remains inert afterwards allowing Admiral to dominate the scene.

On the subject of adolescent sexual subjectivity, Sharon Lamb articulates that a personal sense of authorization is not sufficient to establish real empowerment, as 'many of the images today of a young woman in charge of her sexuality come from the world of pornography and reproduce very old exploitative scenes of male voyeurism and women's victimization and/or oppression' (2010, 300). For Lamb, feeling empowered and being empowered are distinct features that maintain a link with power and autonomy: 'Feeling emboldened sexually is not the same as empowered. And if a girl feels empowered, because she has the power to attract attention and admiration via her sexuality, that may be a kind of power of sorts, but it's narrow. That is, it is a feeling of being empowered to be a sexual person' (2010, 301). Zilayefa could be viewed as a victim of sexual objectification given that her unpreparedness results in her contraceptive risk: 'I admitted [to Emem] that [Admiral] did not use a raincoat as she had advised and [she] promised to get me some birth control pills [...] to make sure I did not buy fakes' (YY 145).

Although Zilayefa is sexually exploited, Agary seems reluctant to view the experience as nonautonomous, reasoning that Zilayefa reflectively endorses the relationship to satiate her paternal void: 'I felt a deep sense of longing for [Admiral], not because of the comfort Emem hinted at, which was money, but because I was hoping that the relationship would give me a taste of close paternal affection that I had never had' (YY 138). Zoe Peterson, on the subject of sexual empowerment, observes that neglecting girls' personal experience of sexual consent, even when it is influenced by male prototypes of desire, seems to undermine girls and thereby conflicts with the aims of empowerment (2010, 307–13). To undermine girls' experiences of sexual authorization is, for Peterson, to propose that their own opinions of sexual control and confidence are untrue, for, 'if we tell girls that they cannot even trust their own perceptions of enjoyable and empowered sexuality, then they are left with no compass to point the way toward healthier sexuality' (2010, 308–9). Unlike Lamb's earlier assertion, it is possible to infer from Peterson's claim that adolescent girls have the right to authorize their sexual actions, and it could be wounding to their ego to assume them wrong. Agary similarly describes a budding sexual experience of a teenager who insists that her actions and inactions be considered as autonomous.

Eventually pregnant, Zilayefa rejects Admiral's safe clinical advice opting instead for self-induced abortion. She carefully selects and chews special plants known to '[wash belle] some were so bitter I had to force them down with water [...]. I did not know what to expect [...] if I would live to see the next day. However, if I lived, it was an opportunity for a personal rebirth along with Nigeria' (YY 177). This indeed is a risky act, a demanding quest for freedom that would have claimed her life; '[m]y chest grew tighter and tighter [...]. I feared that I might die. I cried but could not feel sorry for myself because I had made the choices [even] I had to bite on a towel to keep from screaming as my body pushed out blood and clumps of tissue that had been forming a little person inside me for almost three months' (YY 178). For Friedman, an agent is adjudged autonomous if she determines 'what she chooses and does' (2000, 4). Zilayefa is, for Agary, autonomous given her subjective sense of authority in determining what suits her most.

Zilayefa's preferences for much of the text have been self-motivated, commencing with her repudiation of her mother's instructive anecdotes, her living on her own terms as against Sisi's and Lolo's restrictive relationships, her refutation of Emem's contraceptive advice and her ultimate rejection of Admiral's harmless medical abortion. This is what I recognize as a subversive feminist character: a personality who views autonomy as a core value. Although the abortion scene resonates strongly with the ambivalence of Zilayefa's relationship with her mother and the need to refocus on her studies, 'I promised God and myself that I would focus only on completing my education and making my mother, Sisi, and Lolo proud of me, [particularly as] I wanted the confidence Lolo had [and] if Sisi was right, the choices also that came with an education' (YY 177). However, Zilayefa does also reject her mother's example: 'My life was out of focus, and I wished for the days when my mother planned my life, but I could not go back to what I had rejected' (YY 177). Had Binaebi made the choice that her daughter makes, Zilayefa would not be alive. Zilayefa, then, is not following her mother's wishes entirely through her repudiation of motherhood. This denunciation validates Zilayefa's individuality, suggesting that she does not subscribe to the notion that motherhood intensifies a woman's self-worth, and consequently differs from Stoljar's women who 'accept the norm that pregnancy and motherhood increase their worthiness' (2000, 109). Zilayefa ultimately survives the abortion for at 'daybreak when I woke on the bathroom floor, I was grateful to see another day; that was luxury enough. The rest I would have to figure out' (YY 178). By authorizing Zilayefa's moral capability to carry out an abortion successfully, Agary significantly acknowledges women's full individuality and right to exercise choice, and through this act advances the feminist core philosophical value of women's autonomy.

It is evident that autonomy is fundamental to Agary's women. Here, I have demonstrated that although the issues around the environment are definitely important, with a great impact on some of the opportunities accessible in the text, the female characters' unprecedented drive for self-rule is the prevailing motif that Agary explores in the novel. I have examined self-asserting agents, highlighting that Agary's women play dynamic roles in determining their daily choices. Much like Binaebi's maternal option, her single parenthood and preference for care validate her value-neutral autonomy, Zilayefa's individualistic, self-originating, and to some extent, ambivalent lifestyle with its ultimate repudiation of motherhood authorizes her strong substantive brand of autonomy. Agary upholds that both choices are valid and autonomous, but maintains some degree of reservation towards the maternal option, viewing it as limiting to the overall goal of autonomy, and this necessitates her authorization of Zilayefa's drastic self-induced abortion. This subversive femininity, coupled with the womancentric nature of the plot, I have argued, validates the text as a feminist work.

WORKS CITED

Agary, Kaine. 2006. *Yellow-Yellow*. Lagos: Dtallkshop.

Amadiume, Ifi. 1987. *Male Daughters, Female Husbands Gender and Sex in an African Society*. London: Zed Books.

Awhefeada, Sunny. 2013. 'Degraded environment and destabilized women in Kaine Agary's Yellow-Yellow'. In *Eco-critical Literature: Regreening African Landscapes*. Ogaga Okuyade, ed. Lagos: African Heritage Press, 95–108.

Chukwumah, Ignatius. 2013. 'The displaced male-image in Kaine Agary's *Yellow-Yellow*'. *Tydskrif vir Letterkunde* 50.2: 47–61.

Feghabo, Charles Cliff. 2014. 'Inverting otherness in Kaine Agary's Yellow-Yellow'. In *Tradition and Change in Contemporary West and East African Fiction*. Ogaga Okuyade, ed. Amsterdam & New York: Rodopi, 315–32.

Friedman, Marilyn. 2000. 'Autonomy, social disruption, and women.' In *Relational Autonomy Feminist Perspectives on Autonomy, Agency and the Social Self*. Catriona Mackenzie and Natalie Stoljar, eds. New York: Oxford University Press, 35-51.

Haram, Liv. 2004. '"Prostitutes" or Modern Women? Negotiating Respectability in Northern Tanzania'. In *Rethinking Sexualities in Africa*. Signe Arnfred, ed. Sweden: Almqvist & Wiksell Tryckeri.

Kant, Immanuel. 1785[1948]. *Groundwork of the Metaphysic of Morals*, translated and analysed by H. J. Paton. New York: Harper & Row.

Lamb, Sharon. 2010. 'Feminist ideals for a healthy female adolescent sexuality: A critique'. *Sex Role* 62.5: 294–306.

Mackenzie, Catriona, and Natalie Stoljar, eds. 2000. *Relational Autonomy Feminist Perspectives on Autonomy, Agency and the Social Self*. New York: Oxford University Press.

Meyers, Diana. 1987. 'Personal autonomy and the paradox of feminine socialization'. *Journal of Philosophy* 84.11: 619–28.

Nwangwu, Julie and Ibiene Iboroma. 2018. 'The psychological effects of single parenthood in Kaine Agary's *Yellow-Yellow* and Sefi Atta's *Everything Good Will Come*'. *British Journal of English Linguistics* 6.6: 22–33.

Nwokocha, Sandra. 2017. 'Subversive responses to oppression in Chimamanda Ngozi Adichie's *Purple Hibiscus*'. *The Journal of Commonwealth Literature* 54.3: 367–83. https://journals.sagepub.com/doi/10.1177/0021989417720817

Ohagwam, Uchenna. 2018. 'The Niger Delta crises in the Niger Delta novel: Reflections on Kaine Agary's *Yellow-Yellow*'. *Journal of Arts & Humanities* 7.11: 11–17.

Peterson, Zoe. 2010. 'What is sexual empowerment? A multidimensional and process-oriented approach to adolescent girls' sexual empowerment'. *Sex Role* 62.5: 307–13.

Rawls, John. 1971. *A Theory of Justice*. (rev. ed., 1999). Cambridge, MA: Harvard University Press.

Stoljar, Natalie. 2000. 'Autonomy and the feminist intuition'. In *Relational Autonomy Feminist Perspectives on Autonomy, Agency and the Social Self*. Catriona Mackenzie and Natalie Stoljar eds. New York: Oxford University Press, 94–111.

Uchenna, Azuka-Obieke. 2013. 'Single-parenting, psychological well-being and academic performance of adolescents in Lagos, Nigeria'. *Journal of Emerging Trends in Educational Research and Policy Studies* 4.1: 112–17.

Local Collisions:

OIL ON WATER, POSTCOLONIAL ECOCRITICISM, AND THE POLITICS OF FORM

KATHERINE E. HUMMEL

Helon Habila's 2018 Presidential Address to the African Literature Association conference seemed to confirm what some literary critics have suggested about his 2010 novel, *Oil on Water*: it is not a political text – or, at least, not political *enough*. Balking at the label of 'environmental activist' that has hounded him since the novel's publication, Habila reiterates throughout the address that he has an 'instinctive discomfort at being defined and classified by [my] subject matter' ('The Future of African Literature' 154). In this case, Habila's subject matter is the Niger Delta, the oil-rich region in south-eastern Nigeria that has endured unabated drilling since 1958, producing upwards of 300 oil spills per year, in addition to 35 million tons of carbon dioxide and 12 million tons of methane from natural gas emissions (Watts 196). Curiously, *Oil on Water* does not shy away from these environmental facts. As Habila's protagonists, the Port Harcourt-based journalists Rufus and Zaq, travel throughout the Delta in search of Isabel Floode, a kidnapped British woman, they witness first-hand the widespread environmental degradation, indigenous displacement, and increasingly violent competition for limited resources that have come to characterize the region. Their experiences in the Delta, however, are framed through a detective story, a genre Habila finds appealing because it is 'a form that is the least political', one that 'make[s] the reader believe this is pure entertainment, nothing more' ('Future' 160).[1] In using the detective genre to distance himself from the text's potential political claims, Habila positions himself within a new generation of African artists, including Dambudzo Marechera and Taiye Selasi, who argue that African writers should not bear the responsibility of functioning as their respective nation's conscience. In doing so, Habila not only questions a hallmark of Nigerian literary production – namely, the writer's duty to 'bea[r] witness to Nigerian social conditions' (Griswold 3) – but also contextualizes his anti-activist stance in a longer, and as yet unresolved debate about the relationship of the African writer's politics to aesthetic forms.[2]

While postcolonial ecocritics have not criticized Habila's aversion to activism per se, they have taken issue with the role of witnessing in *Oil on Water*, suggesting the novel pays insufficient attention to the oil industry's transnational reach. For Byron Caminero-Santangelo, the novel prioritizes Rufus' individual acts of witnessing at the expense of 'the *historical* generation of the situation by specific (neo)colonial relationships' ('Witnessing the Nature of Violence' 234, emphasis in original). Echoing Jennifer Wenzel's observation that the novel maintains a 'strange distance' from the Delta's militarized politics ('Behind the Headlines' 14), Caminero-Santangelo concludes that Habila 'implicitly suppress[es]' the representation and critique of structural violence ('Witnessing' 239). Part of this suppression comes, as Leerom Medovoi notes, from the fact that the novel 'concludes with no particular journalistic result, no mediational strategy for representing the environmental condition in a politically efficacious way' (23). For all his idealized statements about the journalist's duty to bear witness, it appears that Rufus 'is admittedly too close to his subject to report its broadest social ramifications' (LeMenager 130). In other words, while *Oil on Water* clearly depicts the environmental degradation of the Delta in all its realist detail, the novel's intensely local focus risks a kind of parochialism, thus appearing to foreclose the multi-scalar interventions that postcolonial ecocritics have come to expect of environmentally engaged fiction.

So, what is the purchase of a text like *Oil on Water* that, on the surface, appears tailor-made for postcolonial ecocritical analysis, but falls short of articulating an anticolonial, anticapitalist, or environmentalist politics? How do we read Habila in light of his own refusal to take up an activist mantle? It seems to me that these frustrations with Habila's political shortcomings reveal the limits of postcolonial ecocriticism's long-standing preoccupation with representation, by which I mean the thematic content of literary texts. As Rob Nixon declares in *Slow Violence and the Environmentalism of the Poor*, the central challenge of slow violence is representational. In working against temporally and geographically dispersed forms of violence, writer-activists must use the aesthetic tools at their disposal to re-route habits of attention toward marginalized groups and phenomena, all while articulating their affiliation with an environmentalist agenda (Nixon 3, 31). The problem with relying on representation as the sole means for change, however, is that it assumes increased visibility will lead to increased action. In her recent book, *The Disposition of Nature*, Jennifer Wenzel, following Stephanie LeMenager, troubles the linear progression that '*seeing* is *knowing* and that *knowing* is a catalyst for *caring*, *acknowledging*, or *acting* to rectify suffering or injustice' (14, emphasis in original). Rather than continue to emphasize visibility as the outcome of representation, Wenzel advocates for a shift in 'thinking in terms of *legibility* and *intelligibility*' as the outcome of aesthetic forms like genre, narration, and rhetorical address (*Disposition* 13, 15). Literary forms offer tools for approaching the conditions under which environmental injustice can be 'read, understood, and apprehended' (Wenzel, *Disposition* 15). With respect to oil, this shift from visibility to legibility is crucial for understanding how, as Imre Szeman writes, '*every* social practice, cultural form and political expression is animated by the sheer energetic capacities and seemingly boundless excess of fossil fuels' (286, emphasis in original). In other words, oil's pervasiveness is so embedded in daily life that representation alone is not sufficient to apprehend it, let alone act in response to it.

Bearing these contexts in mind, I want to suggest that, by averting an explicitly activist stance and working within the supposedly apolitical detective genre, Habila in fact contributes to this shift toward legibility and apprehension. *Oil on Water*, then, stages its political interventions not at the level of representation, but at the level of form. By '*mak[ing] the reader believe* this is pure entertainment'(emphasis added), to return to a quote from his lecture, Habila's detective story does not offer any prescriptive activist messaging, nor promises a solution to environmental injustice, thus resisting the knowledge-action-change structure that Wenzel finds so limiting. In doing so, *Oil on Water* deepens the 'mystery' of the detective story beyond Isabel's kidnapping to question the effectiveness of political interventions that depend, as Griswold discusses, on bearing witness and bringing social issues to light.[3] In this context, how does witnessing need to change at the level of form to reframe the political work of the journalist-protagonists, or the writer-activist? One potential response, I argue, is Habila's use of a strategically local narrative form. By taking our attention to the intensely localized scale of the Delta, *Oil on Water* stages encounters between multiple colliding literary, social, and environmental forms, and produces innovations in narrative structure and voice that seek to amplify the perspectives of those most severely marginalized by petro-violence itself.

In describing *Oil on Water*'s intersecting forms as 'colliding', I invoke the new formalist turn in literary studies, which provides a theoretical framework to explore the ways that forms of power often exceed literary representation. Caroline Levine redefines 'form' to encompass both the aesthetic and the social. Form refers to 'all shapes and configurations, all ordering principles, all patterns of repetition and difference … It is the work of form to make order. And this means that forms are the stuff of politics' (*Forms* 3).[4] Both Levine and C. Namwali Serpell use the concept of 'affordance', first developed by cognitive psychologist James J. Gibson, which concerns the latent capacities of an environment that may make themselves available to human and nonhuman animals (Serpell 21). While Serpell is interested in the phenomenological connections between formal affordances and affective experiences of readers, Levine applies affordances to describe how forms structure and shape different aspects of everyday life, especially when multiple forms 'collide', or encounter each other (*Forms* 18). I find that Levine's theory is particularly relevant for reconsidering the kind of political intervention that *Oil on Water* makes. Responding to sceptics of her argument in *PMLA*,[5] Levine explains that political work does not always involve 'pulling this whole rotten society up by the roots' ('Three Unresolved Debates' 1240). Rather, what looks 'like quietism, like complacency' – or, in Habila's case, like an 'entertaining' detective story – is in fact a new understanding of how literary and social forms can help produce a more robust understanding of how power operates systemically, invisibly, and beyond representation (Levine, 'Debates' 1240).

In my reading of *Oil on Water*, I identify two overarching forms that pervade the literary, social, and environmental in the novel – opacity and circularity. These forms encapsulate and characterize other collisions that occur throughout the text, including the generic clashes of Rufus' never-published newspaper exposé and the novel itself, as well as the titular environmental conflict between oil and water. In the readings that follow, I will first explain how opacity and circularity – though not inherently violent in themselves – shape the particular modes of violence that endure across media platforms, political alliances, and material environments within the Delta's local context. While opacity and circularity contribute to the Delta's oppressive conditions, they also collide with Habila's strategically local narration, which enables a path to agency through the narrative's structure and voice. As Rufus travels throughout the Delta collecting stories of multiple local constituencies, he cedes his role as narrator to provide these speakers with direct access to the narrative itself. The novel's complex narrative structure – which can itself be described as opaque and circular – in fact formally amplifies the voices of local constituencies throughout the Delta. As such, Habila, through Rufus, focuses on the populations that have failed to reach the thresholds of legibility required for recognition on a global scale. Formally amplifying these voices through a strategically local narration thus offers postcolonial ecocriticism an opportunity to move beyond questions of explicit environmental representation and toward an awareness of the forms that shape and structure power.

VIOLENT COLLISIONS: OPACITY AND CIRCULARITY

In *Oil on Water*, opacity and circularity emerge as two significant forms that provide insight into the complexities of the Delta's petro-culture. Although these forms co-constitute and collide with each other, I describe their functions separately to trace how they impact different elements of social, environmental, and political life among the Delta's constituencies. Opacity characterizes the narrative from the novel's opening pages, both in Rufus' description of his memories as 'a fog' and the literal 'fog' that envelops the boat that carries him away from Irikefe Island in search of Isabel (Habila, *Oil on Water* 3–4). The waters of the Delta are similarly opaque from pollution, transforming from clear and easily navigable to 'brackish', 'dense', 'sulfurous', and full of dead birds and animals within a few minutes (Habila, *OOW* 5, 9). Here, oil is both hyper-visible and invisible. Ongoing spillages and leakages from underwater pipelines slowly pollute the waters and poison animals, but these effects are not always detectable as they are occurring. Rather, as Medovoi states, Habila demonstrates that oil is 'not simply a toxin that has poisoned its surroundings … but [is] itself a new and persistent feature of the environment' (22–3).

Beyond these literal manifestations, opacity also characterizes the media narratives that both obscure local constituencies from view on a global stage and that create near-permanent descriptions of Nigeria as irreparably corrupt. This is best understood through the BBC News report playing in the background during Rufus' visit to James Floode, in which he updates James about the status of the mission to rescue Isabel. The BBC report discusses Isabel's kidnapping in detail before transitioning to 'a long, rote-like voice-over about poverty in Nigeria, and how corruption sustained that poverty, and how oil was the main source of revenue, and how, because the country was so corrupt, only a few had access to that wealth' (Habila, *OOW* 102–3). After listening to the report, James comments, 'You people could easily become the Japan of Africa, the USA of Africa, but the corruption is incredible' (103). Opacity shapes this encounter in two significant ways. First, the global visibility of a BBC News report is given to Isabel rather than the multiple local constituencies facing the violent conditions in the Delta on a daily basis. Despite the horrid conditions of her kidnapping, Isabel receives the platform that many local groups – such as the displaced indigenous clan led by Chief Ibiram, or the Doctor struggling to publish toxicity reports – long to have. Instead, these constituencies are homogenized under the label of 'corruption', a narrative that James affirms in his commentary. While corruption certainly contributes to local poverty and ongoing pollution, these media narratives refuse to complicate their understanding of the Delta's inhabitants and keep these groups marginalized and illegible on a global stage. Opacity, then, is more than a characteristic of polluted water; it also shapes the modes of legibility that refuse to see the Delta inhabitants as anything more than victims of a corrupt state.

A second form, circularity, characterizes the temporal rhythms in the Delta that contribute to local constituencies' ongoing opacity to non-local media publics. From an environmental perspective, the networks and waterways of the Delta are materially circuitous. Initially without an experienced guide to lead them, Rufus, Zaq, and other journalists are stuck travelling in circles, unable to read the hostile signs of the Delta's environment to take them to their destination. Socially and politically, however, these circular rhythms involve repeated conflicts between independent militant groups, who are fed up with ongoing oil extraction schemes that give them no share of the profits; government-backed soldiers sent to quell their rebellions; and oil companies, who have no intention of ceasing their operations in the Delta and who also fund the soldiers' efforts. Importantly, local journalists are complicit in this cycle as well. As Rufus explains early in the novel, militant groups – like the one led by the Professor, who holds Isabel captive – typically kidnap individuals from Port Harcourt to lure journalists to the Delta. Once they arrive, the militants 'would make long speeches about the environment and their reasons for taking up arms against the oil companies and the government', eventually exchanging the kidnapped victim for a ransom and a write-up in the local newspapers (Habila, *OOW* 54). Indeed, Zaq's editor Beke views Isabel's kidnapping as the opportunity of a lifetime: 'How often does the oil company come knocking on your door, asking for a favor? We're talking petrodollars here, and a major scoop! ... Our circulation will hit the roof – ' (Habila, *OOW* 36). The expanded circulation that Beke imagines requires journalists to prioritize speed over accuracy. For example, when Rufus and Zaq encounter the aftermath of a gun battle, journalists swarm over a body found in the bushes, 'cameras flashing' to capture a front-page-worthy image to satisfy their editors

(Habila, *OOW* 77). The cycle of the journalistic process complements the broader cycle of what Michael Watts has termed 'petro-violence', in which 'oil as a resource, as a *form* of extraction and transformation, as a *form* of wealth, and as a *system* of meanings are all related' (204, emphasis added). Despite Rufus' understanding of his profession as a noble one, journalism in the novel ensures that circularity, as a form, endures over time and collides with opacity to keep local voices marginalized from transnational platforms.

NARRATIVE COLLISIONS: STRUCTURE, VOICE, PLATFORM

Opacity and circularity not only characterize the forms of violence that shape political life in the Niger Delta; they can also be used to understand the incredibly difficult structure of *Oil on Water*'s narrative itself. Described by Maximilian Feldner as 'complex and disorienting' (519), the novel's structure is extremely non-linear, beginning *in medias res* and employing multiple flashbacks per chapter so that the plot resembles more of a spiral than a chronological timeline. Interestingly, the narrative structure's apparent incoherence distinguishes it from most other examples of petro-fiction, or literature about oil. As Wenzel writes, 'there is something almost antinarrative about the ontology of oil, if narrative is understood as the working out of cause and effect and oil is understood to produce something out of nothing' ('Petro-Magic-Realism Revisited' 212). Because Habila's narrative makes 'the working out of cause and effect' nearly impossible, *Oil on Water*'s formal qualities are thus closer to the ontology of oil, per Wenzel's assessment, than not. This deliberately complex narrative choice again demonstrates how Habila reframes the 'mystery' at the heart of the detective story. By leading readers and critics like Caminero-Santangelo and Medovoi to expect a clear solution to petro-violence through the detective genre, Habila in fact critiques those very expectations when no such solution is provided. Instead, Habila stages his intervention at the level of form, exploring how aesthetic elements like narrative structure and voice can perform a different kind of political work, both by revealing patterns like opacity and circularity, and by providing an unlikely path to agency for local constituencies amidst environmental crisis.

For these reasons, I want to consider how the forms of journalism and the novel collide in *Oil on Water* within the broader categories of opacity and circularity. Recalling Levine, colliding forms produce 'strange effect[s], with minor forms sometimes disrupting or rerouting major ones' (*Forms* 18). I find this definition useful for countering the charges of parochialism against Habila. The collision of the novel and the newspaper, in this instance, produces what I have been calling a strategically local narration, one that formally amplifies the voices of the constituencies throughout the Delta whose stories have been ignored or homogenized by the forms of opacity and circularity I discussed above. By focusing at such an intensely localized level, Habila answers Cajetan Iheka's call to move away from a singular focus on violent forms of resistance in the Delta, as the 'liberatory potential' of violence 'does not mitigate its adverse ecological consequences' (Iheka 87). Ogaga Okuyade agrees; by decentring the violent activities of the militant-soldier-oil corporation cycle, 'Habila not only gives [the local people] a voice, but he also re-humanizes them by rewriting history from the perspective of the displaced and oppressed' (231). Habila's strategically local narration, then, operates by ceding direct narrative control from Rufus to members of multiple Delta constituencies, demonstrating how the 'smaller scale and intimate treatment' of his subjects offers new insights for postcolonial ecocriticism regarding the politics of form (LeMenager 130).

While Rufus interviews many groups throughout the Delta as part of his assignment, I want to focus on two specific instances that best illustrate how the collision of forms amplifies the voices of the most severely marginalized. The first instance of this strategically local narration comes when Rufus and Zaq meet Chief Ibiram, the leader of a clan who has been forced off their ancestral lands. Relating his people's history to Rufus, Chief Ibiram describes how the oil executives, partnering with government soldiers, arrested the clan's previous chief for refusing their offer to buy the village, and then subsequently evicted the people after the chief's mysterious death in prison. On a representational level, Ibiram's story offers insight into one among many indigenous groups who face persecution from the government and oil corporations. However, the formal depiction of this scene raises the stakes further. Rufus synthesizes the majority of Ibiram's story, much as he would if he were writing for a newspaper article. However, the narrative portrayal of this account retains authentic elements of Ibiram's voice. As Caminero-Santangelo points out, Ibiram's people refuse payment from the oil companies because of their commitment to 'an ethic of care for the land' ('Witnessing' 232). Habila writes, 'though they may not be rich, the land had been good to them … What kind of custodians of the land would they be if they sold it off?' (*OOW* 43). The formal intersections between the novel and

Rufus' journalistic ethos are clear here, as the above quote occurs in Rufus' synthesis, but directly expresses Ibiram's environmental ethic at the level of narrative itself.

In the chapter's final paragraph, Ibiram's first-person voice takes over the narration, again discussing his refusal to accept payment for the land:

> We didn't take their money. The money would be a curse on them, for taking our land, and for killing our chief. We left, we headed northwards, we've lived in five different places now, but always we've had to move. We are looking for a place where we can live in peace. But it is hard. So your question, are we happy here? I say how can we be happy when we are mere wanderers without a home? (Habila, *OOW* 45)

By ending the chapter with Ibiram's haunted, unanswered question, Habila makes two formal interventions. First, he reintroduces circularity in a new context – the displacement of Ibiram's people, who are forced to become 'wanderers without a home'. Indeed, later in the novel, the community is once again on the move, abandoning the settlement where Rufus and Zaq spend the night to try to find better accommodations closer to Port Harcourt. Second, the rhetorical openness of Ibiram's question implies that there is no satisfactory answer to this situation from journalists alone. Not only does Zaq's question seem short-sighted given the profound loss of the clan's social, cultural, and environmental home, but it also indicates that there is no easy solution to the ongoing thefts of land, life, and oil in the Delta (Okuyade 227). However, while Rufus does not publish Ibiram's story within the confines of the narrative itself, Habila's novel does bear witness to Ibiram and his people, demonstrating how the formal amplification of local voices expands the representation of Delta peoples beyond monolithic narratives of corruption and poverty.

A second example of strategically local narration occurs later in the novel when Habila meets Dr Dagogo-Mark, the personal physician of a soldier known as the Major. Unlike Ibiram's account, which blended Rufus' synthesis with Ibiram's voice, the Doctor speaks almost entirely in the first person. He discusses the slow obsession with oil in the local villages, and describes how, less than a year after oil drilling began, the community's health began to decline. The Doctor makes three distinct efforts to publicize the toxicity results of the village's water supply and blood levels, both of which have become contaminated. After being ignored by the oil workers and their manager, he seeks attention from bigger platforms:

> [W]hen people started dying, I took blood samples and recorded the toxins in them, and this time I sent my results to the government. They thanked me and dumped the results in some filing cabinet. More people died and I sent my results to NGOs and international organizations, which published them in international journals and urged the government to do something about the flares, but nothing happened. More people fell sick, a lot died. (Habila, *OOW* 153)

Each of the Doctor's attempts to create awareness about the toxicity and pollution in the Delta is met with resistance from the government. Here, we can see how the form of opacity becomes concentrated in the government's ability to silence not only individuals, but also internationally recognized research supported by humanitarian organizations. The fallout from these decisions is both environmental and social. As the landscape becomes further polluted and more villagers die, the Doctor notices how life in the town can no longer sustain itself, transforming the village into one of the many deserted settlements that Rufus and Zaq encounter early in the novel. I find the Doctor's story crucial both for its succinct depiction of how opacity functions to produce violence and for its indictment of the non-local actors that Habila has been accused of ignoring. Because of the government's decisions – motivated by petro-dollars and enforced by the military – local human lives and nonhuman environments remain at risk. Once again, it is the collision of the novel and the newspaper that brings this story to light. Informed by Rufus' journalistic ethos, the text formally amplifies the Doctor's narrative and offers him a similar opportunity to Chief Ibiram – to circulate his story not within the toxic networks of the Delta's media-militant-government complex, but within the broader transnational reaches of the Anglophone novel. Accessing the novel's platform offers a path through the violent forms of opacity and circularity to emphasize the social and environmental stakes of each constituency's struggle to survive in the Delta.

This essay has argued for a revitalized attention to the aesthetic and social politics of form to better attend to systems of power, like the hegemony of oil, that exceed mere representation. By way of conclusion, I want to consider Rufus' conversation with Salomon, which spans over ten pages and is the longest first-person account that Rufus collects in the Delta. Salomon is Isabel's driver who, as the accused architect of her kidnapping, is easily conscripted into the dominant narrative of Nigerians as greedy, oil-addicted, and corrupt. In finding Salomon, Rufus presumes he will also find an answer to the 'mystery' that initiated his journey throughout the Delta, and eagerly promises

Salomon that he can help him tell 'the real truth' (Habila, *OOW* 216). However, as Salomon's story unfolds, it quickly becomes clear that there is nothing here for Rufus to 'solve' in the conventional sense of the detective story 'exorcis[ing] the crime' in its conclusion (LeMenager 126). Salomon's motivation for the kidnapping is personal: Isabel's husband, James, has had an affair with and impregnated Salomon's fiancée, Koko. When retelling his story, however, Salomon connects James' personal affront with the oil industry's pervasiveness. He recalls, 'the money wasn't even coming out of [James'] pocket: the oil company always pays the ransom, and … if you thought about it carefully, you'd realize that the money came from *our oil*, so we would be getting back what was ours in the first place' (Habila, *OOW* 221, emphasis added). Salomon rationalizes Isabel's kidnapping as reparation not only for his own humiliation, but for the decades of neocolonial oil theft that has devastated the Delta region. At the source of the 'mystery' Rufus has been trying to solve, then, is another iteration of the militants' logic to reclaim oil wealth by any means necessary. Salomon is here complicit in the circular forms of media-military-corporate violence that ensnare the Delta's various constituencies. However, as the star villain in the media's kidnapping narrative, he is also a victim of the opacity that keeps the 'truth' of his story and the conditions that led to it obscured. In using his journalistic ethos to amplify Salomon's story at the level of *Oil on Water*'s narrative, Rufus thus faces a political question: what does it mean to tell *this* Delta story alongside those of Chief Ibiram and the Doctor, whose very livelihoods have been threatened by the petro-violence Salomon appears to perpetuate?

In a sense, this question re-emphasizes Wenzel's argument that knowledge about environmental injustice does not necessarily lead to action nor change. Even when Rufus has the 'truth' of Ibiram's, the Doctor's, and Salomon's stories, he is no more poised to offer a journalistic intervention than at the beginning of his journey to the Delta. While it is frustrating to leave his readers with no clear-cut solution, Habila's lack of diegetic resolution as well as his own hesitation to articulate an activist stance reinforce the notion that prescriptive or straightforward answers are impossible, and even naïve, in the context of the Delta. Instead, Habila leverages the politics of form to give narrative authority to the Delta's multiple constituencies, including individuals like Salomon, who further complicate what it means to bear witness to environmental injustice when the outcomes of political work do not extend directly from representation. What remains, then, is a novel that attempts to make marginalized voices more legible by allowing each local constituency to speak on their own terms – an outcome that I find political to its core. By attending to the politics of form, Habila demonstrates that the novel, especially one informed by Rufus' journalistic ethos, can provide tools for apprehending how powerful forms like opacity and circularity fuel petro-violence on multiple scales. In tracing how these forms and others collide across the social, the environmental, and the literary, postcolonial ecocritics can thus begin to make legible both the sites of environmental degradation and the forms of power that structure and enable them to endure.

NOTES

1. Habila's framing of the detective story as the 'least political' genre is, ironically, a common criticism of crime fiction, especially in the post-apartheid South African context. Mike Nicol's work in particular has been accused of 'a pervasive abandonment of the complexities of (permanent) transitional politics in favour of the consolations of genre' (Titlestad and Polatinsky 270). In response to these critiques, Christopher Warnes and Geoffrey V. Davis argue respectively that, in addition to being commercially popular, South African crime fiction by Nicol, Deon Meyer, and Margie Orford enables readers to explore contemporary social anxieties regarding violence, instability, and misogyny (Warnes 981–4; Davis 8–13).
2. Much of Habila's framing in his lecture discusses his frustration with African literature's continued preoccupation with debates on nation, language, and authenticity. Citing Marechera's resistance to the 'African writer' label, Habila aligns himself with contemporary 'Afropolitan' and 'post-national' writers like Selasi, who are 'unfettered by tradition or national expectation', yet still remain influenced by their parents' African languages and cultures ('Future' 157–8).
3. For more on the question of witnessing with respect to literatures of the Niger Delta, see Caminero-Santangelo's 2017 essay, 'Petro-Violence and the Act of Bearing Witness in Contemporary Nigerian Literature'.
4. Levine defines politics after Jacques Rancière, arguing that it 'gives shape to collective life' ('Debates' 1239). Politics for Levine encompasses both disruption and order, the latter of which is imposed spatially and temporally. Her taxonomy of forms – wholes, rhythms, hierarchies, and networks – refers to different types of patterning, shaping, and ordering that illustrate different articulations of politics, both on their own and as they collide.
5. Levine's *Forms* was the subject of a 2017 *PMLA* Theories and Methodologies forum. While she receives positive reviews from several respondents,

critics of her argument cite scepticism about the 'radical' nature of her project. Langdon Hammer calls her argument 'a disciplinary fantasy of empowerment' that seeks to rescue literary studies from the current crisis in the humanities (1204), while Hoyt Long disagrees with her sampling of sociological concepts without a similarly rigorous application of sociological methods (1206). Levine responds to these charges and concludes that literary texts 'know something about how overlapping constraints work in ways that social scientists, precisely because of their methods, do not' ('Debates' 1242).

WORKS CITED

Caminero-Santangelo, Byron. 'Witnessing the Nature of Violence: Resource Extraction and Political Ecologies in the Contemporary African Novel'. In *Global Ecologies and the Environmental Humanities: Postcolonial Approaches*. Elizabeth DeLoughrey et al., eds. New York: Routledge, 2015. 226–41.

——. 'Petro-Violence and the Act of Bearing Witness in Contemporary Nigerian Literature'. In *A Global History of Literature and the Environment*. Louise Westling and John Parham, eds. Cambridge: Cambridge University Press, 2017. 363–76.

Davis, Geoffrey V. '"The Advent of a Genre": Crime Fiction and the State of the Nation in South Africa'. *Journal of Postcolonial Writing* 54.1 (2018): 6–18.

Feldner, Maximilian. 'Representing the Neocolonial Destruction of the Niger Delta: Helon Habila's *Oil on Water* (2011)'. *Journal of Postcolonial Writing* 54.4 (2018): 1–13.

Griswold, Wendy. *Bearing Witness: Readers, Writers, and the Novel in Nigeria*. Princeton: Princeton University Press, 2000.

Habila, Helon. *Oil on Water*. New York: W. W. Norton & Company, 2010.

——. 'The Future of African Literature: ALA Presidential Address, 2018'. *Journal of the African Literature Association* 13.1 (2019): 153–62.

Hammer, Langdon. 'Fantastic Forms'. *PMLA* 132.5 (2017): 1200–05.

Iheka, Cajetan. *Naturalizing Africa: Ecological Violence, Agency, and Postcolonial Resistance in African Literature*. Cambridge: Cambridge University Press, 2018.

LeMenager, Stephanie. *Living Oil: Petroleum in the American Century*. Oxford: Oxford University Press, 2014.

Levine, Caroline. *Forms: Whole, Rhythm, Hierarchy, Network*. Princeton: Princeton University Press, 2015.

——. 'Three Unresolved Debates'. *PMLA* 132.5 (2017): 1239–43.

Long, Hoyt. 'The Sociology of Forms'. *PMLA* 132.5 (2017): 1206–13.

Medovoi, Leerom. 'Remediation as Pharmikon'. *Comparative Literature* 66.1 (2014): 15–24.

Nixon, Rob. *Slow Violence and the Environmentalism of the Poor*. Cambridge: Harvard University Press, 2011.

Okuyade, Ogaga. 'Negotiating Identity in a Vanishing Geography: Home, Environment and Displacement in Helon Habila's *Oil on Water*'. In *Natures of Africa: Ecocriticism and Animal Studies in Contemporary Cultural Forms*. F. Fiona Moolla, ed. New York: NYU Press, 2016: 212–34.

Serpell, C. Namwali. *Seven Modes of Uncertainty*. Cambridge: Harvard University Press, 2014.

Szeman, Imre. 'Conjectures on World Energy Literature: Or, What Is Petroculture?' *Journal of Postcolonial Writing* 53.3 (2017): 277–88.

Titlestad, Michael and Ashlee Polatinsky. 'Turning to Crime: Mike Nicol's *The Ibis Tapestry* and *Payback*'. *Journal of Commonwealth Literature* 45.2 (2010): 259–73.

Warnes, Christopher. 'Writing Crime in the New South Africa: Negotiating Threat in the Novels of Deon Meyer and Margie Orford'. *Journal of Southern African Studies* 38.4 (2012): 981–91.

Watts, Michael. 'Petro-Violence: Community, Extraction, and Political Ecology of a Mythic Commodity'. In *Violent Environments*. Nancy Peluso and Michael Watts, eds. Ithaca: Cornell University Press, 2002. 189–212.

Wenzel, Jennifer. 'Behind the Headlines'. *American Book Review* 33.3 (2012): 13–14.

——. 'Petro-Magic-Realism Revisited'. In *Oil Culture*. Ross Barrett and Daniel Worden, eds. Minneapolis: University of Minnesota Press, 2014. 211–25.

——. *The Disposition of Nature: Environmental Crisis and World Literature*. New York: Fordham University Press, 2020.

'It is the Writer's Place to Stand with the Oppressed':

ANTHROPOCENE DISCOURSES IN JOHN NGONG KUM NGONG'S *BLOT ON THE LANDSCAPE* AND *THE TEARS OF THE EARTH*

EUNICE NGONGKUM

INTRODUCTION

For the past several decades, climate scientists have acknowledged the alarming impact of human actions on the earth system. Atmospheric carbon devolving from greenhouse gases, biotic impoverishment, flooding, soil erosion, extreme weather conditions, and a warming planet are some indicators of this phenomenon. The urgency of the situation has led to the conclusion that the present rate at which the decline of the earth's natural life-support systems is being accelerated by human action is ten to two hundred times higher than the average over the past ten million years (Watts). The Anthropocene, which has come to define this imprint, is 'a twenty-first century term that some scholars use to signal that human activity has attained the scale of a geological force akin to a volcanic eruption or a meteorite changing the Earth as a system' (Deloughrey 2). As a theoretical platform, it transcends geology to engage knowledge from interdisciplinary fields, bringing what Danila Cannamela calls 'a rich variety of proposals that address social and environmental concerns at a planetary scale' (5). Such interdisciplinarity is a convenient yardstick for foregrounding human accountability, thus inviting a crucial dialogue about our earthly circumstances.

This article seeks to contribute to such dialogue through a postcolonial ecocritical reading of selected poems from the Anglophone Cameroonian poet John Ngong Kum Ngong's *Blot on the Landscape* (2015, hereafter referred to as *Blot*) and *The Tears of the Earth* (2018, hereafter referred to as *Tears*). Grounded in the understanding that, in the current ecological crisis, 'acts of cultural representation can wield significant power' (Clark 2019, 2), I seek to show how Ngong's poetry, from a Cameroonian/African prism, intersects the Anthropocene as an emergent global force, inviting humans everywhere to engage with the ever-increasing, complex nature of the culture/nature interaction. Poetry for Ngong, as these two collections typify, can aptly translate scientific results on the phenomenon into forms that will move people to action. In an aesthetic rooted in visionary realism, protest, affect, symbolism and borrowings from oral traditions, Ngong highlights the declensionist perspective of the Anthropocene, witnessed in irreversible change, damage and loss; occasioned, for the most part, by the ineluctable intersection between capital and neocolonial politics. His primary aim is, firstly, to enlighten readers on the unprecedented and dangerous nature of human actions on the biosphere. Secondly, he proposes an ethics of care and repair of the environment as a positive contribution to our ecological futures.

Ngong's aesthetic model is rooted in a traditional African view of the social responsibility of art – a major defining paradigm of cultural productions from the continent. Written African literature, to which category Ngong's poetry belongs, has historically performed this social role, responding, at various stages of the continent's evolution, to the dilemmas besetting it. Simon Gikandi notes that art for the African writer is 'at least one of the ways available to the writer to organize himself and his society to meet the perils of living' (29). The current anthropogenic climate change constitutes one such peril for Ngong and his society. As an 'environmentally conscious poet whose consciousness stems from ecological literacy' (Vakunta par 11), his art becomes a mobilizing idiom meant to give both content and warning to an otherwise complex 'glocal' phenomenon. Indeed, in one of the poems in *The Tears of the Earth*, the poet's/writer's role is underscored in the line 'it is the writer's place to stand with the oppressed' (2). How Ngong does this, in my selection, constitutes the major thrust of this article.

With more than ten published collections of poetry to his credit, John Ngong Kum Ngong is one of the most prolific poets writing in Anglophone Cameroon today. John Nkemngong Nkengasong notes that, while his work 'covers a broader historical spectrum than that of many other Anglophone poets, it is evidently a product of history and of historical circumstances of marginalization [and] assimilation' (52). The poet's commitment to issues of injustice and oppression in his works – injustice and oppression that take the environment as an important site of engagement – is here underscored. In a review of the award-winning *Walls of Agony* (2006), Shadrach Ambanasom notes that 'the Cameroon that the poet examines is a country blessed with many natural resources which are unfortunately mismanaged by a few privileged citizens to the detriment and misery of many'. This concern with the environment undergirds a concern for human life in a damaged world; a position that has evolved over time, crystallizing in the two collections analyzed here. Both confirm Ngong as an ecopoet, conscious of the urgency of 'writing in a world of accelerated environmental change' (Reilly 258).

In reviewing *Blot on the Landscape*, Peter Wuteh Vakunta says that 'the volume is a battle cry, urging everyone to fight back against the forces – including human nature itself – ravaging the earth'. For James Enongene, *The Tears of the Earth* presents 'the poet … deeply touched with noble anger at the plethora of ills that bedevil his society and beyond, especially the [hu]man-induced suicidal threat to his unique habitat – planet Earth' (v). Vakunta and Enongene situate both collections of poetry in the Anthropocene, which is the issue at stake in this article. My analysis seeks to show that Ngong's engagements with the Anthropocene are sited in the postcolonial context and thus, 'do not lay claim to the "novelty of crisis" but are rather rooted in a 'historical continuity of dispossession and disaster caused by empire' (DeLoughrey 2). Vakunta seems to corroborate this when he notes that 'the poet uses poetic license to engage with issues relating to the intersection between poetry, politics and environmental activism' in Cameroon and the world at large. Enongene equally opines that 'the poems [in *The Tears of the Earth*] particularly take to task the local Cameroon/African and even global environmental politics impaled on the antlers of politics of interest, mal-governance and an insidious global materialistic culture' (v). The postcolonial ecocritical paradigm I adopt, here, becomes meaningful in articulating Anthropocene discourses in Ngong's poetry, given its imbrication in postcolonial politics, society, environment, and economics.

As a reading template intersecting postcolonial theory and ecocriticism, postcolonial ecocriticism, Elizabeth DeLoughrey et al. say, involves 'how environmental change is entwined with the narratives, histories and material practices of colonialism and globalization' (2). A postcolonial ecocritical reading of Anthropocene discourses in Ngong's poetry foregrounds lived experiences of ecological degradation, crisis and transformation in Cameroon/Africa as being intimately bound up with colonial and neocolonial capitalist practices. In the selection I analyze, the postcolonial context is one in which the ruling elite perpetuate practices of former colonial powers largely to the detriment of the masses, who, caught up in the situation, become complicit in environmental degradation. Such a position in the poetry gestures towards a postcolonial ecocritical reading, all the more so, if one agrees with Clark that 'Arguably, the rise of debate on a global

"Anthropocene" must now render all ecocriticism "postcolonial" in a broad sense, as the economic systems and lifestyle of any "developed" country necessarily impinge on the material contexts of all other parts of the world' (2019, 137–8).

The Anthropocene is informed by the understanding that the hitherto secure operating zones of human life, namely, the natural systems and processes undergird by the nine planetary boundaries are now under pressure thanks to human activity (see Rockström and Klum). Ngong's poetry sounds the alarm that climate disruption on a planetary scale is not only a future threat but a lived reality that needs to be addressed.

ANTHROPOCENE ENTANGLEMENTS IN VERSE: VISIONARY REALISM AS POETIC FOCUS

As a keen observer of the historical reality around him, Ngong's poetry abounds with vivid pictures of degraded landscapes, devolving from the actions of humans whom he describes as 'eco sworn enemies/ draining the earth of gracefulness' (*Blot* 3). Aptly conveyed through metaphors and motifs, such depictions unite each of the collections in an organic thought pattern, consistent with the poet's position that, while the Anthropocene foregrounds human agency, the outcome of such agency is at best catastrophic. For instance, the collection *Blot on the Landscape* is constructed on the metaphorical 'blot' which refers at once to devastated landscapes (both rural and urban) depicted in some of the poems as 'plastic place[s]', 'knotty country', 'drab dog eat dog city', 'the earth my sore mother', 'slim slippery streets' and 'realm of dust' (10, 17–18, 19, 21). Insensitive humans in poems like 'Breathing with Difficulty' are imaged as 'mouthpiece[s] of carrion' with a 'putrid train of thought/ not cut out for giving rise/ to beauty that clears the mind', they are the 'blot on the landscape' (7–8). The outcome of their actions on the ecosphere are obvious in 'the land [that lies] in waste/ and feeling the itch of decay' with 'the woodlands [...] all gone/ and my ozone layer sheet torn' (7, 11).

In *The Tears of the Earth*, the motif 'tears of the earth', on which the entire collection is built, presents the earth, in anthropocentric terms, shedding tears in anguish as a result of the ruptures – captured in images of tears, destruction, scars, fissures, shock – on its surface caused by humans. For instance, in poems like 'Beyond Recognition', 'Problem Child' and 'The Tears of the Earth', the earth is presented as being 'beyond recognition', 'scared' and 'torn' by 'arrogant man' equally referred to as 'earth's problem child', 'hatchet men' and 'murderers' who, in a 'mad bid/ to dominate the whole world' and 'feed [his/ their] greedy miscreant heart' have 'defiled and disfigured' it, pumped it 'with weed killers and nuclear waste' and 'with potash and insecticides / for a better yield of harvest' to the extent that now the 'soil is no longer fecund', 'its spent ground muddy and bitter' and her features, 'muddied beyond recognition' (*Tears* 1, 4, 6).

The above images are striking in their visionary realist ethos, faithfully representing 'an [anthropogenic] epoch that has thrown our alleged agency over time and memory into disarray' (Cannamela 5). This is allegorical in perspective; allegory being, Elizabeth DeLoughrey argues, 'the fundamental rhetorical mode for figuring the planet as well as the historical rift between part and whole that is symbolized by the Anthropocene' (18).

The visionary realist vision is crucial in Ngong's poetic project of representing the Anthropocene in its scalar and temporal templates. In its allegorical model, it captures the disjunction between space and time and what DeLoughrey calls 'the perceived disjunction between humans and the planet, between our "species" and a dynamic external "nature"' (2). In several poems, the speaking voice of nature or the questioning voice of an overwhelmed human, addressed to nature, communicates a situation, increasingly out of control for the human species. For instance, 'If You were Human' (*Blot* 1–2) situates the reader in the realm of the seasons, which are distinguished by special climate conditions. These periodic divisions, often marked by changes in weather, ecology, and amount of daylight in each hemisphere, have enormous influence on vegetation and plant growth but, current disruptions in global weather conditions trouble the lyrical 'I', whose requests to these times of the year reflect a disturbed mind:

> Seasons, if you were human,
> understanding and forthright
> as you roll across the world,
> if you could communicate
> I would put forward my case
> for fairness and equity. (1)

Questions of justice and fairness intersect this apostrophe as a poetic engagement with an oft critiqued Anthropocene attribution of ecological collapse to an undistinguishable 'humanity' when both accountability and susceptibility are unequally disseminated. The global South, from which the poet comes, contributes minimally to atmospheric carbon emissions, but suffers the brunt of catastrophic changes in weather more than the developed North. Through this example, Ngong's poetry illuminates some of the blind spots of a 'universalizing' discourse of the Anthropocene.

In stanza two, the understanding is that the seasons, which as part of nature 'roll across the world', and 'glide across the globe', have become very 'severe/ as you visit the whole world'. In this stanza, the Anthropocene is engaged at the global level, unlike in stanza one where the focus was much more local. This movement between the local and the global, characteristic of several poems in this collection, reinforces the idea that manifestations of human violence on the earth are both planetary and specific. Together with the use of the apostrophe, such structural patterning constitutes the poet's tools in navigating an ecological crisis of great scale. Together with the realist images in the poetry, they acknowledge the poet's consciousness of the disturbing 'derangement of scale' (Clark 2015) engendered by the Anthropocene.

The above stanza also intimates that environmental conditions, like seasonal change, ebb and flow naturally without human intervention; but, in the current global context, significant environmental issues are traceable to human activity. This is perceptible in the 'floods [which now] devastate our homes and the bush fires [that] fell forests' (1), the handiwork of those 'who cover long long distances/ looking for forests to despoil/ for [their] empires to flourish' (12). The images of floods and bush fires ground the Anthropocene in a typical Cameroon/African context witnessing unusual floods and ravaging bushfires in recent times. The reference to 'empires' hints at how contemporary environment issues, in postcolonial contexts, cannot be divorced from the history of globalization and imperialism. Climate change, in this context, is thus a fallout of empire. These distinct Cameroonian/African topographies are relevant in a poetic enterprise that engages the global and local facets of the Anthropocene, resonating with Tom Bristow's view, as summarized by David Farrier, that 'an engagement with the particularities of local place can expand our sense of affinity with places far distant and therefore cultivate a greater awareness of the distributed nature of what Clark calls the Anthropocene's scale effects' (Farrier 19). In this poem, and in others like 'Our Shame' (*Tears* 30), 'Eco Sworn Enemies' (*Blot* 3), 'Carry Me Away' (*Blot* 3) and 'Stretches of Green' (*Blot* 54), the normalizing figure of the Anthropocene is conveniently grounded or questioned through such engagements with specific frameworks and, in this way, highlight and/or question its global character.

The possessive 'our' underlines the speaker's identification with those suffering the vagaries of weather. This gestures toward the 'us/them' binary, representing hierarchization in postcolonial contexts where 'different subjects are positioned in different ways with respect to humans' geologic reordering of time and space in the here and now' (Braun et al.). Ecological problems are the fallouts of 'structures of hierarchy and elitism [...] geared to exploit both other people and the natural world as a source of profit' (Clark 2011, 2). The poor and their environments in the global South suffer the brunt of the climate crisis more than any other group and place. At a personal level, the possessive equally relates the poet's commitment to the oppressed; a role coterminous with that of the artist in traditional African society, which I have highlighted above.

Stanza three employs images of luxuriance, fruitfulness and abundance to underscore traditional knowledge about the seasons' role in sustaining human life. For instance, one learns that, in the rainy season, 'a green carpet' bejewels 'the bumpy surface of my land', 'many fruit trees ... bud' and 'the scent of life ... mushrooms'. 'Fed' by the 'clement sun' until harvest time, these elements of nature are 'gather[ed] for survival' by humans who, paradoxically, have now endangered their very source of life. Angered by such unconscionable behaviour, the speaker seeks to liaise with the seasons to 'blot out blot on the landscape' – the 'blot' image here reinforcing humanity's negative activities on the biosphere. A recollection of the seasons' role in human survival here is an engagement with the category of deep time of the Anthropocene, namely, 'the vast time scales that shape the Earth system and all life forms that depend on it' (Farrier 6). While seasons, from time, are a natural occurrence of a somewhat positive disposition, the present context of floods and atmospheric carbon emissions with effects on the ozone layer, are recipes of an eerie future disaster of incalculable proportions. The poet calls this fallout 'an ecological stroke', in 'Eco Sworn Enemies' (*Blot* 3); a poem whose thematic and formal ethos, enhances one's understanding of the deep time dimension of the Anthropocene.

In the piece, a place-based poetics of climate change serves not only to delineate its devastating effects, but also to show how time past, time present, and time future are entangled in the Anthropocene. The place is Buea – capital of the South West Region of Cameroon and erstwhile capital of former West Cameroon and German Kamerun, and the place of the poet's formative years. In the poem, therefore, Buea is a place of entangled histories – colonial, neocolonial and biographical.

The specific locale is the G.R.A., otherwise the Government Residential Area, reserved for government functionaries during colonial times, a practice continued by post-independence governments. The evocation of a specific environment, laden with historical significance, eloquently underlines how, in postcolonial contexts like Cameroon, 'ruptures to social and ecological systems have already been experienced through the violent processes of empire' (DeLoughrey 7).

Through the prism of collocation, this poem of four equal-length stanzas intersects the past and present to foreground how humans, otherwise 'eco sworn enemies', have transformed an ecologically viable past into an environmentally threatening one for its inhabitants:

> I remember G.R.A.
> Buea, once so green and clean
> now so brown and repulsive
> thick with unsavoury smells
> and infectious diseases. (3)

In the last three stanzas, one would have thought that 'The green hedges of yesteryear' and the carpet grass', part of the heritage of this place, would have been destroyed by, say, natural 'floods' but this is not so. The agents of destruction are identified as unconscionable humans who 'drain the earth of [its] gracefulness'. The consequence now is that G.R.A. Buea's 'beautifully trimmed lawns,/ the gardens and flowers/ that made [the poet-speaker] beam like a child/ each time he visited them/ are now blots on the landscape'. The poem ends with the voice of an ecologically conscious individual longing for change, while also warning of a dire future if no concrete action is taken:

> I burn for a new G.R.A.
> not exclusively in Buea.
> I burn for it in the nation
> for greenery to protect us
> from an ecological stroke. (3)

The image of a looming 'ecological stroke' – the word 'stroke' lending itself to geological and medical interpretations – shows how the protrusion of a time of calamities into human life is both a sign of the rupture provoked by the Anthropocene and of the 'violence of ecological harm' which Richard D. G. Irvine says 'is a confrontation with the potential of a deep time in which we are no longer at home' (207). The lyrical 'I' is clearly uneasy with the situation and his anxieties are reinforced by the regularity in stanza pattern and the repetitive 'I burn for', which convey a sense of urgency in the call for change of attitude in his nation and beyond. It is an urgency informed by the awareness of how the temporality of the Anthropocene is signalled in its demanding of us, David Farrier says, 'to accept the fact that the ethical proximity between the most fleeting act in our present and planet-shaping effects that will play out over millennia, is deeply menacing' (2).

Tracking toxic waste is another way of understanding anthropogenic climate change. In poems like 'The Garbage Bags are Full' (*Blot* 4), 'Death Waits in the Wings' (*Blot* 5), 'Breathing with Difficulty' (*Blot* 7), 'Your Heart's Trademark' (*Tears* 15) and 'Beyond Recognition' (*Tears* 1), Ngong engages these categories as markers of the Great Acceleration, a term coined by Will Steffen and his colleagues to indicate the material 'fallout' of globalization. In 'Beyond Recognition', for instance, the reader is confronted by an unhappy earth, 'bowed in deep sorrow' consequent on the degradation of its biophysical and biological spheres by 'plastic bags and arrogant man'. 'Foul smelling deadly waste' literally 'choke her' and man's 'darkening thoughts' (a hint here at climate change denialism and the wanton global dispersal of waste) have 'muddied her' beauty. The consequence is that 'the purity of green is gone' (green symbolizing luxuriance, beauty, and the life-giving attributes of the earth), 'forests [are] butchered for crude oil' and she is 'filled 'with/ everything impure and deadly'. The verb 'choke' is particularly significant here if one understands that plastics mark the excesses of the global age, especially as their non-degradability literally 'chokes' the earth, affecting its mass and energy flows.

The reference to 'forests' being 'butchered for crude oil' resonates with a Cameroon/ Africa where a neocolonial politics of self-aggrandizement, in league with foreign capital, abets large-scale deforestation in the search for mineral wealth. In the poem, the understanding is that this wealth ends up in the pockets of a few, while the masses, with whom the poet identifies, and who aid in 'tearing up the earth' for such extraction, never get anything as the line 'the petrol never gets to us' underscores. The cutting down of trees as a prelude to oil exploration destroys the forest ecology, releasing large amounts of carbon dioxide into the atmosphere. That is why, in the poem, the earth 'today' is said to be 'in tears, filled with/ everything impure and deadly'.

In this two-stanza poem of unequal length, anthropomorphism captures an earth in the throes of human engendered destruction while also emphasizing its embodiedness; a perspective informed by a traditional Cameroonian/African environmental ethos that recognizes nonhuman nature as living entities. It also underlines affect, namely, the poet's empathy for the decaying earth with whom he shares affinities as victims of global capitalist exploitation. Such exploitation is traceable to imperialist politics, whose major focus was, and remains, located in the exploitation of bodies and environments for profit. Ngong's 'Paradise Lost' (*Blot* 32–3) underscores this as it draws from biblical and Miltonian antecedents to foreground former colonial spaces as continuous resource spaces, namely, zones of privileged access for imperial powers.

In this poem, a remembered beautiful and harmonious environmental past – a paradise of sorts, conceived in utopian terms – serves, through the technique of juxtaposition, to better illuminate the present degradation caused by 'the parasites' who came and 'chose to blow to pieces/ our life and our happiness'. The 'parasite' image aptly defines capitalist predators who live off others without their consent. This is further reinforced by references to them as 'lewd leeches [who] appeared/ and chose to live on our blood/ to refill their treasuries/ with dollars from our felled trees'. The consequence for a land where harmony existed between animal and bird species, where everything 'was green, ever so green', are enormous; the exquisite balance of ecosystems has been disrupted; 'birds and butterflies / that used to grace our Eden', have now taken 'to the air / in the clutches of panic' while 'all the animals are dead and the trees are felled daily'. In disrupting a once viable ecological setting, imperialist forces have become a geologic force.

Ngong's place-based and global representations of the Anthropocene, in the preceding paragraphs, uniquely underscore the multiple and often contradictory discourses that attend it. Through a visionary poetics, the poetry captures the complex planetary drama of human existence against geological time. It is a situation that urgently necessitates the development of responsible ways of dealing with the earth as the next portion of this paper will underscore.

ENGAGING ECOLOGICAL RECUPERATION: POETRY AS ACTIVISM

Ngong's chronicling and interpreting of our ecological present constitute a poetics of confrontation with humans meant to raise awareness about the Anthropocene. Known as consciousness-raising in ecocritical circles and rooted in didacticism and activism, this prelude to concrete action for change serves to 'facilitate the process of conscientization by promoting a reflective awareness and thoughtful understanding of the environment' (Ngongkum 151).

In the second place, a discourse of activism, in the poetry, promotes palpable action such as tree planting, to ensure a radically viable future for the earth. Poems such as 'Let Me Plough with You' (*Blot* 73–4), 'Time to Clean' (*Blot* 77–8), 'Take A Stand' (*Tears* 38), and 'Do Not Back Off Mate' (*Tears* 44), intervene in this light, espousing an ethics of care and repair by their call to protect and restore living ecosystems as a way of responding positively to the climate crisis. In 'Take A Stand', for instance, the speaker enjoins his audience not to be cowed by 'death's head', that is the climate crisis, but to 'take your stand on the pathway/ away from the Cobra's base/ under the light of the moon/into any empty plot/ to replant uprooted blooms/ and give your kind a name' (38). Deniers of global warming are likened to 'Cobras' because, in the poet-speaker's estimation, such a mindset is simply dangerous and evil. The injunction to take a stand is informed by the urgency of environmental repair; which is not a future action but one in the here and now as 'Time to Clean' intimates:

It is time to clean the land
and plant evergreen windbreaks
to deal deforestation
disciples a deadly blow
for stars not yet come to light
to bring to light the bright green
face of a brutalised land
and a corrupted landscape.

For the poet, however, such concrete action must be the fruit of a heightened consciousness, which is why, in poems like 'The Darkness Inside Kills' (*Blot* 67–8), 'Make Melody' (*Blot* 75–8), 'Stoke The Fire' (*Tears* 39), 'Words Should Shout Conscience Awake' (*Tears* 49), and 'Out of the Red Zone' (*Tears* 50), the role of poetry and that of the poet is shown to be primordial. 'Words should Shout Conscience Awake', for instance, draws from gastronomy to underline the poet's belief in art's effective role in ecological recuperation. The reader learns that 'words' can effectively awaken consciences 'to give us a human face' and cause us 'to bind the tears of the earth'. The writer's 'words like seasoning spices', literally ground together in the creative enterprise, is a recipe that can 'touch the heart/ and nourish the wanting head'; a crucial issue if 'our Earth [is] to smile again'. The poet's role as gadfly in 'Stoke the Fire' is highlighted when he says:

I have come out of the ashes
to stoke the fire within us.
I have come out of the ashes

to make you feel beyond the pain
piercing through the lobes of your brain.
Sunrise will water our dry roots
and the notes from my flute like shafts
run Earth's uncontested foes through. (39)

Repetition of the line 'I have come out of the ashes', shows the speaker's own awakening to the reality of climate change. The fire symbol, representing emotion, zeal, creativity and motivation, shows that 'science alone', Bill McKibben rightly observes, 'can't make change, because it appeals only to the hemisphere of the brain that values logic and reason'. Emotion is needed because 'we're also creatures of emotion, intuition, spark' (8). The poet believes that his logic, namely, his diction, together with the music of song, highlighted in the 'notes from my flute', can effectively move human hearts and souls to action for the environment at risk. In 'Out of the Red Zone', the intimation is that solving the climate crisis is achieved by changing individual behaviour. At the forefront is the poet-speaker who, having 'cut down trees for warmth/ and received gifts from friends', has realized that 'the warmth and gifts last not'. He has now left that 'red zone/ sparkling with sweetmeats and wine' to become an activist, enjoining fellow humans to 'stop being cold' and take a stand for the environment as a way of rebuilding their lives. Human life, as it were, depends on the planet, and humans must respond urgently to the call to fight for it.

CONCLUSION

While the nexus between poetry and the environment is not immediately self-evident, this analysis of Anthropocene discourses in John Ngong Kum Ngong's poetry reveals a poet who is conscious of the art's effectiveness in humanity's response to the planet's intensifying biodiversity crisis. By investing his poetry with daily lived experiences of anthropogenic change from the spaces of Cameroon/Africa, he unearths the entanglements of the Anthropocene at the local and global levels and, in this way, helps the reader to better understand its dynamics to respond adequately. The poetry reveals that while the effects of climate change may be slightly different everywhere, the consequences tend to be the same. That is why, through affect and activism, the poet makes a 'glocal' call for environmental stewardship, grounded in accountability and maintenance of the planet.

WORKS CITED

Ambanasom, Shadrach A. Book Review. *Walls of Agony*. John Ngong Kum Ngong. https://www.postnewsline.com/2006/06/book_review_2.html#more, accessed 11 August 2019.

Braun, Bruce, Mat Coleman, Mary Thomas and Kathryn Yusoff. 'Grounding the Anthropocene: Sites, subjects, and struggle in the Bakken Oil Fields'. 2015. https://antipodeonline.org/201314-recipients-2/iwa-1314-braun/, accessed 12 August 2019.

Bristow, Tom. *The Anthropocene Lyric: An Affective Geography of Poetry, Person, Place*. London: Palgrave Pivot, 2014.

Cannamela, Danila. '"La poesia dopo la fine della poesia": Visionary Realism and the Ethics of Playful Care in Aldo Nove's Twenty-First Century Poetry'. *California Italian Studies* 8.1 (2018):1–23.

Clark, Timothy. *The Cambridge Introduction to Literature and the Environment*. Cambridge: Cambridge University Press, 2011.

——. *Ecocriticism on the Edge: The Anthropocene as a Threshold Concept*. London: Bloomsbury, 2015

——. *The Value of Ecocriticism*. Cambridge: Cambridge University Press, 2019.

DeLoughrey, Elizabeth. *Allegories of the Anthropocene*. Durham: Duke University Press, 2019.

——, Jill Didur and Anthony Carrigan, eds. *Global Ecologies and the Environmental Humanities: Postcolonial Approaches*. London: Routledge, 2016.

Enongene, James Njume. 'Foreword'. *The Tears of the Earth*. John Ngong Kum Ngong. Bamenda: Langaa RPCIG, 2019. v–viii.

Farrier, David. *Anthropocene Poetics: Deep Time, Sacrifice Zones and Extinction*. Minneapolis: University of Minneapolis Press, 2019.

Gikandi, Simon. 'Chinua Achebe and the Post-colonial Esthetic: Writing Identity and National Formation'. *Studies in 20th & 21st Century Literature* 15.1 (1991): 29–41.

Irvine, Richard D.G. 'Seeing Environmental Violence in Deep Time: Perspectives from Contemporary Mongolian Literature and Music'. *Environmental Humanities* 10.1 (2018): 257–72.

McKibben, Bill. 'High Ice and Hard Truth: The Poets Taking on Climate Change'. 2018. https://www.theguardian.com/environment/2018/sep/12/high-ice-hard-truth-a- poetry-expedition, accessed 15 September 2019.

Ngong, John Kum Ngong. *Blot on the Landscape*. Bamenda: Langaa RPCIG, 2015.

——. *The Tears of the Earth*. Bamenda: Langaa RPCIG, 2019.

Ngongkum, Eunice. *Anglophone Cameroon Poetry in the Environmental Matrix*. Frankfurt: Peter Lang, 2017.

Nkengasong, John Nkemngong. 'Interrogating the Union: Anglophone Cameroon Poetry in the Postcolonial Matrix'. *Journal of Postcolonial Writing* 48.1 (2012): 51–64.

Reilly, Evelyn. 'Eco-noise and the Flux of Lux'. *((eco(lang) (uage) (reader))*. Brenda Iijima, ed. New York: Portable Press/Nightboat Books, 2010. 255–74.

Rockström, Johan and Klum, Mattia. *Big World, Small Planet: Abundance within Planetary Boundaries*. Yale: Yale University Press, 2015.

Vakunta, Peter Wuteh. 'Cry of the Environment: A review of Ngong's *Blot on the Landscape*'. June 2015. https://www.pambazuka.org/land-environment/cry-environment-review-ngong%E2%80%99s-%E2%80%98blot-landscape%E2%80%99, accessed 21 July 2015.

Watts, Jonathan. 'Biodiversity Crisis is About to Put Humanity at Risk, UN Scientists to Warn'. 2019. https://www.theguardian.com/environment/2019/may/03/climate-crisis-is-about-to-put-humanity-at-risk-un-scientists-warn, accessed 20 June 2019.

Black Atlantic Futurism, Toxic Discourses and Decolonizing the Anthropocene in Nnedi Okorafor's The Book of Phoenix

MICHELLE LOUISE CLARKE

INTRODUCTION

and in the salt chuckle of rocks
with their sea pools, there was the sound
like a rumour without any echo
of History, really beginning.
The Sea is History, Derek Walcott (1986)

The last lines of Derek Walcott's poem *The Sea is History* sets the tone for a close reading of *The Book of Phoenix* by Nnedi Okorafor (2015a). The sea as 'history' asserts that the Atlantic ocean's sinister history is not past-tense, but resounds into present day. Nestled within this highly charged narrative, an ecocritical reading can tease out an interweaving of both racial and environmental histories. Okorafor's dystopian novel is layered with narratives of waste, and reverberations of the slave trade, set against a science fictional world in which African-Americans are used for a neoslavery which involves cyborgian, transhuman transformations, organ trade and other cruel genetic experiments. This text is far from pastoral narratives of nature, as it traverses racial geographies, using the Atlantic as its anchor point in a speculative oceanic imagining. The Afrofuturist[1] aesthetics of the text collapses past, present and future, 'interlinking historiographical and mythical rhetoric not so much in order to reconstruct a lost history, but to dismantle the established one and give scope to altogether different, highly fantastic scenarios instead, which are as much of the future as they are of the past' (Mayer 2000, 566).

'Green' criticism has been the defining position of ecocriticism since its formation as a discipline. The discourse has been plagued by 'wilderness fetishism' which Ross (1999, 16) refers to as 'almost wholly devoted to nature worship in "the cathedral of pines"'. Definitions of 'Nature' remain tied to wilderness in the Western imagination, excluding narratives from beyond this tradition, often both aesthetically and geographically. Literature which contains dirt, pollution, and defiled ecosystems has had little place within the discourse. However, beyond this, it is the cultivation of such wilderness narratives which have served to legitimate and racialize processes of conquest and imperialism through a preference for sublime aesthetics. Ecocritical scholarship has a tendency to lean towards texts which address wild spaces and landscapes where either 'positive collaboration', refuge or the idyllic are presented, even if they are disrupted by degradation or disaster. This need to strive towards harmony with nature, or our recognition of nature's intrinsic importance to our survival as a race, is almost always the desired or hopeful outcome. *The Book of Phoenix* is a text which could easily be overlooked or defined as devoid of ecocritical content in this regard, as the novel defies pastoral conventions.

Just as the wilderness imaginary is subject to amnesia of colonial violence, so too is oceanic space. William Slaymaker (1999) has argued that there has been little literary production by black Atlantic writers which might be called environmental or ecological. This is, of course, aligning texts with a rigid sense of what defines environmental writing, in accordance with Western notions of nature and ecological literary tradition. Nature in *The Book of Phoenix* is instead an entity 'that was forced to collude with oppressive systems' (Wardi 2011, 13), and the novel explores racialized topographies and geographies, with both nature and blackness as a constructed 'other', connected by a biological and green imperialism. In direct opposition to Slaymaker's claims, Nixon (2005) writes that, 'Black Atlanticism stands as one of the most energizing paradigms to have emerged in literary and cultural studies' (244), with a role to play in exploring intersections of environmentalism and postcolonialism.

The Atlantic Ocean has long been a site of radical scholarship and artistic expression, pertaining to Africa and its diaspora. Far from a blank desolate space, the Atlantic is a space haunted by its past as the Middle Passage. The second leg of the Atlantic slave trade reverberates through history. The 'Black Atlantic' was first theorized by Paul Gilroy (1993) as a space which connected Africans and the African diaspora, emphasizing 'routes' instead of 'roots' which connect and influence hybridity and identity. The ocean becomes loaded with a complex and terrible history. A watery aesthetic is often present, especially in African-American literatures, mapping lived geographies, and 'unanchored memories'. This literary tradition often charts both alienation and interconnectedness as bodies of water become repositories of collective memories, baring witness to a shared past (Wardi, 2011). Afrofuturism in particular has followed this aesthetic, exploring lived realities of racial hierarchies from past and present, and allows us to connect the body of water that encompassed the Middle Passage, with racialized bodies of past and present. Although Brayton (2011, 180) notes that the ocean's 'intellectual history has been long constructed as a non-place, an extra-social nowhere that lies eternally outside – or on the margins of history', within Afrofuturist discourse, the sea not only becomes the site of a shared past, but entangles current realties and futurist imaginings.

We can read *The Book of Phoenix* through a trans-Atlantic lens, exploring entangled and forgotten ecological histories. This is a retelling of history which also pays attention to both ecological and human violence and can be read in response to Chakrabarty's (2009) call for geological or ecological history to be incorporated into human history. Yet, this is not a novel which universalizes human history as so much of Anthropocene discourse has. Instead the novel decolonizes[2] Anthropocene narratives, allowing for a re-examination of how we read such texts and how we define both history and ecology. As Trevathan (2017, 43) portends, 'There is a need, then, for narrative and analysis to descend into the depths, to submerge in ecological devastation in the hopes of contemplating other future alternatives'. The Atlantic haunts the pages of the novel, reminding us of the violence of the Middle Passage, but also becomes a space beyond ancestral memory, allowing for an understanding of the historical processes which are constantly negotiated by the human and nonhuman (Deloughrey, 2017). The environmental legacies of imperialism and global capitalism are revealed in the ocean (Connery 1996; Helmreich 2009) and it is within the legacies of violence and rising sea levels of a future world on the cusp of apocalypse where Okorafor demonstrates the complex and inextricable consequences of racism and the commodification of black bodies.

BLACKNESS AND WASTE: TOXIC DISCOURSES IN *THE BOOK OF PHOENIX*

> To them I was like a plant that they grew for the sake of harvesting (9)

In *Wasted Lives* (2004), Zygmunt Bauman proposes that the border politics of globalization designates many people as human waste. These 'wasted lives' are the 'superfluous' populations of migrants, refugees, residents of urban ghettoes and other outcasts who are the product of a modernity driven by an economic system which seeks order and progress, casting out those who are deemed out of place and undesirable. Where there were once frontier territories which served as 'dumping grounds' for the human waste produced by processes of modernization, globalization has added a new and complex face onto this territorialization, creating refugee crises and 'security fears' in the emergent power struggles. Okorafor's *The Book of Phoenix* allows us to trace the 'wasted lives' through the history of capitalism and modernity, from the wasted lives lost in the Atlantic to the neoslaveries of the genetically altered humans in her future world, to those marginalized by rising sea levels. Okorafor employs what Lawrence Buell (1998; 2001) has called 'toxic discourse': a mode of writing that invokes images of toxic spaces, places, and bodies. An ecological reading of the novel must consider race and the biophysical environment, as Okorafor infers black bodies as 'other', exploited by neocolonial powers, akin to waste in their commodification throughout history. She draws parallels in this commodification to be read alongside environmental racism of her future marginalized humans in an aesthetics of waste which adds ecocritical dimensions to the link between racialized others and the ecological other.

The novel explores the reverberations of the slavery and racial hierarchies in place today, within the multilayered and complex text. Okorafor pays attention to the historical and current geographies of racism. The novel is set around seven research towers, as Phoenix explains, 'Research. This was what all The Towers are about. There were seven, all in American cities, yet they were not part of the American government. Not technically' (7). The 'Big Eye', an oppressive group of scientists run the research tower (named as such because they are always watching their imprisoned subjects). Each tower, we come to understand, has 'specializations', such as genetic modification, cloning, disease research (we understand that AIDs has been eradicated, but New Malaria is a threat), space exploration (for the Mars colonies), climate change and buoy technology for floating cities, and organ harvesting. The research subjects, known as 'speciMen', are modified humans, but more specifically they are almost exclusively African, or of African descent. The term 'speciMen' even adheres to the understanding that Phoenix and her kind are classified as sub- or non- human, as an animal or plant would be, for purely scientific study and without other purpose or agency:

> To them, I wasn't human enough to be a threat. I was their tool. I was nothing to worry about or to fear. They saw me as they saw the Africans made slaves during the Trans-Atlantic Slave Trade hundreds of years

> ago. They saw me as many Arabs saw African slaves over millennium and how some still see Africans today. The Big Eye didn't think they needed to put a leash on me because my leash was my DNA. (136)

This neoslavery narrative emphasizes the black body as a commodity. Camae Ayewa (2016) writes that, 'The black body is the first technology in which man gathered and traveled from far and wide to finance to torture and control … and were used to jumpstart the Industrial Revolution' (12). Okorafor's speciMen are an extension of this concept, produced to serve as experiments for research or for organ harvesting. The hierarchal dynamics of power are still very much entrenched as black bodies are objectified and marginalized for profit, functioning only as technologies of production and reproduction, just as historically took place during the slave trade. Okorafor very directly emphasizes these issues within the text, for example with her reference to Henrietta Lacks. Phoenix attempts to rescue another speciMen from the clutches of Tower 4, and discovers the woman's name is HeLa, named after Henrietta Lack's immortal cells. Lacks was an African-American woman whose cancer cells were taken without her knowledge or consent and used in medical research. 'HeLa cells were the first human biological materials ever bought and sold, which helped launch a multi-billion-dollar industry' (Zielinski 2010). By Okorafor's reference to Lacks in the text, we can understand her attention to the black body as material and disposable. The speciMen HeLa's blood is sold to seven wealthy business men so they can achieve immortality, pointing to the wealth and power of the few, over the oppression of the many. History repeats itself as Lack's immortal cells are constantly resold and reproduced, just as her ancestors were as slaves.

Phoenix herself is an 'accelerated organism, born two years ago, Yet I looked and physically felt like a forty year old woman'. Her body becomes weaponized as she realizes that she has been raised for use in biological or nuclear warfare. Okorafor applies an aesthetics of waste to highlight Phoenix's and other African and African-Americans' disposability and inferiority as a sub-human other. Phoenix states that, 'I was nothing but the result of a slurry of African DNA and cells. They constructed the sperm and the egg with materials of over ten Africans, all from the West African nations of Nigeria, Ghana, Senegal and Benin' (146). The use of the word slurry here is particularly poignant, as Phoenix realizes the brutality and reality of her enslavement, is due to an inherited ancestry of slavery. Towards the end of the novel, Phoenix finds her mother, who was imprisoned after giving birth to her. She too is of African descent and is compared to waste as she is tricked into carrying the 'special' embryo used to create Phoenix. 'She was like radioactive refuse – she was waste, but needed to be disposed of carefully. Jail was perfect' (203). She is thrown away and left in a cell, under the guise that she is in a vegetative state. However, although dying when Phoenix arrives, she is still aware of the evils committed against her, calling the Big Eye, 'Modern day slavers!'

Capitalist modes justified the exploitation of nature and black bodies through a history of oppression. Okorafor's novel links the experience of the commodification and othering of black bodies to an aesthetics of waste, allowing us to examine the history of the Atlantic alongside environmental racism. As Deloughrey (2010) emphasizes, the Atlantic's waters are the 'heavy waters of ocean modernity' where the past wasted lives of slaves are akin to the toxic waste presently found in our oceans, a reminder of the 'process and product of the violence of Atlantic modernity'. In other words, this waste is 'constitutive', a product of past and present processes.

The history of racism then is bound up with environmental history in many ways, and as Merchant (2003, 380) notes, 'Slavery and soil degradation are interlinked systems of exploitation, and deep-seated connections exist between the enslavement of human bodies and the enslavement of the land'. Slavery was the commodification and exploitation of both black bodies and nature. The frontier of Africa and the Atlantic Ocean became the forefront of the expanding world market and capitalist modernity. Further, a historical pattern of environmental marginalization and inequality can be traced back to the inhumane conditions of the Middle Passage (Washington 2006). African slaves were forced into excruciatingly small spaces in the holds of ships, with black bodies treated as cargo, worse than chattel. The air was noxious and the floor doused in bodily fluids, and these environmental conditions drove diseases and a high mortality rate. Those that did survive the long ocean crossing were then forced to work in marginalized areas which white settlers would have avoided – swamplands and plantations full of mosquitoes – or industries with harsh working conditions, most likely with little shelter from the natural elements (Washington 2006). After slavery ended environmental conditions did not get much better, as African Americans were forced into 'voluntary' racial segregation within urban areas, where they found themselves, 'living among diseased people in a crime-ridden geography where city services of water, sewerage, garbage-removal, street cleaning, lighting, noise and traffic regulation, schools and hospitalization are usually neglected or withheld' (182–

3), according to W. E. B Du Bois' (1940) famous *Dusk of Dawn* essay on racial segregation. Du Bois also noted that there was no ability for social mobility out of these areas due to racist legislation, which was only to become exacerbated by the Jim Crow laws through the nineteenth and much of the twentieth centuries.

It has been the taming of 'wilderness' and the 'othering' of nature that has sustained environmental racism. Indigenous peoples were forcibly removed from 'colonized Edens' and 'Sublime nature was white and benign, available to white tourists; cities were portrayed as black and malign, the home of the unclean and the undesirable' (Merchant 2003, 385). It is still those living in the global south, indigenous communities and predominately black neighbourhoods that bear the brunt of environmental degradation and inequality. We only have to look at those affected by global climate change and natural disasters such as New Orleans' Hurricane Katrina to see how such events are 'decidedly raced' (Wardi 2011). Toxic pollution and waste disposal are also unevenly distributed. Europe has been accused of 'Toxic Terrorism' (O'Keefe 1988) for exporting toxic wastes, including radioactive wastes both illegally and legally to Africa, whereas a recent study has shown that the percentage of African-Americans living in the fence-line zones of chemical facilities is 75 per cent greater than for the US as a whole, and so are more vulnerable to toxic chemicals (Environmental Justice and Health Alliance 2014).

The novel pays attention to these geographies of racism. The dystopian landscape of the novel draws attention to the marginalized poor, who are subject to a slow violence as temperatures and sea levels rise, leaving some areas uninhabitable and the most vulnerable at risk:

> I was flying above the submerged parts of the city. The tops of the once majestic, now wobbly skyscrapers peeked above the dark, slow-moving water like trees in a swamp. I'd read that a species of nocturnal, dog-sized rats lived in the portions of the building right above the water, and they fed on fish. They were probably out now, fishing the shallows. I'd read that these buildings were inhabited by the poor and illegal. Hardworking people who commuted to the city using boat services provided by New York's government. (56)

This insight into the everyday lives of the marginalized in the city of New York belies the catastrophic future consequences of the modes of capitalism laid out by Bauman (2004). This part of the novel, although fantastical, offers us a glimpse into the eco-spatial realities of the local and global systems in operation. It is suggested that a large-scale catastrophe has submerged the city, and yet we can see the microlevel effects on the local nonhuman nature. Further, the government provides infrastructure in order to safeguard the commodity of cheap labour while also sustaining the uneven societal structures, where the poor and illegal are marginalized. Okorafor allows us a glimpse of these 'wasted lives' woven amongst her neoslavery narrative. She exposes us to a new normality where the vulnerable and marginalized become the majority. *The Book of Phoenix* dwells on a slow racial violence which repeats and manifests itself no matter the era. This is underscored if we trace the racial geographies of neoslavery in the novel, which duplicate the geographies of the Atlantic slave trade, and comments on new racial inequalities of the twenty-first century. The novel connects nodes of temporality in order to demonstrate both immediate crises and past violences of the Anthropocene era.

RUPTURE AND CONNECTION IN *THE BOOK OF PHOENIX: DECOLONIZING THE* ANTHROPOCENE

> Rebellion. I whispered to myself. And the word blossomed from my lips like a flower. (11)

As Mitchell (2015) and McAfee (2016) remind us, the Anthropocene is not the product of all humanity, but a small corner that has dominated the 'ecosocial' order. While Žižek (2010) contends that we live in an era of 'apocalyptic time', Grace Dillon, in her studies of Native American speculative fiction, argues that 'the Native … Apocalypse has already taken place' (2012, 8). This chimes with Mark Fisher's (2013) discussions of the 'hauntological', where our late capitalist modernity is haunted by spectres of lost futures, as those who already encountered 'postmodernity' with the introduction of the slave trade were denied futurity. The waters of the Atlantic have thus emerged as a paradoxical site of both erasure and new histories. These histories traverse between fact, fiction, and myth as 'black history is both there and not there, evident in countless traces, scars, and memories, yet largely submerged when it comes to written accounts and first person documentations of the past from the viewpoint of the victims' (Mayer 2000, 558). Christine Sharpe (2016) in her work *In the Wake: On Blackness and Being* likens the epistemic violence of the Middle Passage to being in the wake of a ship. Just as the wakes of ships are tracks left on the water's surface, the disturbances and currents and 'semiotics of the slave ship continue', from forced movements of slaves to the current refugee crises in the Mediterranean, to the 'weaponized sidewalks' of America today, where black bodies are considered armed anytime whilst walking down the street, to worldwide structures of neocolonialisms and imperialisms, such as structural adjustment programmes, and the continued slow violence of environmental racisms.

Through Okorafor's Afrofuturism in *The Book of Phoenix*, the ocean is not passive space, or a 'connector' but instead becomes a 'hydroterritrialiser' (a word used by Eshun 1998), where aspects of identity and history are played out through the aquatic surroundings. Okorafor's retelling of the 'Flying African Myth' within *The Book of Phoenix* is particularly poignant. The main character, Phoenix, is described as a winged being who flies back and forth across the Atlantic. 'Traditionally, the Flying African myth has reflected the desire for freedom and cross-Atlantic return shared by generations of African descendants who inherited the trauma of forced displacement and enslavement throughout the Americas' (Thorsteinson 2015, 259). These stories about slaves who could fly back to Africa were common in folktales and popular culture, from the eighteenth century to the present day. While Phoenix is subjected to a form of neoslavery by geneticists and subsequently escapes, her understanding of her ancestral ties to the trans-Atlantic slave trade is indicated in the novel. Her abhorrence of ships is evident: '"Of course. I'll be flying." I paused, anxious to get going. "I can't believe I even set foot on this ship. It's only for you two that I do. If you two were black Americans, you'd understand better"' (156–7).

As discussed, with her blend of myth and science fiction, Okorafor traces the seismic shockwaves of the Atlantic slave trade and positions this against present ecological realities within the text. The author invokes 'ecological thought by employing pluralist perspectives and recombinant spatial logics' (Geier 2016, 57). By simultaneously focusing on local environmental issues, and examining the role of humanity on a planetary scale, Okorafor uses a narrative encompassing the multiplicities of scale as a method of examining the racialized histories of environmental crisis. Many characters in the novel have experiences of marginalization and ecological crisis. For example, amongst the other SpeciMen, Mmuo is involved in a Sci-Fi version of the Niger Delta oil crisis, whereas Saaed spent his childhood living off refuse tips to keep from starving.

Beyond this, the novel can also be read temporally, exemplifying how Afrofuturism can address what Yusoff (2018) terms the 'White Geology of the Anthropocene'; the myth which positions the Anthropocene as 'a cautionary tale of planetary predicament, which fails to identify its own histories of colonial earth-writing, to name masters of broken earths, and to redress the legacy of racialized subjects that geology leaves in its wake' (Yusoff 2018, 2). The role of such literature from both sides of the Atlantic in deconstructing and establishing other narratives of the Anthropocene cannot be understated in this regard. Okorafor's use of an oceanic, Afrofuturist aesthetic, where myth and collective memory disrupts a linear history, ultimately rejects dominant Western epistemologies. As Braziel (2005, 122) notes, 'Historical memory suffuses past, present and future, reflecting on past historical violence, even as it projects future hopes and dreams'.

The novel features a creation myth, an allegorical re-reading of human history:

> Thousands of years ago, when the world was nothing but sand and dry trees, Ani looked over her lands. She rubbed her dry throat. Then she made the oceans, lakes, rivers, and ponds. Her lands breathed and then danced. Water is life. And from the oceans. she took a deep drink and was refreshed. 'One day', she said, 'I'll produce sunshine. Right now, I'm not in the mood.' She turned over and slept. Behind her back, as she rested, human beings sprang from the sweetest parts of the rivers and the shallow portions of the lakes (219–20)

As well as individuals, then, humans are portrayed as 'bodies on a scale', which can be read as being in line with Anthropocene narratives of humans as geological actors. Anthropocene discourse has been widely celebrated as a way of reframing humanity's impact on Earth, which Bruno Latour refers to as 'our common geostory' (2014, 3). However, the predominant theoretical narratives of the Anthropocene portray humanity as a 'universal geology' which has a tendency to see humanity as a universal 'we', situating us as unintended 'destroyer' or 'maker of worlds' (Yusoff 2015). In direct criticism of this, Okorafor's myth positions humans as 'aggressive like the rushing rivers, forever wanting to move forward, cutting, carving, changing the lands. As much time passed, they created and used and changed and altered and spread and consumed and multiplied' (220). The author avoids the universalist post-racial 'we' in her origin myth, as she refers to an 'exclusive group' which – as a nod to colonization and also her ongoing discussion of neoslavery and neocolonialism in the novel – are a privileged select few who manipulate the Earth. There are no unintended consequences here, instead Okorafor exemplifies the 'racialized ruptures' and 'geosocial rifts' that make up the Anthropocene (Yusoff 2018, 58) through her narratives of toxic discourses.

The book's ending is apocalyptical. After finding out the cruel truth about the experiments, and as she understands humans, animals and the landscape itself are all disposable to the 'Big Eye', Phoenix decides to 'wipe the slate clean' (221) by destroying all humanity, hoping to give the Earth another chance. Okorafor uses the apocalypse narrative, not just as an end of humanity and the Earth as we know it, but as a way of exploring seismic shockwaves of capitalism and modernity. Her mythmaking, which writes a longue durée of history from the beginning of ecological time to its apocalyptic end, reminds us of the violence which can occur with grand narratives which remain oblivious and unwilling to examine epistemological framings. The novel's prologue and final chapters narrate a time after the apocalypse where an elderly man named Sunuteel finds a recording in a cave. The recording turns out to be Phoenix's memories, which Sunuteel is inspired to rewrite after his memory of reading an essay entitled 'Author is Dead'. This is an evident nod to Roland Barthes's 'The Death of the Author' (1967) which advocated the liberation of the author's identity and intent from a text. 'Let it all be rewritten' (221) states Phoenix as she is destroying the Earth. Her story is rewritten, but it is changed and manipulated beyond recognition. The old man instead uses the recording to retell *The Book of Phoenix into The Story of the Okeke and Why They are Cursed* or *The Great Book* (229). The transformation of Phoenix's story into a narrative which privileges an ethnic group whilst ostracizing another is an act of epistemological violence. We can compare this to the geostories of a 'White Anthropocene' which privilege a collective humanity, whilst erasing racialized and ecological violences of the past (Yusoff 2018).

However, we find hope in lost futurities, as Phoenix appears to Sunuteel, and warns 'I know what you think … you can rewrite a story, but once it is written it lives. Think before you do; your story is written too and so is the map of consequences' (228). Okorafor is at once pointing to the danger and violence which shapes such narratives, but also to our ability to revise such myths.[3] Okorafor strikes into the very heart of something that Édouard Glissant (1997) terms as an 'aesthetics of rupture and connection' (151). Glissant equates the historic ocean journeys of slaves to an abyss which must also be traversed by future generations. The abyss at once haunts, disrupts or ruptures the present, as well as creating a connection and relation for shared memories, experiences and exchanges. He writes, 'For though this experience made you, original victim floating toward the sea's abysses, an exception, it became something shared and made us, the descendants, one people among others. Peoples do not live on exception. Relation is not made up of things that are foreign but of shared knowledge. This experience of the abyss can now be said to be the best element of exchange' (1997, 8). Glissant has argued for an ecological vision of relation (1997, 146), which encompasses lost histories of both the human and nonhuman. Okorafor negotiates this as she uncovers and negates a myth of return to a pristine nature which has been a hereditary myth of environmental discourse. The novel continues to unravel, destroy and renegotiate our very ideas and values of nature and our relationship to it, as its textual violence demonstrates real world violence: the slow violence handed down incrementally throughout history collides with a narrative of neoslavery. Glissant describes the Atlantic Ocean as a 'beginning' for modernity, where 'time is marked by . . . balls and chains gone green' (1997, 6). Glissant's Middle Passage has a double meaning: it is at once a 'tautology' that haunts the ocean spaces, a deep abyssal wound, with a silent history of suffering, and at once a space of 'metamorphosis' where 'this experience of the abyss can now be said to be the best element of exchange' (1997, 8), the best way to imagine and build anew. The Middle Passage haunts *The Book of Phoenix* at every page, but like Glissant's abyss, the ocean is at once a space of empowerment and a reminder of the past which has had direct consequences on the lived experiences of the present.

CONCLUSION

The Book of Phoenix understands the hierarchal and geographical legacies of race, and the futurism employed speculates on the present and future of racial topographies. As Okorafor examines the black body as a site of violence and environmental racism, *The Book of Phoenix* ruptures and connects histories of racial and ecological oppression, uncovering past violences and juxtaposing them against the 'wasted lives of modernity'. Her black Atlantic ecologies are an important reading, attending to an ecology which makes us aware of our estrangement from nature, yet understands a return to 'nature' heralded by scientists and environmentalists as impossible given it would mean an ignorance of the embedded racial hierarches that were rooted in the splitting of man from nature (Kovel 2003). Oceanic imagery floods the pages of *The Book of Phoenix*, the catastrophic rising sea levels is juxtaposed against the heredity violences of the Middle

Passage, leading us away from a normalized ecocritical reading of such texts. Such readings understand a ripple effect leading to the ecosocial realities of present violences, in the wake of the past, and how world ecologies link racial geographies of the Americas and Africa across the Atlantic. Okorafor reminds us that nature has never been separate from human histories, and our present and even futures continue to be haunted by violent histories of ecocide and genocide.

NOTES

1 *The Book of Phoenix* stands alongside other giants of literature which have explored Black Atlantic Futurism, including Octavia Butler's *Kindred* (1979) and Toni Morrison's *Beloved* (1987). These texts explore the neoslave narratives, which confront not only the histories of slavery but also its ongoing legacies (see Vint 2007). Nnedi Okorafor differs slightly from these two authors, as she has been classed as both an African writer and as an African-American author. She was born in the USA to Nigeria parents, and spent much of her childhood on both sides of the Atlantic, and defines her 'flavor of sci-fi' as 'evenly Naijamerican' (Okorafor 2015b). She has commented on the label of Afrofuturism for her work as something she accepts, but has issues with the label, due to its roots in the African-American tradition, rather than African.

2 By the phrase to 'decolonize the Anthropocene', I mean to understand the current ecological crises of our late capitalist modernity, not as a product of 'unintended consequences' due to globalization and industrialization, but instead as a process of systemic violences stemming from as far back as the Columbian Exchange. Through the lens of a decolonized Anthropocene discourse we can begin to understand the 'continuities' of colonial violence, and the temporal and spatial entanglements between 'power, technology, violence and politics' (Mitchell 2015). Davis and Todd (2017) argue that we must link colonialism and the Anthropocene for two reasons. The first is to recognize how our current ecological crises are intrinsically linked with an ideology bound up with accumulation and extraction, of an ontological rift between man and nature. The second is to question and explore the realm beyond Western epistemologies – the Anthropocene 'systematically erases difference'. This erasure happens through genocide and displacement, as well as through universalist ideas embedded in its very discourse. By allowing for other voices in the Anthropocene we can reshape and undermine these regimes.

3 *The Book of Phoenix* is a prequel to *Who Fears Death* (2010) when the protagonist Onyesonwu is living in the world that *The Great Book* created, as her ethinic group Okeke are oppressed by the Nuru. The novel revolves around her trying to defeat the sorcerer Daib and attempting to rewrite *The Great Book*.

WORKS CITED

Ayewa, C. 2016. 'Sights and Sounds of the Passage'. In *Spac- Time Collapse: From the Congo To The Carolinas*. R. Phillips et al., eds. Philadelphia: AfroFuturist Affair.

Barthes, R. 1967. 'The Death of the Author'. *Aspen* 5–6. http://www.ubu.com/aspen/aspen5and6/threeEssays.html#barthes, accessed 11 February 2020.

Bauman, Z. 2004. *Wasted Lives: Modernity and its Outcasts*. Cambridge: Polity Press.

Brayton, D. 2011. 'Shakespeare and the Global Ocean'. In *Ecocritical Shakespeare*. L. Bruckner and D. Brayton, eds. Farnham, Surrey: Routledge, 173–190.

Braziel, J. E. 2005. 'Caribbean Genesis: Language, Gardens, Worlds (Jamaica Kincaid, Derek Walcott, Édouard Glissant)'. In *Caribbean Literature and the Environment: Between Nature and Culture*. E. M. DeLoughrey, R. K. Gosson and G. B. Handley, eds. London: University of Virginia Press.

Buell, L. 1998. 'Toxic Discourse'. *Critical Inquiry* 24.3: 639–65.

Buell, L. 2001. *Writing for an Endangered World: Literature, Culture and the Environment in the U.S.* London: The Belnap Press.

Chakrabarty, D. 2009. 'The Climate of History: Four Theses'. *Critical Inquiry* 35: 197–222.

Connery, C. L. 1996. 'The Oceanic Feeling and the Regional Imaginary'. In *Global/Local: Cultural Production and the Transnational Imaginary*. W. Dissanayake and R. Wilson, eds. Durham: Duke University Press, 284–311.

Davis, H. & Todd, Z. 2017. 'On the Importance of a Date, or Decolonizing the Anthropocene'. *ACME: An International E-Journal for Critical Geographies* 16.4: 761–80.

DeLoughrey, E. 2010. 'Heavy Waters: Waste and Atlantic Modernity'. *PMLA* 125.3: 703–12.

DeLoughrey, E. 2017. 'Submarine Futures of the Anthropocene'. *Comparative Literature* 69.1: 32–44.

Dillon, G. (2012. 'Imagining Indigenous Futurisms'. In *Walking the Clouds: An Anthology of Indigenous Science Fiction*. G. Dillon, ed. Tucson: University of Arizona Press, 1–12

Du Bois, W. E. B. 1940. *Dusk of Dawn: An Essay Toward an Autobiography of a Race Concept*. Piscataway, N.J: Transaction Publishers.

Environmental Justice and Health Alliance for Chemical Policy Reform. 2014. 'Who's in Danger? Race, Poverty, and Chemical Disasters'. https://comingcleaninc.org/assets/media/images/Reports/Who's%20in%20Danger%20Report%20FINAL.pdf, accessed 11 February 2020.

Eshun, K. 1998. *More Brilliant Than the Sun: Adventures in Sonic Fiction*. London: Quartet Books.

Fisher, M. 2013. 'The Metaphysics of Crackle: Afrofuturism and Hauntology'. *Dancecult: Journal of Electronic Dance Music Culture* 5.2: 42–55.

Geier, T. 2016. 'Noncommittal Commitment: Alien Spaces of Ecocosmopolitics in Recent World Literature' In: Tally, R. T. Jr., & Battista, C. M, Eds.) Ecocriticism and Geocriticism: Overlapping Territories in Environmental and Spatial Literary Studies London: Palgrave Macmillan 55–73.

Gilroy, P. 1993. The Black Atlantic: Modernity and Double Consciousness London: Verso.

Glissant, E. 1997. *Poetics of Relation*. Translated from French by B. Wing. Ann Arbour: The University of Michigan Press.

Helmreich, S. 2009. *Alien Ocean: Anthropological Voyages in Microbial Seas*. Berkeley: University of California Press.

Kovel, J. 2003. 'Racism and Ecology'. *Socialism and Democracy* 17.1: 99–107.

Latour, B. 2014. 'Agency at the Time of the Anthropocene'. *New Literary History* 45.1: 1–18.

McAfee, K. 2016. 'The Politics of Nature in the Anthropocene'. In: Emmett, R. & Lekan, T. eds, 'Whose Anthropocene? Revisiting Dipesh Chakrabarty's 'Four Theses'", *RCC Perspectives: Transformations in Environment and Society* 2: 65–72.

Mayer, R. 2000. '"Africa As an Alien Future": The Middle Passage, Afrofuturism, and Postcolonial Waterworlds'. *American Studies* 45.4: 555–66.

Merchant, C. 2003. 'Shades of Darkness: Race and Environmental History'. *Environmental History* 8.3: 380–94.

Mitchell, A. 2015. 'Decolonising the Anthropocene'. *Worldly*. https://worldlyir.wordpress.com/2015/03/17/decolonising-the-anthropocene/, accessed 2 February 2020.

Nixon, R. 2005. 'Environmentalism and Postcolonialism' In: *Postcolonial Studies and Beyond*. A. Loomba, S. Kaul, M. Bunzl, A. Burton and J. Esty. Durham, North Carolina: Duke University Press.

O'Keefe, P. 1988. 'Toxic Terrorism' *Review of African Political Economy* 42 84–90

Okorafor, N. 2015a. *The Book of Phoenix*. London: Hodder & Stoughton.

Okorafor, N. 2015b. 'Insight into the Lagoon'. Nnedi Wahala Zone Blog . http://nnedi.blogspot.com/2015/09/insight-into-lagoon.html, accessed 11 February 2020.

Ross, A. 1999. 'The Social Claim on Urban Ecology (interview by Michael Bennett)'. In *The Nature of Cities: Ecocriticism and Urban Environments*. M. Bennett, ed. Arizona: University of Arizona Press.

Sharpe, C. 2016. *In the Wake: On Blackness and Being*. Durham: Duke University Press.

Slaymaker, W. 1999. 'Forum on Literatures of the Environment'. *PMLA* 114.5: 1100–1.

Thorsteinson, K. 2015. 'From Escape to Ascension: The Effects of Aviation Technology on the Flying African Myth'. *Criticism* 57.2: 259–81.

Trevathan, J.H. 2017. 'Submergence: On Transatlantic Ecocriticism, Islands and Archipelagos'. *Ecozona* 8.1: 42–60.

Vint, S. 2007. '"Only by Experience": Embodiment and the Limitations of Realism in Neo-Slave Narratives'. *Science Fiction Studies* 34.2: 241–61.

Walcott, D. 1986. *Collected Poems, 1948–1984*. New York: Farrar, Straus and Giroux.

Washington, H. S. 2006. '"My Soul Looked Back" Environmental memories of the African in America, 1600–2000'. In *Echoes from the Poisoned Well: Global Memories of Environmental Injustice*. H. S. Washington, H. Goodall and P. C. Rosier. Lexington Books.

Wardi, J. A. 2011. *Water and African American Memory: An Ecocritical Perspective*. Florida: University of Florida Press.

Yusoff, K. 2015. 'Anthropogenesis: Origins and Endings in the Anthropocene'. *Theory, Culture and Society* 33.2: 3–28.

Yusoff, K. 2018. *A Billion Black Anthropocenes or None*. Minneapolis: University of Minnesota Press.

Zielinski, S. 2010. 'Henrietta Lacks' "Immortal" Cells'. *Smithsonian Magazine*. https://www.smithsonianmag.com/science-nature/henrietta-lacks-immortal-cells-6421299/, accessed 2 February 2018.

Žižek, S. 2010. *Living in the End Times*. New York: Verso.

Readings into the Plantationocene:

FROM THE SLAVE NARRATIVE OF CHARLES BALL TO THE SPECULATIVE HISTORIES OF OCTAVIA BUTLER AND NNEDI OKORAFOR

JAMES McCORKLE

Octavia Butler's *Parable of the Sower* and Nnedi Okorafor's *Who Fears Death* consider environmental catastrophes structured as narratives of captivity and escape, and propose a problematized feminist teleology. Reading Butler again in the age of Trump with economic disparities, the denial of the global climate crisis, and the backdrop of the extended fire season (stretching into nearly the entire year) in southern California, continent-wide brush fires in Australia, and years-long drought in southern Africa makes her all the more prescient. Commenting in 2017, Okorafor stated, 'After everything that happened, I'm not reading *1984*, I'm not reading *Fahrenheit 451*, I'm not reading *A Handmaid's Tale*. I'm reading *Parable of the Sower* by Octavia Butler. I feel like if we're looking for any answers or where we're going, it's definitely in Octavia's work' (*Modern Ghana*). Okorafor's novel – regardless of its use of the fantastic – explores the violence consuming a world that has undergone an undisclosed but cataclysmic event. Or perhaps it is the world that many are currently facing, and have faced. Belonging to different generations, and occupying different spaces within the diaspora, Butler and Okorafor examine the world as depleted spaces, ones which have been written by the histories of enslavement and colonialism, and where those histories have become the very terrain and time we move in. These novels provide urgent responses to what Kathryn Yusoff argues is the erasure of blackness, the 'lack of recognition of race', from the Anthropocene, and 'a prioritization of white biopolitics' (17). Butler and Okorafor thus intervene in the narrative of the Anthropocene, expanding the presumed 'we' reflective of 'a specifically racialized territorialization of the earth' (Yusoff 105).

Butler and Okorafor share specific genealogies: not only do they draw upon the narrative constructions found in slave narratives, but their work foregrounds reading slave narratives as also narratives of the Plantationocene.[1] Here Charles Ball's narrative *Slavery in the United*

States. A Narrative of the Life and Adventures of Charles Ball, A Black Man is most illustrative. Butler and Okorafor, while writing into the future, also demand a re-reading of the past. Christina Sharpe proposes that individual black 'lives are always swept up in the wake produced and determined, though not absolutely, by the afterlives of slavery' (8). The two protagonists and narrators, Butler's Lauren Oye Olamina and Okorafor's Onyesonwu, extend the dystopian antiblack narrative, whose origins are most acutely expressed by chattel slavery, into a future that is still bound by the effects of dislocation and migration, the depletion of resources, and the threat and exercise of violence most acutely felt by black women. Harriet Jacobs' admonishment that 'Slavery is terrible for men; but it is far more terrible for women' in that 'Superadded to the burden common to all, they have wrongs, and sufferings, and mortifications peculiarly their own' (77) is re-inscribed and reiterated in the future by Lauren and Onyesonwu.

Both speculative novels offer future histories that are always and already present. *Who Fears Death* is not only a future but also a retelling of the complex violence of Darfur, the systematic impoverishment of colonialism, multiple histories of enslavement, and the specific violences enacted upon females in each of these histories. Butler's novel, published two years after the brutal police assault on 3 March 1991 on Rodney King and the subsequent rebellion, addresses the racialized economic displacements that affect education, housing, and health. Butler presciently understood that the rise of 'sea levels ... with the warming climate' corresponded to the cascading social and political violence (118). While neither novel has as its protagonist an enslaved person, the novels describe slavery's spectral haunting – it is not merely the potential of chattel slavery's return, but new formations of slavery as well as a remembering of slavery's continental and diasporic histories.

Parable of the Sower and *Who Fears Death* reflect the continuation of the *Maafa*, the Ki-Swahili term for the disaster of the displacement and forced removal of African peoples and the subsequent unfolding disasters to both the continent and those swept away. The novels create the sensation of being in a creased time, both future and past, describing our present conditions and a future that is still in the process of formation. While both novels are framed as first-person narratives – speculative autobiographies, personal narratives set as either a journal or a dictated narrative of a captive – they are not strictly personal stories, bildungsroman, or coming-of-age novels, but auto/graphs of historical and social processes. They depict, as though from archives, the particular violence rendered upon black women including rape, dismemberment, female genital mutilation, exile, and childbirth in isolation. Both works, to evoke Saidiya Hartman's words, 'rewrite the chronicle of a death foretold and anticipated, as a collective biography of dead subjects, as a counter-history of the human' (3). As Hartman writes, in regard to the silence of the archives, 'loss gives rise to longing, and in these circumstances, it would not be far-fetched to consider stories as a form of compensation or even as reparations, perhaps the only kind we will ever receive' (3–4). These speculative autobiographies of the future (and the past folded back into the future, where the horror of five hundred years are, to use Toni Morrison's term in *Beloved*, *re-memoried*) are the historical recordings of past passages of black women. Their intention is to unravel the silence of the archives; thus they serve as interventions to provide significance – and I use 'provide' in the sense of provisioning and distributing. That Butler and Okorafor create speculative autobiographies underscores James Olney's observation that the person engaging in autobiographical production is not 'a neutral or passive recorder, but … [is] a creative and active shaper [whose] memory creates the *significance* of events' (149). Thus these narratives are a form of re-provisioning the archive; they are also a form of 're-centering' of the first person so as to implicate oneself as dependent upon the collective.

This re-centering of the self is a distinguishing element of the slave-narrative from Olaudah Equiano's narrative, to that of Harriet Jacobs, to Toni Morrison. Butler's and Okorafor's speculative narratives are further articulations of dystopian histories extended into the future. Storytelling within the *Maafa* acts as resistance as it asserts one's own and collective presence. To write was prohibited for the enslaved; to write one's own story would be doubly jeopardizing. With their foregrounding of narrative agency, Butler and Okorafor reflect and extend the slave narrative. Similarly Charles Ball's 1836 narrative *Slavery in the United States. A Narrative of the Life and Adventures of Charles Ball, A Black Man*, a little-known narrative, offers two significant elements that not only foreshadow the concerns of Butler and Okorafor, but also remind us of the dystopian condition the doors of the barracoon opened to. First, Ball's account of his own dislocations embeds a narrative of an unnamed (both individually and ethnically) 'African' who is captured by fellow Africans in presumably the Sahel and sold to Europeans on West Africa's coast. Told to Charles Ball, who belongs to a third generation of enslaved blacks, the narrative serves as Ball's past even as Ball maps his own future. Ball's narrative thus enfolds the oral history; the narrative provides a methodology that inscribes the process of maintaining archives (as historiography it provides for or provisions sources) and of the literary structures of storytelling.

Secondly, Ball maintains meticulous observations of his environment throughout his narrative. Sold and forced to march in shackles south from a Maryland plantation to a South Carolina plantation, and ultimately to Georgia, Ball describes the ecologies (soil, vegetation, and human conditions) and records the destruction of the environment by inept European plantation owners who exploited both humans and the arable land for short-term profits:

> [The land] had originally been highly fertile and productive, and had it been properly treated, would doubtlessly have continued to yield abundant and prolific crops; but the gentlemen who became the early proprietors of this fine region, supplied themselves with slaves from Africa, cleared large plantations of many thousands of acres – cultivated tobacco – and became suddenly wealthy … but regardless of their true interest, they valued their land less than their slaves; exhausted the kindly soil, by unremitting crops of tobacco … Virginia has become poor by the folly and wickedness of slavery. (39)

Ball's narrative is significant as it is the first dystopian work that explicitly enfolds the *Maafa* into a sweeping ecological disaster. Had the land been 'properly treated' it may have flourished. Thus Ball proposes a future that is not the Plantationocene. Ball's narrative, even as he recounts the precarity of land and the enslaved, observes the creation of, in Sylvia Wynter's words, 'a counter-culture through the transplantation of their old cultures onto a strange soil, its reinvention in new and alien conditions. It was in this transplantation … that the blacks made themselves indigenous to their new land' (quoted in Yusoff 35). Similarly, at the conclusion of their novels, Butler and Okorafor offer the possibility of an Afro-future that emerges from the dystopia of slavery's afterlives.

Both novels are structured around the transmission of texts. As Ball's narrative is both an argument for abolition and a warning of the effects of Plantationcene, Butler's and Okorafor's works are cautionary narratives. Butler presents two interwoven texts, the diary of Lauren and her meditative poems that express the vision of Earthseed. Okorafor positions the reader as if not the amanuensis, then one looking over her shoulder as her twin transcribes on a laptop the narrative of Onyesonwu: 'It's a long story. But I'll tell you … I'll tell you. You're a fool if you believe what others say about me. I tell you my story to avert all those lies. Thankfully, even my long story will fit on that laptop of yours' (6). The reader/transcriber (thus implicating us in the transmission of the narrative) serves as a griot who makes a claim on our present moment to rearrange the elements of accepted thought into a new narrative. Furthermore, positioned as we are, we become part of the genealogy of the narrative and we still possess critical literacy, thus potential agency. In Butler's landscape, literacy has largely disappeared. Cory, Lauren's brother, in fact is prized by the unknown group he has fallen into because he can read. 'So you read for a living – help your friends learn to use their stolen equipment', Lauren exclaims when Cory describes his activities (106). While Onyesonwu goes to school – indeed her classmates Luyu, Diti, and Binta who all underwent the Eleventh Rite, or ritual female circumcision with Onyesonwu – the idea of literacy is not foregrounded, except in terms of the narrative's transmission. In both novels the production and transmission of the texts is most central as the text is the means toward agency. The presence of the performance of writing prompts the desire for literacy, as Butler demonstrates when Zahara asks Lauren to teach her to read and write: 'I was surprised, but I shouldn't have been. Where, in a life like hers, had there been time or money for school' (186). The loss of literacy is a form of colonial 'dismemberment' and points to the wider destruction of culture as Ngũgĩ wa Thiong'o has argued (5; 17–21). In Okorafor's novel, the porous frontier line between the darker Okekes and the expansionist Nurus marks an improvisatory violence, primarily directed against the Okekes, where the weapons are scooters, automatic rifles, and kerosene. The threat of rape is not only a means of brute terror but also a form of cultural dismemberment. Okeke women who bear children as a result of being raped by a Nuru man will be ostracized and their children, labelled as Ewu, are scorned.

Literacy, or its lack, is a form of 'slow violence', to evoke the complex of impoverishment and environmental crisis described by Rob Nixon, ensuring the destruction of human community. Literacy is also a means of transmitting trust, as Harry demands of Lauren to 'show me something of you that's real' (Butler 195). In this episode literacy, trust, and empathy (for it is at this moment that Lauren must reveal she suffers from hyperempathy) are linked with Lauren and, through her, transmitted. Lauren's hyperempathy offers a further meditation on the 'slow violence' of our socialization. Here the idea of the post 9/11 'new norm' is echoed: empathy is transformed into a medical condition or aberration in need of control. Cruelty ironically becomes painless, while empathy induces paralysing pain.

The dystopia of the slave narrative, as in Ball's descriptions of how torture has become normalized on the plantations he has been sold to, foregrounds the question of who is human. Contemporary speculative fiction, such as the work of Butler and Okorafor, enjoins that same question with the narrative arc of the journey out of captivity and toward provisional freedom. Butler's novel invokes the iconic journey north of Lauren. Okorafor situates the movement on an east–west axis: Najeeba flees east after the decimation of her town, and then her outcast Ewu daughter, Onyesonwu, travels west in a quest to confront not only the sorcerer Daib and the seer Rana, but her own death and the spell of enslavement. Beyond the narrative arc of captivity and freedom, Butler and Okorafor explore the conditions of frontiers. Butler's novel, sited on the California coast, plays on the metaphor of the ever-expansive American frontier: here we have reached the historical dead-end of capitalism, there can no longer be an expansion driven by the myth of the open horizon. We have also reached the end of technology, as an expansive promising and emancipatory frontier; it has become, as we are experiencing, part of a surveillance state, whose very panoptical condition, as Simone Browne argues, begins with the Door of No Return, that is the barracoon, where the 'violent regulation of blackness as spectacle and as disciplinary combined in the racializing surveillance of the slave system' (42). One of the possible afterlives of slavery, Butler suggests, is the closed city of Olivar, where the inhabitants trade freedom for security, and are required to work maintaining solar farms and desalination plants, and fend off the ever-encroaching Pacific Ocean (119).

The backdrop to both novels is one of a depleted future that has already been cast by the present and the legacies of the past. Butler's Los Angeles of 2025 has fallen into dysfunction – there is no gas, water scarcity is acute, housing is limited, the electrical grid is faltering, the necessities of food and clothing are difficult to acquire. Survival depends upon living within fortressed enclaves, such as the walled compound of Robledo where Lauren and her family lived. Individual gardens, much like slave gardens at the beginning of the Plantationocene, provide what cannot be gleaned from the increasingly depleted metropolis of Los Angeles. Against this, the novel proposes the need to re-vision the meaning of community. Okorafor's novel, drawn from the civil wars in Sudan and, specifically, Darfur, describes a landscape that is drought scarred, littered with portable CD-players, laptops, scooters, digital imaging, and flash drives. The landscape that once existed was flush with late twentieth-century technology, but it has proven unsustainable and insubstantial to technologies of the sacred that the West would label as magical or the fantastic or primitive. The sacred technologies (the ability to shapeshift or to induce mass visions for example) and the knowledge of the land (the ability to survive in the desert or to hear the desert) are those that provide Onyesonwu with agency. In both novels, there is an implicit understanding that the late capitalist technologies have failed humans in the most fundamental ways – that is to preserve a sense of humanness. As each work explores precarity through depletion as it affects populations of colour, they question how we can remain human under such depletive regimes.

Late in *Who Fears Death*, Onyesonwu finds, stashed in a cave filled with white spiders and antiquated computers (a cross between an electronics waste dump and a tomb for purged talismanic objects), a momentarily operable e-reader that had on its screen the title *The Forbidden Greeny Jungle Field* (an intertextual reference to an e-book that appears in Okorafor's 2005 novel *Zahrah the Windseeker*, where the e-reader is a consistently malfunctioning provider of information). An image flashes before Onyesonwu's eyes of 'a place of plants, trees, and bushes' which she recalls 'Just like the place my mother showed me ... The place of hope' (335). This memory of a recounted place, a double displacement, signals the loss of an Edenic landscape. Similarly, Lauren has saved, from her father's library, books on survival, including one that described 'California Indians, the plants they used, and how they used them' (59). The father of the friend Lauren has loaned the guide to, returns it; Lauren's father admonishes her for scaring her friend, asking Lauren if she thinks the world is about to end. Of course she responds 'yes' and thinks '*your* world is coming to an end, and you with it' (62). These lapsarian visions imply a previous condition of beneficent environments that in effect exist only as archives. As such they are textualized slave gardens – but they also thrust the past into the future, much as Ball's lament that had the land been 'properly treated' – and hence those who laboured on it – the future would have been far different.

Importantly, the economic structure of modern slavery necessitated the invention of new technologies, whether it was logistical technologies (tracking shipments), new financial instruments (insurance and lending institutions), or medical technologies (for example, the minimal caloric requirements for human survival during the sequestering in barracoons and during the Middle Passage). Both Butler and Okorafor imply the structures that these technologies emerged from, inextricably bound as they were to the Atlantic plantation economy beginning with the Portuguese sugar plantations on the islands of São Tomé, were not sustainable practices, and were, in fact, doomed to failure due to their fundamental disregard of human-ness. This is not a rejection of technology per se; indeed, in *The Parable of the Sower* Lauren declares,

> 'The destiny of Earthseed is to take root among the stars … That's the ultimate Earthseed aim, and the ultimate human change short of death. It's a destiny we'd better pursue if we hope to be anything other than smooth-skinned dinosaurs – here today, gone tomorrow, our bones mixed with the bones and ashes of our cities, and so what? … Beyond Mars,' I said. 'Other star systems. Living worlds.' (222)

Lauren acknowledges that her vision 'won't be possible for a long time,' but her mission is one that is foundational, to build 'foundations – Earthseed communities – focused on the Destiny' (222). Reaching an environment beyond the reach of pillaging and fires, of deprivation and destruction, is Lauren and her small group of Earthseed followers' immediate goal; but a new dispensational techne is expected to emerge, as a historical necessity; Lauren reflects 'Earthseed is being born right here on Highway 101 – on that portion of 101 that was once El Camino Real, the royal highway of California's Spanish past' (223). California's Highway 101 cuts through Silicon Valley. The past prefigures the future.

At the end of *Who Fears Death* – though Okorafor puts into question 'ending' – we are given a glimpse, a literal bird's eye view as though through shape-shifted Onyesonwu's vision, of the future:

> If Onyesonwu had taken one last look below, to the south, with her keen *Kponyungo* eyes, she'd have seen Nuru, Okeke, and two Ewu children in school uniforms playing in a schoolyard. To the east, stretching into the distance, she'd have seen black paved roads populated by men and women, Okeke and Nuru, riding scooters and carts pulled by camels. In downtown Durfa, she'd have spotted a flying woman discreetly meeting up with a flying man on the roof of the tallest building. (386)

Okorafor invokes at the conclusion of the novel the use of the traditional *Kponyungo* mask, found among the Sene and Senufo cultures in Mali, Burkina Faso, and Côte d'Ivorie. A fusion of different animals, the zoomorphic mask – a visualization of Onyesonwu's shape-shifting abilities – when worn during funerary rites, ensures that the community will not be haunted by the inopportune dead, which may unleash chaos upon the community. Okorafor, however, does not assure us of that harmony, for she concludes, 'But the wave of change was yet to sweep by directly below'; instead the Nuru are still waiting to seize Onyesonwu and dismember her (386).

Butler questions the possibility of a salvageable planet – whether considered in terms of political or environmental destiny. During Lauren's description of the teleology of Earthseed, she 'nodded toward the burned area' (222), thus gesturing to the irredeemable destruction that has been wrought. While the fires that Lauren witnesses have been intentionally set – often by addicts of Pyro, an addictive synthetic drug, ironically created to forestall the ravages of Alzheimer's but that also induces pyromania – the land has already been drought-stricken and over-developed, paralleling the landscape Ball travelled through some two-hundred-and-fifty years earlier on the East coast. Butler's critique of capitalism is premised on the claim that the origin of capitalism is slavery; enslavement is the always present origin or that which is persistent in its own reproduction. 'Slavery again,' Lauren comments as she realizes that she and her companions have 'become the crew of a modern underground railroad' (292). Her companion Taylor Bankole responds that 'none of this is new', noting that in the 1990s growers held migrants and blacks in California and the south and forced them to work without pay, and that in the future-present 'children were sold like cattle – and no doubt into prostitution' (292). Not unlike current workfare mandates and convict labour, Butler indicates that new laws were being formulated to force 'people or their children to work off debt that they can't help running up' (292). As Lauren makes her way northward gathering her Earthseed community, she collects stories of escaped captives, beginning with Zahra, her neighbour, whose history, like that of many, she had not known:

> Her alien past again. It distracted me for a moment. I had been waiting to ask her how much a person costs these days. And she had been sold by her mother to a man who couldn't have been much more than a stranger. He could have been a maniac, a monster. And my father used to worry about future slavery or debt slavery. Had he known? He couldn't have. (184)

As Lauren and her companions slowly migrate north, she collects and archives their journey and their stories of origin. Her act of transcription and transmission is the replenishment and reparation of the silence of the archive that Hartman has advocated, and a resistance to the very silences that the Plantationcene systematized.

For both Butler and Okorafor, environmental knowledge, and knowledge in general, is under contention, for there is both an impetus for archiving as well as interrogating. Lauren has saved not only old maps and survival information, but also has kept an archive of seeds for future cultivation. Her action recalls the various origin stories of the trans-Atlantic dispersal of African rice in the New World (the hiding of grains of rice in a girl's hair to carry not only knowledge of cultivation but also the social and cosmological structures that insure the survival of cultures) as well as depictions of Maroon women in Suriname and Brazil, carrying sacks of seed, who flee colonial forces that seek to destroy their hidden communities and re-enslave the escapees (Carney and Rosomoff 76; 94–6). The text that Lauren generates also conveys this sense of organic transfer:

> Well, today, I found the name, found it while I was weeding the back garden and thinking about the way plants seed themselves, windborne, animalborne, waterborne, far from their parent plants. They have no ability at all to travel great distances under their own power, and yet, they do travel …
>
> Earthseed.
>
> I am Earthseed. Anyone can be. Someday, I think there will be a lot of us. And I think we'll have to seed ourselves farther and farther from this dying place. (77–8)

Lauren re-names herself, which parallels her father and Bankole's assumption of African names, as she subsequently notes after meeting Taylor Bankole: 'Our last names were an instant bond between us. We're both descended from men who assumed African surnames back in the 1960's. His father and my grandfather had had their names legally changed, and both had chosen Yoruba replacement names' (Butler: 230). Lauren carries forward the recuperative process begun during the Black Power and Black Consciousness movements – but she also revisions the Pan-Africanist that motivated her forefathers, implicitly challenging that patriarchal structure. She uncovers her name or more precisely the name of her thinking as she is weeding her family's garden, which bears similarity to the provision and subsistence gardens, memory gardens in fact, found in the quarters of the enslaved, whereby they were able to give 'material expression to the ways exiles commemorate the past and shape new identities amid alien cultures' (Carney and Rosomoff 185).

Butler and, to a lesser extent, Okorafor concede that the cataclysms that have befallen the planet are irremediable. Onyesonwu's vision looks over the edge of the horizon toward a cooperative human environment; Butler, however, finds Lauren already at the start of her diary, concluding that the astronaut who has died in space, 'can be a kind of model for me. She spent her life heading for Mars – preparing herself, becoming an astronaut, getting on a Mars crew, going to Mars, beginning to terraform Mars, beginning to create sheltered places where people can live and work now' (21). Onyesonwu's sight line is taken from space, wearing the mask of *Kponyungo*, acting as a protecting spirit from the past; Lauren is looking at the stars, once hidden, through the death of an astronaut, whose very name, Alicia Catalina Godinez Leal, is a shape-shifting manifest, toward possibility. Yet, that she has died in space and thus her own funeral rites are disregarded, suggests that possibility is already foreclosed. Hartman writes, 'the *history* of black counter-historical projects is one of failure, precisely because these accounts have never been able to install themselves as history, but rather are insurgent, disruptive narratives that are marginalized and derailed before they ever gain a footing' (13). Butler's and Okorafor's speculative fictions of the unfolded Plantationocene, but posited as histories of the future, cannot become installed as requisite counter-narratives; instead they inscribe a dire and insurgent, an already-made, yet to-be, history.

NOTE

1 Donna Haraway on the origin of the term Plantationocene: 'In a recorded conversation for *Ethnos* at the University of Aarhus in October, 2014, the participants collectively generated the name Plantationocene for the devastating transformation of diverse kinds of human-tended farms, pastures, and forests into extractive and enclosed plantations, relying on slave labor and other forms of exploited, alienated, and usually spatially transported labor' (162). In their 'Plantation Legacies', Sophie Sapp Moore, Monique Allewaert, Pablo F. Gómez and Gregg Mitman place 'this emergent concept in dialogue with long-standing traditions of Black, Caribbean, and Indigenous radical thought confronting the enduring legacies of plantations and the transformations of land, labor, bodies, and systems of value that have accompanied their making. Invoking the Plantationocene … helps to make visible power relations and economic, environmental, and social inequalities that have made ways of being in a world undergoing rapid climate change, accelerated species extinction, and growing wealth disparity more precarious for some human and nonhuman beings than others. It is also an invitation to see, in the words of geographer Laura Pulido, "the Anthropocene as a racial process", one that has and will continue to produce "racially uneven vulnerability and death"' (Moore et al.).

WORKS CITED

Ball, Charles. *Slavery in the United States. A Narrative of the Life and Adventures of Charles Ball, A Black Man*. Pittsburgh: J. T. Shryock, 1853, reprinted from John W. Shugert, 1836.

Browne, Simone. *Dark Matters: One the Surveillance of Blackness*. Durham: Duke University Press, 2015.

Butler, Octavia. *Parable of the Sower*. New York: Grand Central, 1993.

Carney, Judith and Richard Rosomoff. *In the Shadow of Slavery: Africa's Botanical Legacy in the Atlantic World*. Berkeley: University of California Press, 2009.

Haraway, Donna. 'Anthropocene, Capitalocene, Plantationocene, Chthulucene: Making Kin'. *Environmental Humanities* 6 (2015): 159–65.

Hartman, Saidiya. 'Venus in Two Acts'. *Small Axe* 26 (2008): 1–14.

Jacobs, Harriet. *Incidents in the Life of a Slave Girl, Written by Herself*. Jean Fagan Yellin, ed. Cambridge: Harvard University Press, 2000.

Modern Ghana, 'Parable of the Sower – Not 1984 – Is The Dystopia For Our Age – Nnedi Okorafor'. 17 February 2017. https://www.modernghana.com/news/756213/parable-of-the-sower-not-1984-is-the-dystopia.html, accessed 23 December 2019.

Moore, Sophie Sapp, Monique Allewaert, Pablo F. Gómez and Gregg Mitman. 'Plantation Legacies'. *Edge Effects*. 12 October 2019. https:// edgeeffects.net/plantation-legacies-plantationocene/, accessed 23 December 2019.

Morrison, Toni. *Beloved*. New York: Knopf, 1987.

Ngũgĩ wa Thiong'o. *Something Torn and New: An African Renaissance*. New York: Basic Books, 2009.

Nixon, Rob. *Slow Violence and the Environmentalism of the Poor*. Cambridge: Harvard University Press, 2011.

Okorafor, Nnedi. *Who Fears Death*. New York: DAW Books, 2010.

——. *Zahrah the Windseeker*. Boston: Houghton Mifflin, 2005.

Olney, James. '"I Was Born": Slave Narratives, Their Status as Autobiography and as Literature'. In *The Slave's Narrative*. Charles T. Davis and Henry Louis Gates, Jr., eds. New York: Oxford University Press, 1985.

Sharpe, Christina. *In the Wake: On Blackness and Being*. Durham: Duke University Press, 2016.

Yusoff, Kathryn. *A Billion Black Anthropocenes or None*. Minneapolis: University of Minnesota Press, 2018.

Kenyan Novelist, Yvonne Owuor,

INTERVIEWED BY

NG'ANG'A WAHU-MUCHIRI, 16 JUNE 2017

Yvonne Adhiambo Owuor's *Dust* (2014) scrutinizes carefully the multi-generational cycles of violence that have featured in Kenyan history. Rather than posit this in atavistic notions of tribalism, however, Owuor is interested in how tyranny can itself become a ritual: an act that is repeated seemingly with its own momentum. Kenya, as a nation-state that gained political self-rule from European colonial masters, nurtures a deep residue of state violence. *Dust* takes seriously the idea that human and ecological events are connected; that in fact these two influence each other. Without presenting a voyeuristic attitude towards violence, Owuor deftly invokes human mortality. The novel's plot, however, shows that death is not haphazard, either. Habits of impunity can be strongly entrenched, whether this is for colonial forces stamping out a peasant Land & Freedom (Mau Mau) rebellion, or twenty-first century crime-fighting units in Nairobi that shoot to kill. Impunity. Mortality. Habits. These three elements haunt the text. Owuor's *Dust* stretches its canvas from Turkana, Northern Kenya, to Brazil. Her characters occupy these spaces in ways that increasingly get us to question contemporary representations of lands and landscapes. The eponymous dust develops into a motif that connects humanity to the ecosphere. In *Dust*, landscapes come alive. Topographical features are portrayed as living entities, which I think greatly advances our ongoing discussions on how to mitigate climate change. Owuor asks that we re-imagine the oceans, polar ice caps, deserts, lakes, and rivers not as inanimate objects that we act on, but as subjects – and agents – in their own right. In this wide-ranging conversation, Owuor threads together the binary thinking developed during the Age of Reason with a long history of separating culture from nature, arts from sciences, body from soul. In this sense, her writing seeks to undermine an ontology of dualism. Owuor's second novel, *The Dragonfly Sea* (2019), is an expansive and lyrical ode to the cultural, spiritual, economic, and migratory patterns of the Indian Ocean. A third novel, tentatively titled *The Long Decay,* is in progress.

NWM: So, a little about myself. I've been working on land rights in Eastern Africa. And I think I've approached *Dust* from that perspective, too. I'd love to hear a little bit about how the novel came about? Was there a specific moment of 'inspiration?'

YAO: The referendum of 2005, and the disconnect between the media and official narrative and the rage on the ground. It found its 'voice' in the season of the 2007/8 PEV (Post-Election Violence).

NWM: Yes, I was thinking about that PEV part, too. Since you brought up violence, let's start there. There is such a range of violence in the text: post/colonial, Mau Mau, Shifta, cattle raids, crime, etc. How do you as a writer work with/around violence without adopting a voyeur perspective? And also, how do you ensure your reader doesn't do the same? (Is that even something you can attempt?)

YAO: Challenging question that. But I imagine the space opens because of the questions that compel a person who is also an artist: what does it mean to be human? Who worries about the darkness and shadows of the human being but seeks to look at these as a means of also gaining insight into the things she could get up to? No acts of violence are alien to me, because I share the same humanity as those for whom violence is the only means of communications.

NWM: So, looking away is simply NOT an option – despite the ugliness.

YAO: Not anymore, Ng'ang'a. Not after my own small witness of what we, a country of 'siblings', could do to each other.

NWM: That makes sense. But then, I wonder, is violence a discrete event, which happens once and it's over, or can we also talk about remnants of violence? In other words, what, if anything, ties together the moment Nyipir's son is gunned down to the kinds of acts Nyipir himself might have been involved in … perhaps even perpetrated?

YAO: I would be interested in your perspective … but my hypothesis about this is that it has many forms, acquires many shapes, and each distinct character has its particular cycle, life and method of exorcism. Some types of violence are supernovas;

they erupt and fade. Others, the more personal kind of the sorts humans visit upon each other, grow, expand, metastasize, and become monsters if they are not uprooted by daring acts of courage, humility and atonement.

NWM: Thinking back to the process of writing, were there any significant developments in how you view/ed violence from the beginning to the end? Some revelations along the way?

YAO: There is something visceral and profound about the betrayal of life, I believe. And that is what violence visited on another being is and does. Developments? Let us see: at first it terrified me, its overwhelming power and seeming ceaselessness. I judged it as an aberration. By the end of the story, I understood it as human, as part of the broken in the human, and its vulnerability to love, to those human values we have stopped talking enough about: listening, apology, acknowledgment, forgiveness, re-naming, truth. It dies before truth. What is your opinion?

NWM: Violence dies before truth?

YAO: It seems to lose its will.

NWM: That sounds point on. There's a way in which secrecy, darkness, fear, etc. empower violence. and the opposite weakens it.

YAO: Beautifully put, Ng'ang'a. Exactly that.

NWM: Thanks. Then perhaps that might 'explain' the subtle hints in the text about the creative process: singing, painting, sculpting, etc. or what else was going on for you in those scenes/moments?

YAO: The muse made me do it. Now that you point that out, I see it. You are right. Reaching, questing, searching ... that is exactly what was going on. Ways of speaking that are not the familiar.

NWM: Which is the great thing about the book; that yes, violence is very present, but there's definitely more. How then, does human violence translate into environmental violence? The kind of landscape that Akai-ma walks into is dry and arid, barren even? How are humans tied in to that kind of environmental space?

YAO: I cannot separate these, Ng'ang'a. The environment, seemingly unable to fight back, suffers most from that odd, broken impulse to destroy life, to destroy that which is good, beautiful and true, and then create justifications for the aberration. What are these that soil the very source of their living and do so in a manner that devastates its core? I suspect that one can tell a people and who they are, and how they treat each other by the state of their surroundings. And what they elevate as iconic and meaningful in their landscape.

NWM: Yeah, but does that mean the ecosystem is our victim ... perhaps in the same way that colonial projects feminized the global south in order to justify domination? When you say 'I suspect that one can tell a people and who they are, and how they treat each other by the state of their surroundings', I like that because it suggests that the logical effect of capitalist/imperialist economic projects is exactly what we're seeing now.

YAO: We have turned the ecosystem into our scapegoat and victim without realizing that we are sawing off the branch on which we stand. It is exactly the same shit the colonial project put forth to justify their own will to violence and greed. The consequences of the paradigm that was valorized and elevated after the so-called Age of Reason has driven us to this crisis point. The whole paradigm, the ideological bent with its pretence to objective reason needs to be microscopically examined.

NWM: Yeah, and that it almost doesn't make sense to worry about environmental degradation whilst humans cannibalize each other. *And*, that once human relations are truly egalitarian, the immediate effect will be positive *even* for the environment. So, perhaps human violence versus environmental violence is a false dichotomy. There's just violence and its adverse effects are visible on both human and physical geographies ...

YAO: I agree with you, Ng'ang'a. We may struggle with egalitarianism though, but surely we can at the very least start by a will to see the human and the humanity of the one we call 'the other'? To approach that with the delicacy and wonder it deserves ...

NWM: True. OK, then what's the role of the state in all these?

YAO: To my mind, that is not a useful dichotomy. The character of violence is one and the same. The so-called modernism, post modernism, post-post modernism and its framing is for me a continuation of the voodoo practices of the paradigm's ancestral icons (Kant, and his ilk), the French schools and all those thugs from the Age of Reason and 'Enlightenment' who atomized the world; separated body from soul, arts from sciences; divided human beings into racial categories (can you believe a more stupid framing of humanity), divide, divide, divide in order to study in a special silo. The state ... *do* not get me started ... I have come to the point of asking what the state is and what it is for.

NWM: In the novel, the state appears as a malevolent force: shooting down young men, electoral violence, etc. Is the state redeemable?

YAO: Is its primary role as that of trustee of a people and their territory of influence? In which case, certainly in Kenya and other examples, it should have started by asking, who are we (and 'we' includes the environment) and what do we stand for in the world? In the absence of all this, why can't the state dare to define an 'elevated' position from which to speak and articulate its vision for the common good of its people and ecosystems?

NWM: Right, and of course, the state on its own is empty. It only comes alive once the president, district officers, district commissioners, state officials, animate it. So what responsibility do we as humans have for this structure that we've created and which has seemingly turned into something we can no longer control?

YAO: Created by humans, it can be re-imagined by these same humans. Perhaps, then, the idea of the interconnectedness of all things, including the state to us citizens. We are of that ecology. Is there a critical number who have a clear and visionary orientation that has the sense of an encompassing common good? Can that citizenry articulate their vision so that it is understood, and has a buy in? I don't know anymore, Ng'anga...

NWM: Yeah, tough questions.

YAO: A bit like your questions about violence; the overarching governing paradigm and its structural inclination to eviscerate, uncover, exploit in the name of 'development' feels like a runaway train.

NWM: The basic idea of development is that someone else *always* has to pay for it: slaves for the development of US/Europe, global South for global North, lower classes for political elites ... etc.

YAO: It is such a lie.

NWM: I have a question about the book's title. What's the significance of 'dust' as a motif in the book? As well as its variants: earth, soil, land, landscape?

YAO: Among other things, it does speak to the 'truth', the culmination of all human striving and madness: *Memento*, homo, *quia pulvis es, et in pulverem reverterisi*. Inspired by the landscape of Northern Kenya. The immensity of earth; the starkness of nature unveiled; the truth that I was not the first to stop by this land, nor would I be the last, and most of those who have traversed it, are probably as dust in the wind ... as we each shall ... 'Remember man, that thou are dust and unto dust thou shalt return!'

NWM: Which is a humbling truth that we strive our best to forget: monuments, statues, etc.

YAO: But the book did go through a few other titles. Strangely enough, they all had to do with earth, soil and dust.

NWM: Oh, interesting!

YAO: Our wars, our petty hatreds ... Dust.

NWM: How about movement? There's a lot of motion in the text: bodies, winds, water, words? Where is all that leading?

YAO: I wish I knew! But it is interesting that you found, saw and followed these. Fascinating.

NWM: And a good part of that has to do with rhythm. The references to music are numerous ...

YAO: The pulse of this story is fuelled by the things one loves about life, about an awareness of its progression, I guess. That seeped into the story. You know that I 'hear' the story before I can write it.

NWM: I like the idea of the story's pulse!

YAO: And the story has a sound track in the heart ... Unless I hear the 'song' of the story ... there is no story. Strange, eh?

NWM: And fascinating! How does that work?

YAO: I have no idea whatsoever ... It is like a sliver of song in the wind that makes you turn your head to look ... that is how a story visits me. Hope it doesn't sound so strange ... And then once it starts it finds its sound track.

NWM: Strange? No. But I love the idea.

YAO: I am glad you also found the music in the story. Fascinating. Not everybody does, you know.

NWM: So, for instance, when you say 'song', is it like a song from another musician or a whole new creation?

YAO: Yes ...

NWM: Does it have lyrics? Instruments? Beats?

YAO: Snippets of lyrics, but mostly melody; and always a beat.

NWM: Really?

YAO: Aha.

NWM: That is so fascinating

YAO: Synesthesia, another interviewer suggested.

NWM: That definitely gives a whole new level of significance to the songs shared by the herdsman.

YAO: Have you heard the songs of our desert lands, Ng'ang'a? Camel songs, the herdsmen whistle songs … The northern Kenya space is a territory of secret concerts.

NWM: You know, I'm embarrassed to say I've not.

YAO: Since you care for land and landscape … do go when you can … and go with one who knows the land, and go and just listen.

NWM: Our time is almost up. Before you go, what's next: projects? novel?

YAO: New novel coming out later this year, *The Dragonfly Sea*. Indian ocean story.

NWM: Awesome, I can't wait! All the best, and many thanks for your time.

Literary Supplement

Maiming

JULIANA DANIELS

Once I met this couple
On my way back from visiting the aged fellas of my kinfolk
She and he both stooped as though to pick from ground
No! But bent over from years of bending to till
What toil to take a peasant meal home?

Twice I met this miner lad
The kid of the couple
Dressed in mud from crown to soul
What ceremony I wanted to ask?
For school bells for lads his world went hours before. That I am sure
This young earth dressed lad
Bent sideways as though to scratch a rib
No! He too, what toil to take home a paltry mine to fend a world of
mouths?

Thrice I met this bent over farmer and mud-dressed miner
In this house of ailment
Here some coughed and others puffed
Here some peed and others pooped
Here some healed and others ailed worse
And here the farmer and the miner both came
Bent over to the fore and to the side
Both peed and pooped and coughed and puffed
For the miner's mine maimed the earth
And the farmer's farm maimed the belly

I am Set in a Burden to Sing

UCHECHUKWU UMEZURIKE

I am accustomed to sing of love
Among the pristine marigolds of dawn,
Like some poet would serenade beauty
Cushioned by the surf caress of women.

Between the emerald boulevard of obeche,
I am set in a burden to sing
Of the pastoral poetry of my kindred
Slaving hungry in the savannah of foods.

I am set in a burden to sing
Darkness overriding our homes,
Like the howl of pipelines beneath our
Earth dense with barrels of crude excess;

I am set in a burden to sing
The behemoth belch of fumes
Cramming the nostrils of Escravos,
Choking the lungs of Nun and Forcados;

I am set in a burden to sing
The dirge of barren fields and barns,
The murmur of slick-smeared mangroves,
The sour breath of fish steaming the shore.

I am set in a burden to sing
Hacked dugout canoes drifting
On the salted spine of scorched creeks,
And bones of frogs fossilised for future;

I am set in a burden to sing
The limping cock, the mangy dog,
The one-eyed goat, the wounded pig;
All the graffiti of sickness and sadness;

I am set in a burden to sing
Boys and girls in sore scramble
For rusted pipes spewing yellowed
Water like gonorrhoea-pained penis;

I am set in a burden to sing
How mothers torment their brow
At the slightest warble of wings above,
Like Heaven's bread will plop in their laps;

I am set in a burden to sing
The haste of fathers breeding waifs;
Their wait like Simeon's pregnant
Like their dissolution of time in alcohol;

I am set in a burden to sing
Gaping, black effigies of houses
Cuddled by the careless arms of fire
Of the froth-clouded, hot-headed ruler;

I am set in a burden to sing
Ugly swell of bodies strewn about,
Limbs and arms mashed in the mud
By the toothed tread of military tanks;

I am set in a burden to sing
The hunched histories of Oloibiri,
Ogoni, Odi, Umechem and Egbema;
The looming hurricane in their slow rebirth;

The nebulous Niger, the foaming flood,
The chains to bear Africa's shame –
But my voice is cracked, the feeble flute;
Its timbre wafted as ash on time's wind.

Poems from the Oil Archipelago

DOKUBO MELFORD GOODHEAD

TROUBLE IN THE OIL ARCHIPELAGO

The classrooms are deserted.
The playgrounds have turned into
ghost fields where the gunfire
of militia and government troops
echo and re-echo again.

The curse of the great curse is upon us.
The curse of oil is upon us.
The once happy archipelago
is in the midst of a great dying.
The seabirds are gone, the fish are gone.
The river is red with the blood of the slain.
An ancient seagull, woken up from
a thousand years of slumber,
flies over the dying archipelago,
crying to sky, crying to earth,
mourning the death of everything.

MINOR AND THE OIL

This archipelago,
My blood.
My mother
Watered it
With her tears.
When I was born,
I was called Minor,
And treated like

A nobody.
When I howled
Against the infamy,
I was cut down
Like a thing
That this blood-
Stained sea,
My birth water,
May continue to roll
Out to sea
The killing oil barrels.

ODE TO A CHILDHOOD FRIEND

I remember you,
O singing river,
river of my childhood,
haunting river, river of the singing creeks,
where Nature made of me a hunter,
a young fisherman hunting crabs
at the ebb of your mighty tide

I remember you
O sweet childhood friend,
wandering bard that sang to me
of adventures beyond the dancing banks
of the arching sunset, where sweeping tides
meet with the great sea and carry
the brave fisherman to seas
where waves tower over the earth
like Mount Kilimanjaro

I remember you
O playful elf, mating between the roots
of the mangrove trees and murmuring sweet sounds
with the water crabs, mating too and burrowing
deeper into sodden caves, where colonies of crabs
arise like columns of armor-clad Roman soldiers,
march down the banks in serried formation
at the hemline of your laughing skirt.

I remember you. I remember you.
I remember you, O fallen friend, blood-stained river,
river drunk with the black crude of death,
river drunk with the vomitus of dying pipes,
river blind from the death touch of smoldering pipes.

I remember you. I remember you, O childhood friend,
and weep and weep upon these deserted banks,
where, now, laughters come to die, the seabirds crying,
The night, the night, the night is upon us.

THE DARK NIGHT

I see columns
upon columns
  of gray pipes
reaching into the sky,
        the remnants
        of the followers
        of the great idol,
spewing curses
  into the gray sky.
  The sea is dead.
        The land is dead.
  The people are dead.
        Every form of life is dead
  and lie gray
        in the bleaching rain.
  And yet
        I see columns
                                        upon columns
of gray pipes
  standing sentry
upon
  every atoll,
  spewing curses into
        the sulfurous sky.
The great idol has fallen,
    the pipelines dry and rusty.

The nightmare is
upon us. The nightmare is upon us. The nightmare is upon us.
And
now
only
the gray pipes
remain.

THE OLD MAN OF THE OIL ARCHIPELAGO

OLD MAN

Son,
I was here before the oil men and the oil barges landed
on this archipelago.
Son, I was here before the grizzled shark hunters
took to the high seas and never returned.
Son, I was here before the leaping flames were planted here
and the singing archipelago became the oil archipelago
and the oil flowed in the veins of the river
and death and dying came upon everything.

Son, I have been here counting the stones on the shore
these countless seasons
waiting for her who was taken from me by the swamping waves
of the great oil barges.

The sea has left bruises on my back.
The wind has left furrows on my face.
The sun has burnt my flesh to cinders.

The hippopotamus once ripped a hole in my stomach;
I fought him back with my bare hands and the ungainly beast
has not seen these parts again.

The crocodile once held me fast in its jaws but I sent him
into the depths of the boiling sea and have been telling
the tale
ever since.

When the horde of elephants came like a trampling tide, I was one
of the warriors
that sent them into the roaring sea.

Son, I have been counting pebbles here ever since and my name
is minor,
so no one knows my name.

Son, I have been counting pebbles here ever since, waiting for my
beloved,
Ibiere
to return to me from the sea
and my name is minor, so no one knows my name.

My heart beats like a fist in the belly of a water-filled dream.
I think it will burst its banks. I think it will overflow the riverside
take to the sea like the mourning tide of dead fish and sea
birds,
ripped from the sea, ripped from the air by black crude from burst
oil pipes.

O dead sea kingdom! O dead bird kingdom! O dead sea! O dead sea!

Son, my heart is a fist and a hammer, a fist and a hammer,
threatening
to burst upon the riverside
like the broken oil pipes,
dying blood taken to sea like dead fish and sea birds.
But son, here I will remain, here I will remain until my beloved
returns
from the sea.

O wife of my youth, o canoe woman of the oil archipelago, o wife
of my youth!

O son, here I will remain, here I will remain until the guardian of
the four portals
of my being returns from the sea.
O son, here I will remain, until she returns from the sea.
O son, here I will remain until she returns from the sea.

YOUNG MAN

I left him by the sea, his hair gray, his eyes gray, his ancient beard
gray and falling
like a pencil of mystical light onto his bony chest. I could see his ribs.
I could count every one of them.
He must have waited by the riverside for his dead wife for ages.

The sea came to the shore and beat upon him with an incredible
fury.
I saw him disappear in the roaring surf and emerge again
from its unhappy folds like a weather-beaten sea bird
drenched to the bones. He resumed his position by the sea
like a lone palm tree,
as if nothing had happened, as if the world no longer spun
on its course,
as if time itself had lost all meaning.

Suddenly, I cried with all my might. I cried with every fiber of my
being.
I cried like an angry child, protesting his banishment
from hearth and home:

'Let her go, let her go, let her go';
the sea has taken her.

But the old man sat cross-legged by the sea, a lone palm tree,
as he had sat for ages.

The sun had completed its voyage in the silken sky. The moon
and stars
were already peeping out from behind their shutters
in the silken dome.
The crickets were already alive, raising a cacophonous song
in the belly of the dusk.
An owl cried and flew against the leaping flames from the oil pipes
and disappeared into the night spewing curses at the flames.

I saw a flock of bats heading into the newly-born night,
& I heard the cry of mother bat to infant bat:
'Little ones, do not fly into the flames. O little ones, do not fly into

the flames.'

The night had come alive with a million creatures and I too began
to head home,
far away from the brooding sea, far away from the old man.
My bed beckoned, my pillow beckoned, and sweet sleep was
already alighting
like fireflies upon my tired eyes.

I was heading home, the flames from the oil pipes lighting my path,
when suddenly I heard the old man cry with all his might,
with every fiber of his being,
with all the mortal power he could summon to his trembling lips:
'Here I'll be, here I'll be, until she returns from the sea.'

Thrice I heard him repeat the cry, like the sorrow song of a hapless
fugitive
from home and hearth. & suddenly the night swallowed him,
the sky turned suddenly dark, despite the flames from the
oil pipes.
The sea birds of the oil archipelago were heading to another clime,
to another archipelago, to another home away from oil flames
and the restless sea turned the color of night by oil from
burst oil pipes.

In all my journeys around the world, I still hear the haunting cry
of the old man, see images of giant oil barges and a
drowning woman.
& in those moments when time seems to flow like
a silken river, I hear myself crying:

'O love, have mercy. O love, have mercy on your acolytes,
give reprieve long before the final hour.'

Man is Dead

KELVIN NGONG TOH

I

I am just an old man
Caught in a revolution
That makes my mind to
Wonder and ponder
What my children will be –
After I should have cross
Sowe's gate never to return –

Without the sweet
Melodies of the birds,
Without the frightening beauties
Of snakes seeking
The fowl and eggs for
A sumptuous daily delicacy.
Shall these ones know
When rain comes and when
The sun comes?

The confusion is right
Here in front
Of me as I set out with
An umbrella and the
Sun almost melts my flesh.
I get out only the next
Day without an umbrella
And the rain soaks me
To shivering points.
Where has the forest gone?
Can sky-scrapers shelter like the forest?

II

Man is dead;
Nature now fights
From hurricane to mount Fako
Quarrelling and reminding west
Africa of her great authority
Where Epasa Moto along
With the spirits at Oku
And Boyo demonstrate their majesty.

Man is dead;
The sacred voice's order
And ordination to stewardship
Never meant destruction.

Man is dead;
The refusal of birds to sing,
The rain and sun confusion
Only plunges man to object
Of pity.

III

Holes were made
For rats and snakes
To abode.
Stones beneath
Were made to
Beautify and to hold
The foundations of the earth.

Man. Your digging of holes
In search of stones and liquid
Has shaken the foundation
Of the earth. And Fako
And Oku and Boyo
And Nyos and the twin lakes
Are speaking and you are deaf.
Deaf to Mongo's mournful flow;

Lamenting the history of a people
Stricken by violence and hate.

IV

God created the earth,
It was beautiful.
He gave man for stewardship.
Man decided to know
More than his creator.
The creator has given man
His most cherished peace,
And man has ruined the earth –
All alone
And instead of returning
To God for help,
He now blames God
For ordaining him with stewardship powers.

V

Man! What a creature?
And sure all other creatures are
Pondering like me.

Nature's shelter shall prevail
And my children's children
Will enjoy the songs from
The forest and feel
The taste and the feel
Of the scintillating sun rays
Clad in the many
Colours of the rainbow.

VI

Nature's shelter shall prevail
And my children's children
Will enjoy the songs from

The forest and feel
The taste and the feel
Of the scintillating sun rays
Clad in the many
Colours of the rainbow.

Art Pub / City Life

GUZAL AKRAM

ART PUB

Art's Bar – a tavern
That serves pizza and beer

With a furbishing of crimson, yellow and gold.
It has a hold on clients that
Bustle like bees and clamor
Of people having a good time.

Behind the door that says
Employees only
Is a world of clinking spoons
And clanging pots.

On this side of the door
I see wrinkled faces like crinkled fries
Along with those who are
Absent of those lines that
Reflect time.

That's Art's Bar – a tavern
That serves pizza and beer

CITY LIFE

We live in a jungle of concrete and steel
Malls that display
What we want, what we think.
But,
No place to sit without the
Sounds of calamity and strife.

Too much investment in the hustle
With no gain in return
Preoccupied with tensions and worries
Of what tomorrow may bring.

It has taken from us,
The precious element of time
That rare gem that takes a
Lifetime to find.

Indian Ocean is Crying

ALEXANDER OPICHO

I stand at the silver sand beaches
Where Francis Xavier was buried,
Looking at Pillar of Vasco da Gama,
The point at which this son of Spain
Hopped to the land mass at city of Malindi,
I look at my dear love, the beauteous Indian Ocean,
As her tidal face struggles under the soft rays,
Of the tired sun on the verge of its soonest set,
She looks annoyed and down cast, O! My love,
What happened to you there in deep seas?
Cheer up love, for you're the anchor of my heart,
Regret not a little of those who vilify your face,
With tanks of oil leaking into your heart,
As they scamper here and there, like mad ones,
In search of Dolphins, squids and octopus,
To kill them merciless for money and power,
They know not how you cry and shed torrents,
Of grievous dears as they kill your sires,
Forgive them dear sweet heart,
They know not what they are doing,
Already they gave you a miserable name;
This name *Indian Ocean*, as if you are proud of it,
Or as if happily in love with castes of India,
I have re-named you the *love ocean*,
With a promise never to pollute you,
Neither will I give way to ships of slavery,
To cross your body with the crying slaves
Captured from hinterland of poor Africa,
In transit to Arabia for hard labour,
I will keep you clean and save my love,

For all the days I will be with you,
I pray you preserve your volcanic anger,
Lest you foment *Tsunamis* and Tornadoes,
To the innocent island and seaside dwellers,
I pray darling you don't go ahead,
With the foul idea of swallowing Mombasa islet,
Forgive her for the sake of our love we have,
Between you and me, as asunder we go not

My Pet Bee

JEROME MASAMAKA

Waggling at rare hours of sunrise
Whirring at first sight of twilight
Glowing at whiff of unseen light
And yet no hive in sight
What bright briar
must have brought you to my littered lair?

I know not what love, I see no flower
No showers even at the usual hour
Only dead leaves dumped on this foyer
by thirsty stems. Bumblebee
drifting free
You left lush shrubs
for a dead courtyard littered with stubs.
I may have smelled green or nipped a forbidden flower
Away to the sanctuary for an early prayer
If I go
will you follow?

But oh, incessant bee flying free
pursued in speed to circle me
gliding closer, a hushed hover
You perch on my shoulder
I smile hands cupped
for a friendly hug or frustrated swipes
yet you spy
in multiple lenses of colourful eyes.
Golden insect, what do you inspect
if there is no honey to expect?

She sniffs my perfumed neck
a Calvin Klein has done the trick
But no, not my armpit
A daring wriggle closer, sniffing and oh, a spit
followed by a sting. You slap me!
Foul odour masked by choicest fragrance
Human delusion to elegance
No insect is fooled by this ruse
How will I be of use
in this subterfuge
to an honeybee?
What decay has she felt or see
in me?

So I rushed to pluck the finest flower
to deck my foyer
with fresh spray
Perhaps she will stay
and not stray.

She flew back secretly
surveyed and sniffed quietly
the old kitchen lingered in smoke
Beware, lest you choke.
Yet, no dismay
as she flew away.
A rotten food
must have fouled her mood
I am no lover, nor do I flower
in this dirty foyer.

A lone harbinger bee surveying courtyards
What message have you brought?
On whose land have I trespassed?
What shrub did I burn down?
What trees did I cut and which birds did I displace?
On whose house did I build mine?

I will clean this old land, plant fresh flowers
and leave room for new lovers.

How do we bring life to a dead cold farm,
light up old homes to let love blossom?
I'm still searching for answers
to lure back the pet bee
who wanted to hive with me.

The Homecoming

BETTY IGE

The day she returned home was the worst day of your life. You were mad. Mad at her for despising you. Mad at her for taking off all these years and coming back at her convenience. You were mad at everyone who rejoiced at her homecoming; and you gave a fire and brimstone tongue-lashing. You hated her.

They begged and cajoled you to forgive her but you refused to budge from your high horse, where you perched like the mistress of the manor. They clasped and unclasped their hands; they pleaded with moist eyes and quivering lips but you were resolute.

'Please, go and look at her,' they implored.

You were mortified. No. You were enraged!

What gall!

'Why would I want to look at her?' you queried. I've not forgotten what she looked like!'

You recoiled at the memory. You hated her looks; not because she was unattractive. She was beauty in human form. You remembered they called her Omalicha, the beautiful one. She was the Akwanwa, the golden child. Imagine that! And what did they call you? Well, nothing significant.

You were embittered.

Oh, how you whined and complained. You desired to be the golden child, the Akwanwa. You coveted her beauty. You wanted to be the one they admired and fawned over. You disliked her comeliness. You wanted to be the beauty queen all the more because they were blind to Omalicha's arrogance. You saw her ungratefulness for her awesome beauty and you loathed her.

You remembered the dazed look on their faces the day Omalicha made her announcement. It was your eighteenth birthday anniversary. What insolence! Their eyes glimmered with fear as they pleaded with the beautiful one. You could have sworn they were overwhelmed with her beauty.

'Are you out of your mind?' they blustered.
'You can't just decide to leave those who love you.'
'Love? That makes me feel better and oh, I will miss you my sweet people,' Omalicha drawled and rolled haughty eyes to convey her scorn.
You mentally blocked your ears to stop the sarcasm dripping from her voice.
Adjusting the ruffles adorning her high-end, boutique-shopped blouse, Omalicha produced a somewhat realistic-sound of sniffle, gathered her flashy belongings and with a click of her stiletto heels, she was gone from your lives without as much as a backward glance.
Then you started hearing the long stories. They said Omalicha was seen in Lagos and Abuja. They said she moved with the high and mighty and frolicked with Casanovas. They said she had become a serial dater who wined and dined with dandies easily identified by their abdominal obesity. You even heard she gorged herself on *isiewu* which she enjoyed with cold beer. The rumour said she was sighted in Dubai, then London and even Saudi Arabia. You heard she feasted on American cheese and Greek yogurt. They said Omalicha smoked cigarettes. That she did drugs and things and has become a psychedelic dancer.
They told you Omalicha's beauty was the topic of every discussion; that men swooned at her beauty and wanted a slice of that renowned beauty. They reported she was alluring at night when they heard her giggling behind closed doors. They said she rode luxury cars and travelled the world first class. You heard she lived life in the fast lane and was robed like exotic women featured on Hollywood movies. You were green with envy.
You found it difficult to understand why Omalicha was having all the good time. You blamed it all on them. All of them who loved and admired Omalicha, and never threw a pinch of admiration your way. And now they wanted you to welcome the prodigal. Mtcheeeeeww!
Then you heard the knock on the door.
'Who?' you demanded.
'It's me.'
The hoarse voice found its way into your room before the owner appeared. You appraised the figure that darkened the doorway. Then you stood, tottered on your feet and gawked at the stranger. You noticed the gray hair bursting from a head that looked a bit too big for the thin neck. The creature smiled uncertainly at you and tried to curtail the abrasive cough that threatened to sever her already

emaciated neck. Her eyes pleaded for mercy.

You gasped and beat a hasty retreat as recognition dawned. Where was Omalicha? Who was the stranger in your room? You tried not to shudder as you watched the effigy rocking on her heels right in front of you. You grimaced at the faded orange dress that clashed loudly with the worn red shoes on dusty feet. Combined with the purple bag on her skinny shoulder she appeared like an artist's nightmare.

Your heart bled at what used to be the Beautiful one. Gone was her mane, the colour of which she changed with the audacity and quickness of a chameleon. Sometimes it was dyed gold; at other times purple or coffee brown. In the place of the once-upon-a-time luxuriant hair was a shaggy growth of gray. You noticed that the luscious lips that were perpetually painted a red colour have been replaced by charred doors, maybe the handiwork of harmattan. Gone were the high and structured twin towers on her chest. What was left looked like … like … Well, you were unable to see anything.

You were besieged by disorderly thoughts. Omalicha has been stripped of her golden splendour. You felt weightless at the thought. You closed your eyes and told yourself that it was a passing dream. But you quickly opened them to discover she has moved and sat on the only chair in your room. You observed the deep exhaustion etched on her forehead. You felt the warm night breeze blowing through the window and whipping her straggly hair across her face. She sighed and her eyes drooped. You closed your own eyes and knew there will be healing when you opened them again. That day Omalicha returned home was your awakening.

**isiewu*: a traditional eastern Nigerian dish that is prepared with goat head.

The Power of Bribe

ALEXANDER OPICHO

She loved him that is why she wanted him to accompany her to the VCT center for voluntary counseling and testing. She was born in America, she is a Mexican, and she only came to Kenya in the company of her father and mother, a diplomatic family, her father was posted there as a consul. The man she loved was tall and slender; he spoke no other language but English, strictly non-kitsch English. He was born in Tanzania two decades ago. He is the only son of the first Attorney General of the Republic of Tanzania. He was born and brought up in the Wasigura sub-urbs of Dar es Salem. The capital city of Tanzania. He is not sure if he is gay or not. It is now that he is seriously feeling like not lose her, come sunshine or come rain. And this is the only reason he will not go for the HIV test at the VCT center. He will not go for the VCT not for anything but as the only surest way of protecting his love for her. Her love for him is so strong that she even feels for her parents, she prays for them as she does for him. It is her wish that God takes care of such delicate situation, the only son to the old aged couple in the times where the harms of the world are marauding around, looking for chance to hurt the sweet love in the arms of the owner. She really prays, in English, Kiswahili and Mexican. She has paid for the most posh VCT service in, Karen, Nairobi, the poshness that bestrides geographies and times of the East and Central Africa; she paid for both of them, him and her. The will to love. Her name is Lupita. Her maiden names weigh on her mind heavily like a sack full of cancer tumors. She is impatient, she longs for the day of adapting herself to the new names. Marital names, his surname. He was called Abu. A short version of Abubakar. He was also a Muslim. He loves his early adult-hood hirsute with sensation. He loves it with religious fervor. It is biology for religious greatness. Eugenics of the Prophet. Dissonance. He does not understand himself; gay love, Islamic terrorism and Lupita attract him with equal force,

Lupita's lubricity above all, it does him down to a feat of mad jealous, fear of losing her. He is ever in bad moods. Lachrymose. Every time he imagines chewing an un-peeled raw cassava, it is un-toothsome; he wants it peeled naked to its white nudeness, watery and sweet. The gift of nature. More natural than the selfish love administered to him by his Italian boy-friend in Malindi, that night managing man, Toffoli Marcello, the son of Napoli. He deserves a song or the sun in us. Karen, the poor-rich estate in Nairobi, have more in store; science before love. She feared giving him a phone call, no, a twitter message, no, inbox him on the Face-book page, no, scan the payments receipts and forwards them to his mail, no, it is better to give him a WhatsApp text. She did one of these things. But she does not remember, what it was, she is only feeling good. Tomorrow they will be together, in Karen. Testing their HIV status. What a sweet day to be in the shadow of a sweet man, two of you in the privacy that cement and stones give, somewhere in the city. The sweetness that verges on transformation. Willy-nilly, good or bad, but the transformation, which grows out of premonition that good things are coming. A kiss. He cannot afford to be mechanical enough to turn down the trip. Better hold the handle for a girl who wants to swallow the axe, he mused the Fulani proverb. And indeed, he held the handle for her. He drove the latest tortoise from Japan; it still smelled newness and novelty. Imagine novelty in the city. The VCT management threw the ivory beads of their career into the abyss of distant future. They saw it, charged him, judged him, understood him, felt for him and they acted Kenyan; having their elbows greased after thinking globally in order to act locally. Their heart went soft. Like a squab. They declared him a virgin and spotless in the blood, virus free and HIV negative even before the test. Power of the bribe. They were both masters of their liberty, but time, the mistress of their mastery, woman-hood the victim of feminine callowness. They were both spot punctual, Lupita and Abu. It was him then her. She was clean with no virus. Just as what the money has done to the truth about the blood of Abu. The falsehood which came as lightening on thick fleshy smiling lips of Dr Kibagenge. 'My *frens*, you are both HIV free.' He cooed like an owl, the harbinger of death, out of his culture of sadism, love for bribery and obviated incompetence of a person brought on the diet of the rotting milk. Abu kissed her, she kissed back. An earth quake of kisses ensued. It destroyed all the fabrics on their bodies, God bless the stony walls and curse the power of money. The cassava was peeled and eaten un-boiled but toad the poet crooned its in-famed piece; '*We Are Dying Tomorrow/ Myself, my wife and my two children will die tomorrow/ Lucky, my first born daughter died last month/ I and my wife we had Aids viruses/ We have no immunity to take us forth/ We are all dying tomorrow. My wife is thin like a ghost/ I breathe with sound like a train/ my kids look ugly like ghouls of Loudon/ Drugs are all over my room like alchemist's domain/ O! Surely my children are dying tomorrow/ Let man of honesty come forth and say/ Not only my succor but world in total/ Tell the world of who really made HIV viruses/ Tell the world of who can cure HIV aids/ But I and my family we are dying tomorrow.* 'They blamed the masters of secret art, crusaders envy and all the blameworths. They whooped with a cough and wheezed with a breath. They made love to each other on that day, they fell asleep. Angels lured them not to go back to the un-slept world. They woke up when they are already in a coffin. Abu then Lupita. None wanted them to jerk out of the coffin; forces against their will to *de-coffinize* themselves reigned supreme.

An African Literary Colossus on Ancestral Journey:

A TRIBUTE TO PA GABRIEL OKARA

PSALMS EMEKA CHINAKA

'Na wetin happen?', 'Person die?', 'Take am easy oo, you hear?' Each of these consolatory reactions in pidgin was laced with 'sorry'. They were actually some of the traditional strings of sympathies that were meant to console me the day Prof. Ernest Emenyonu broke the news that Gabriel Imomotimi Gbaingbain Okara had started the journey to join his forefathers. As at the time of the call I was on a busy street in Port Harcourt, these strings of consolations were apparently triggered by my involuntary exclamation that loudly suggested pain and regret for losing a loved one. These sympathizers were fellow Nigerians within earshot. Though most of them never bothered to inquire whose death it was, they were instinctively responding to the Nigerian traditional ethos at the slightest indication that someone lost someone. In other words, the 'sorry' is not the exclusive condolence ritual of close relatives, it can come from strangers who are just meeting you for the first time in the south-eastern part of Nigeria. My involuntary exclamation that day was natural since only a few weeks earlier I had accompanied Prof. Emenyonu on a visit to Okara's residence at Yenagoa, the capital of Bayelsa, his home State, while he was still alive. I could still almost touch the warm reception his daughter Timi Schiller gave us on that memorable day. But now when I think of the above drama (quite amusing, I suppose), which I would not mind entitling 'Sorry,' I am compelled to wonder aloud: *What an interesting intellectual site it will be for researchers as to the various dramatic ways people instinctively react to death news!*

Indeed, it is a reality that we lost another of Africa's literary legends when I was, incidentally at the time of his death, studying his collection of articles: *As I See It*. One of the remarkable things I had noted in my study of these stories, extracted from the *Sunday Tide* of the then Rivers State Newspapers Corporation, is that each comes with a certain degree of humour capable of concealing the author's message. In each, Okara tells Nigerians and Africans, in a soothing manner, of their precarious socio-political predicaments without necessarily tickling that corner of their psyche where fear and hopelessness reside. His writing technique is in a sense antidotal as it attempts to unburden or relieve Africans from weighty socio-political and economic issues. Sometimes one is compelled to qualify some of his stories as artistic relaxants, in as much as many critics will prefer to adjudge them as experimental artistry or satire, which they are, actually. Such humorous imaginative disposition attracts and sustains the elasticity of his readers' interest in works consistently infused with symbols, imagery and lyricism. In an experimental manner, it helps to transport the same peculiar African themes but with a customized departure from the popular. It is an artistry that appears simplified yet has the capacity to effectively engage, question, resist, agitate or/and sensitize those who Frantz Fanon regards as the 'wretched of the earth'.

Those who knew him well, knew he had a kind of tailored mien of a simple but self-styled African. Attired in the elegance of his Afrocentric fabrics, coupled with the air of humility and a soft-spoken voice, one is bound by fascination to further inquire of his full personal dispositions. To match this rare etiquette was his intellectual niche with strong connection to poetic excellence which, as Chidi Maduka once put it, resonates with simplicity of diction and pleasurable textures of imagery. Underneath his custom-made demeanour lurked the reformatory impulse of an African culture-oriented advocate simply qualified again by Maduka as 'Okara's cultural nationalism' or 'Okara's forceful affirmation of his cultural identity'. A critic who had studied him carefully might arguably posit that Okara did not really exploit his full potential as an artist. This is because he pursued the course of artistry with humility and a tinge of indifference to publicity. He once confessed to Bernth Linfors in an interview about this attitude: 'I've not had my works published in one volume before. I didn't really care much whether I had a volume of poetry or not, so when I finished writing a poem, I think I was very careless about keeping a copy.' In other words, Okara explored art more like an art-for-art phenomenon though with a difference. It is apparent that he insisted in utilising it as a corrective tool in an African world full of catastrophes. He was always in a natural way discharging a tranquil air of contentment.

Talking about his critics, I must note that some have not been able to find a valid critical canon with which to critique his works. It is historically important to note that in 1964 ,when *The Voice* was published, the African theoretical canon had not been clearly defined.

At the time, African intellectuals were yet to properly adopt a lingua franca, colonial or native, that would give expression to African literary creativity. They were still saddled with critical methodologies alien to the African worldview and experience without an Afrocentric alternative. Some of the critics who feasted on *The Voice* as an unsuccessful novel due to its language failed to understand that they were wrongly standing in judgement over, or adopting the Western theoretical framework in the assessment of a work typical of African art-culture, cultural sensibilities and general African world view. They failed to understand that such African-oriented artistry was in dire need of an African-oriented canon. They failed to understand what Prof. Brenda Marie Osbey meant when she asserted, during Okara's burial ceremony, that 'he made English pass through the sieve of his language'.

In other words, *The Voice* is actually guided by the functional or pragmatic use of language which must reflect the socio-cultural typology in which it is structured. This means there is a preponderance of lexical coinages in the text that reflect the linguistic milieu of the source language which is apparently a product of Okara's strategy of transliteration. This strategy precipitates a phenomenon of multi-word units or compound neologisms, which abound in the text. Invariably, meaning is traceable to the source language, though the constituent lexical choice is English. This implies that Okara's narrative devices in the text include linguistic borrowing as well as semantic shift or extension in the mode of standard English. The case of borrowing linguistic properties from the native language entails the narrative expertise of adopting features which differ from those of the main tradition of standard English. In most rational cases, what precipitates this device is basically the non-availability of a lexical equivalent of a native concept in the L2. This departure from the colonialist's narrative mode, as I have argued elsewhere (2016), may be seen as part of Okara's questioning of the imperialist's language and narrative tradition adopted in order to help decolonize and create an African creative identity.

In all, in spite of the volume of criticisms that greeted *The Voice* when it was published, it is safe to say it assuredly survived all its critical validation. Indeed, the few but very significant imprints of Okara's literary legacy have been remarkable, yet he could have achieved more, as I earlier noted, were it not that he was not ambitious for publicity. His case was like that of a very gifted artist who was not necessarily propelled by the accolades from those who appreciate his artistry. Such simplicity, such humility!

After his death, Pa Okara's final burial was scheduled for 22 June 2019. When I attended the chains of events preceding the final burial ceremony, including the Requiem of 9 Verses in Yenagoa, the Bayelsa State capital, I learnt a lot about his Ijaw ethnic group in Nigeria. Apart from my newly found knowledge that Izon is the language while Ijaw is the name of the ethnic group, I also realized that these are about the most hospitality-oriented people in Nigeria. In addition, I noted that Okara was not only a household name in the African literary milieu, but was even more household in a secular sense beyond literature in Bumoundi, the hosting community in the state. Truly, the name is so revered by his people, just as its bearers occupied key positions in the state government. I also enjoyed a bit of education about one of Okara's middle names which is quite phenomenal and rhythmic. It is complemented with the pleasant musicality of a sort of rhyming fashion – Gbaingbain. I desire to unselfishly share this education with my fellow non-Izon speakers about its phenomenal nature.

From visual articulation, the name could be deceptive in pronunciation. The phonetic paraphernalia that constitutes the only vowel sound is actually */ai/* as derived from words like kind, line, pine; not */ei/* as may be suggested by the conventional English pronunciation mode through visual articulation. 'It is wrong to associate it with the sound of a church bell,' one of Okara's kinsmen whispered to me during the 'Ceremony of Poems, Songs and Tributes' at the Okara Cultural Centre – a massive auditorium named after him by the Bayelsa State Government.

The kinsman continued, 'it suggests a rejection against something abominable, I didn't do it, or no, it can't happen.' Overhearing what I was told in a hushed tone since we were in the auditorium, another kinsman added, 'It can also mean don't go away, stay with me.'

Well, we had to break off our hushed conversation and join in the standing ovation as someone with the microphone recognized Prof. J. P. Clark Bekederemo, another literary giant of the same Ijaw extraction. We were then informed of the next programme on the list: a play composed by Okara on the creation myth of the Ijaw people. Hardly had the director of the play finished her announcement that it would be focusing on the major character Ogboinba, than the stage exploded with the battle cries and ululations of warriors, complemented by sounds of spontaneous attacks, thuds of presumed fallen warriors through some very imposing loudspeakers connected to a piano instrument at one side of the decorated stage. You could hear gasps of bottled fears involuntarily uttered by spectators who were not in the least expecting such sudden outburst from the characters on stage. What was before us resonated a typical African-oriented drama stage; its penchant for spontaneity, the jerks, intensity, ululations and all manner of eerie onomatopoeia. There were short-lived reliefs full of uncertainties within the audience. The next minute, new battle cries tore through the air again. Intermittently, the stage was interspersed with momentary calmness when warriors of Woyengi, the mythic Ijaw creator, quietened to allow her and Ogboinba continue their battle through boastful statements and invectives against one another. The plot portrayed Ogboinba, who had earlier conquered every god she met on her way in order to be recreated by Woyengi as a fruitful mother. But she became arrogant at some point in her journey and was finally disarmed by Woyengi. Ogboinba takes flight in fear and has continued to hide till this hour in the eyes of a pregnant woman where she hopes to be safe from Woyengi's wrath since she (Woyengi) earlier swore that no pregnant woman should be killed. According to this Ijaw myth, the play can ultimately be interpreted to mean that the person who looks back at you when you look into someone's eyes is Ogboinba.

This is one of the glimpses of much of the well-organized events I witnessed during Okara's burial programmes. While many of us were apparently thrilled during this memorable drama, I momentarily toyed with imagining that Okara might be somewhere amongst us, also watching the display in his honour before continuing his journey. My imagination became mischievous, I must confess, when I looked at the empty seat by my immediate left, hoping of all places he did not choose that spot. The battery of fearful imagination was so charged in the auditorium especially with those costumed weird faces of Woyengi and her warriors that I noticed the conspicuous absence of smiles on the faces of nearby spectators.

Later when I thought about the significant qualities of the drama, I observed that it resonated that kind of African epic display, highly rhythmic, with breath stops, accentuated by tonal patterns. The intensity of the chanting mode grew at some point in the display to such a crescendo that the audience never knew when and how the chanters swiftly slid into songs with their chant. More so, we only became conscious of the musical dimension by the intervening musical instrumentation with quite exciting rhythm. I also observed that the whole effect generated from these colourful acts helped to delineate the characters of the gods who unbelievably appeared physically on stage among men.

Okara's personality stands taller than I had earlier imagined even over the massive auditorium built by the Bayelsa State Government which did not go unnoticed by Emenyonu in his highly applauded speech after his keynote address: 'Gabriel Okara: A Life in Writing'. The profundity of the paper does not only provide the audience a rare glimpse of Okara's unsung relationship with Emenyonu in the United States during the Nigerian/Biafran civil war, it does not only show his personal perception of Okara's life in writing, but it equally questions the declining nature of criticism in the Nigerian literary canon. The delivery of the paper was punchy, critical and quite creative, especially as it is embroidered with the refrain or interlude that thus runs: 'tell me what I don't know already about Okara and I will …'

Pa Okara is survived by his children, brothers, family members and some of the following legacies:

AWARDS AND HONOURS:

1953: Best All-Round Entry in Poetry at the Nigerian Festival of Arts, for 'The Call of the River Nun'
1979: Commonwealth Poetry Prize, for *The Fisherman's Invocation*
2005: Nigeria Prize for Literature for *The Dreamer, His Vision*
2009: Pan African Writers' Association, Honorary Membership Award

BOOK PUBLICATIONS:

1964: *The Voice* (novel)
1978: *The Fisherman's Invocation* (poems)
1981: *Little Snake and Little Frog* (children's story)
1992: *An Adventure to Juju Island* (children's story)
2005: *The Dreamer, His Vision* (poems)
2006: *As I See It* (collection of articles)
2016: *Collected Poems* (edited by Brenda Marie Osbey)

WORK CITED

Chinaka, Psalms. 2016. 'Reinvigorating Black Vision Amidst Controversy: Chinua Achebe's Linguistic Forte in the Decolonization of African Literature'. *Currents in African Literature and the English Language (CALEL)* 7: 107–18.

Reviews

Helon Habila, *Travelers*

W. W. Norton & Company, 2019, 295 pp.
ISBN: 978-0-393-23959-1, hardback

The Nigerian US-based writer Helon Habila has distinguished himself as one of Africa's important creative writers. He is the celebrated author of the following fiction works: *Waiting for an Angel*, *Measuring Time*, *Oil on Water*, and the non-fiction, *Chibok Girls*, to name a few. In recognition of his writing, he has been awarded several prizes, some of which include: the 2015 Windham-Campbell Prize, the Commonwealth Writers' Prize, and the Caine Prize for African Writing.

Habila, who teaches at George Mason University, United States, is known for tackling pressing issues in his writing (*Chibok Girls* about the Boko Haram scourge, *Oil on Water* about destructive extraction and oil assemblage in the Niger Delta). In *Travelers*, the author is valiant as he narrates a gripping tale of the appalling migrant reception in Europe. This unsettling narrative reveals a desolate portrait of African refugees/migrants – travelers – in their search for safety and a new home in Europe. It is a tale of horror and trauma which implores urgent political redress. But the author offers no easy way out of this dilemma. Broken into six books, each book unveils the entanglement of the unnamed protagonist (and sometimes narrator) – an American-green-card-carrying Nigerian migrant – with undocumented African migrants in Europe. As the protagonist probes their world, the lines blur, and the reader is forced to confront the grim realities of the unmitigated refugee crisis in present day – an indictment of our failing political structures and world order. Its light-hearted cover design of six different houses may resonate with the sections of the book for some, but does little justice to its depth.

The events in *Travelers* unfold as the life of the unnamed narrator intertwines with migrants from diverse socio-political backgrounds and regions of Africa. A commendable wide canvas, this literary technique tasks the writer's narratology and sequence of presentation. Habila's adept handling of narrative and rhetorical strategies move the reader from the first person to the omniscient and the third person. Although this style individualizes each story, evokes affects and urgency, it may disorient some readers. The one flaw of this brilliant novel could be that the unnamed protagonist in some instances comes across as an artificial cohesion that ties the stories together. But you will be quick to forget this as the beautifully told story is way more captivating, and the connective tissue is a crucial lens. *Travelers* is thought-provoking, evocative and haunting because it illuminates the often ignored yet pivotal aspects of refugee crisis.

The travelers we encounter are diverse and complex in distinct ways. The eclectic mix comprises a group of dauntless and passionate activists who reject the status quo, a former doctor turned bouncer, a businessman striving to reunite his family, an asylum seeker on hunger strike in immigration custody, a queer migrant activist and the undocumented. Through their varied experiences, Habila recounts the stories with an unwavering focus, empathy, and pathos. He ought to be praised for his sensitivity to sexual politics and inclusive vision of portraying both heterosexual and homosexual relationship in *Travelers*. Habila continues the trend common to recently published Nigerian novels written from the West – Chinelo Okparanta's *Under the Udala Tree*, Uzodinma Iweala's *Speak No Evil*, and Julie Iromuanya's *Mr and Mrs Doctor* – in the attempt to explore queer sexuality and life. The author's intimate understanding of the migrant condition is no less enhanced by his positioning – he is a Nigerian, living in the West. The triumph thereof is the successful humanization of refugees and those who look different.

When the unnamed protagonist mistakenly boards a train full of deportees in Frankfurt, he arrives at the border of Italy, in a refugee camp by the sea. The sea is a ferocious monster in this work. The macabre imagery of the hungry and bottomless Mediterranean sea filled with 'bodies floating face-up, limbs thrashing, tiny hands … Hundreds of tiny hands, thousands of faces' (234) is gruesome, yet evocative of the transatlantic slave trade. As Karim (book four) narrates the ordeal and the harrowing journey across deserts and the Mediterranean sea, what is undeniable is the mark the journey bestows on those the sea belches out alive, only to be further alienated and imprisoned in camps. Karim explains: '[t]his place used to be an actual prison, but now is empty so they use it for refugee but it is really a prison' (181). Beyond the structure, the inhumane treatment of refugees and the elimination of human dignity inscribes the space as a prison. Through various events and scenarios, the author exposes the deplorable conditions of the refugee centres in Europe. It is in such a brutal space that those who survive the Mediterranean seas are often broken beyond help in the prisons. Reading these experiences, one comes away with the realization that there is no salve for any broken human spirit.

In *Travelers*, Habila is a witness not only to the exodus of African migrants to the West, but to the West's timid reception and othering. With a setting that spans countries and continents – it begins in Berlin in 2012, and moves to Italy, other parts of Europe and Africa – African migrants confront the West, disoriented to discover that it is quite unlike the West of their dreams. *Travelers* explores the interface between the search for home and humaneness, belonging, and the harsh realities of the West and the disconnect thereof. The protagonist tells us of 'the already unbridgeable gap between me and this city' (8), a lacuna so deep/wide it resonates with all the migrants he encounters in his travels. With the looming threat of deportation, the characters navigate uncertainties and survival as they face shocking forms of discrimination, racism, and protests from nativists. Indeed, '[t]here is no loneliness like the loneliness of a stranger in a strange city' (43). Habila is a wordsmith and a journalist who blends motley yarns to deliver a riveting narrative quilt.

KUFRE USANGA
University of Alberta
Canada

Greg Mbajiorgu & Amanze Akpuda (eds), *50 Years of Solo Performing Art in Nigerian Theatre 1966–2016*

Ibadan, Oyo State, Nigeria: Kraft Books Limited, 2018, 614 pp.
ISBN: 978-978-918-514-6, paperback

Since the 1970s, performance art has championed site-specific artists conceptualizing singular visions as non-traditional theatre practitioners throughout the globe. The collective international rise of solo performances that utilize open spaces as diverse as street corners to shop windows has brought us revolutionary artists whose messages, offered to the people, are not for sale. Challenging and discarding many conventional theatre aesthetics, this minimalist theatre style began as a vehicle for agitprop, in your face performances to bring spectators into a raw engagement with the performer. *50 Years of Solo Performing Art in Nigerian Theatre 1966–2016*, is the first anthology to provide an overview of this practice as it has developed in Nigeria. Edited by Greg Mbajiorgu and Amanze Akpuda, this important addition to the study of performance art includes over 30 essays from Nigerian scholars and theatre artists, providing a definitive and up-to-date study of solo performance in Nigeria.

Organized in nine sections, the anthology begins with three essays from Moses Oludele Idowu, Emeka Nwabueze, and Chike Okoye that lay the historical foundations of performance art from a West African cosmology. Chapter 1, Idowu's *Words of Power, and the Power of Words: The Spoken Word as Medium of Vital Force in African Cosmology* leads off the edition with an essay on spoken word that captures the mystical root of 'The Word' in traditional African, Judeo-Christian, and Muslim religious belief systems, before narrowing in on *Ase* in Yoruba cosmology. Nwabueze (Chapter 2) continues to trace the origins of performance art in his essay through a narrative on the traditional griot as storyteller and guardian of the people that would also be of interest to African American spoken word artists. Throughout American streets and college campuses, countless young '*Neo-griots*' rhyme and recite their poetry unaware of the African roots in their aesthetic. Okoye (Chapter 3) then takes us into sacred rituals surrounding Igbo masks/masquerade and the evolution in scholarly arguments that identify the Igbo Mask as an example of solo performance. The first three essays are vital in locating the foundation of performance art in Nigeria far beyond twentieth-century Western avant-garde theatre.

Section B targets 'Meta-Theoretical, Comparative, Analytical, and Generic Studies' to pinpoint various approaches to the solo performer, from the American comedian Lily Tomlin to Greg Mbajiorgu.

Unfortunately, this section falls short, losing an important opportunity to cross the Atlantic by not mentioning Ana Deavere Smith, whose one-woman performances (portraying over 30 characters in each performance) of *Fires in the Mirror* (1992), *Twilight: Los Angeles, 1992* (1994), and *The Arizona Project* (2008) have brought international acclaim to solo performance art. Throughout the text references to numerous Western artists – Shakespeare, Jean-Paul Sartre, George Bernard Shaw, Mark Twain, Bertolt Brecht, and Virginia Woolf, to name a few – are made; to not include the foremost African American performance solo artist, Ana Deavere Smith, leaves Section B with a major omission that would have added dimension and scope.

'The Pioneer Nigerian Soloists: Betty Okotie, Tunji Sotimirin, and Funsho Alabi' are captured in nine essays in Section C. Tracing the rise of solo performances and the issues in crafting a solo play, the essays consider how various pioneers in the discipline, Okotie, Sotimirin, Alabi, and Mbarjiogu have responded and claimed this theatrical genre in postcolonial Nigeria to give voice to their own creative force.

'Directing the Monodrama Script' includes four essays that target the real-world issues a director encounters working with a solo performer to flesh out authentic character/s. This section provides a fascinating discussion of a director's challenge in capturing the distinct physical, intellectual, and emotional nuances of each character that is brought to life on the stage through one performer (since a solo performer may take on numerous characters in his/her monodrama). The transitions from and to each character are tackled in the direction and enhanced working with other theatre practitioners to mount a one-wo/man production. Section D is also a testament to the evolution of this art form as technical designers (lights, sound, set, and costumes) are considered to enhance the vision of the director.

It is midway through the book that we are introduced to the creators of Nigerian performance art in Section E, 'Encountering Dramatists/ Actor-Dramatists'. This is one of the most important sections of the book, highlighting interviews with Tunji Sotimirin, Greg Mbajiorgu, Tunde Awosanmi, Inua Ellams (arguably Nigeria's most renowned performance artist in England), and Benedict Binebai. What makes these interviews so engaging is their universal appeal to theatre artists throughout the globe seeking to take risks and forge fresh vision as they create new works for the stage. Additionally, personal reflective essays by Akpos Adesi, 'My Heritage as a Dramatist and My Monodrama Creations: Reflections', and Benedict Binebai, 'My Monodrama: The Vision and Philosophy', allow the reader deeper insight into the process by which individual theatre artists forge into the dramatic landscape of monodrama as technique and craft continue to evolve. These artistic statements offer a wealth of primary material for future theatre practitioners and scholars of theatre performance.

Greg Mbajiorgu (the editor whose original vision and dedication to monodrama brought this text into fruition) is prominently highlighted in Section F. Seven theatre scholars offer essays that seek to deconstruct Mbajiorgu's theatre practices in his definitive piece *The Prime Minister's Son,* a modern sorrow song that takes the audience through the harrowing tale of a homeless and bereft young man. An examination of Mbajiorgu's monodrama and his non-binary performance considers the layered subtexts he crafts to bring to the stage the consequences of war, sexual abuse, and shameful discarding of street children in this singular piece through dialogue, poetics, and music. Short excerpts from the play *The Prime Minister's Son* are incorporated into the essays, although including the entire script in this section would provide added weight to the criticism. Incorporating essays on one singular play (moving dangerously close to a 'vanity press' chapter by the editor) from seven scholars demands the reader has the opportunity to access the script under scrutiny. An additional section with a sampling of the major dramatists' works (Okotie, Sotimirin, Alabi, Mbajiorgu, Awosanmi, Ellams, and Binebai) would carry this volume to a wider audience.

Two essays on Inua Ellams' work, bringing magical realism to the stage through the voice of the outsider, are highlighted in Section G, while Benedict Binebai, (who was interviewed and provided a personal essay in Section E) is considered in three distinct essays in Section H beginning with a discussion of *Karina's Cross* and feminist aesthetics in Nigerian monodrama. Chidi O. Nwankwo's Chapter 38, 'Idiomaticity of Feminist Aesthetics in Binebai's *Karina's Cross*', locates this piece as the first monodrama in Nigeria to incorporate feminine consciousness and empowerment. Section I concludes this epic study with two essays by Kenneth Efakponana and Emeka Aniago placing feminist theory at the forefront of their examinations of Akpos Adesi's '*Whose Daughter Am I?*', a one-woman play originally staged by the Department of Theatre Arts at Niger Delta University in 2015. Efakponana considers how identity is presented in Adesi's work (who defines the identity of the female gender controls the identity of the female gender) as a major theme at the core of this one-woman drama. Aniago goes on to consider the layers of victimhood in Adesi's main character, Tarilayefa, who believes her descent into prostitution is the result of misery, poverty, and inequalities, blaming society as her oppressor.

The book concludes with short bios of all 36 scholars and theatre practitioners who contributed essays and conducted interviews. At 614 pages, this project is a monumental undertaking that began in 2015. Documenting in one volume the first practitioners in postcolonial Nigeria to create solo performance as a viable stage practice, makes this work the foundation of all future studies in solo performing art in Nigeria. Since none of the monodramas were included in this book, a second volume that provides the major works in one anthology is recommended. This edition should not be confined to Nigeria. *50 Years of Solo Performing Art in Nigerian Theatre 1966–2016* widens the discussion of this innovative art practice to solo performance artists, scholars, and students of African drama throughout the globe.

CAROLYN NUR WISTRAND
University of Michigan-Flint/Dillard University
New Orleans

Sadia Zulfiqar, *African Women Writers and the Politics of Gender*

Newcastle-upon-Tyne: Cambridge Scholars Publishing, 2016, 223 pp.
ISBN: 978-1-4438-9747-1, hardback

This book comprises an introduction, five chapters, a conclusion, and bibliography. It is a compendium of oeuvres by African women, with the introduction providing an extensive background of vibrant oral traditional performances by African women, and how those evolved to constitute credible foundations for the literary consciousness by certain renowned African female writers. The introduction offers an insightful panorama of traditional renditions – such as songs, recitals, chants – which women necessarily performed from pre-literate times to authenticate scenarios, situations and processes that prevail in various African societies. Unfortunately, despite this robust array of women's active contributions to literary forms, women did not feature on the modern African literary platform through much of the 1970s. Notably, after few of them had started publishing creative works, the early critics (who also were male) either did not acknowledge them, or deliberately disregarded their works as unserious, immature, inferior and undeserving of any attention. It was apparent that the early critics – Eustace Palmer, Gerald Moore, Eldred Jones, and others – could not imagine women writers enjoying critical responses alongside such writers as Chinua Achebe, Ngugi wa Thiong'o, Wole Soyinka, Cyprian Ekwensi.

Evidently, Flora Nwapa's *Efuru* and Grace Ogot's *The Promised Land* were published in 1966, but from the early 1970s when there was a proliferation of critical responses to African literary works, the women's writings were not given any attention. Zulfiqar notes that the condescending treatment of the women writers by the male critics did not deter the women. By the mid 1980s, there were several forms of inquiries on, by and about women, which have steadily increased over the decades. In *African Women Writers and the Politics of Gender*, Zulfiqar undertakes a close assessment of the different literary works by women, and indicates that the works reveal women not as perpetuators, but creators, who envision an egalitarian society that transcends the myopic and repressive tendencies which operate among many readers, scholars and critics of African literature.

Essentially, Zulfiqar evaluates the corpora of African female writers who have emerged in the last forty years. They include Mariama Ba (Senegal), Buchi Emecheta (Nigeria), Chimamanda Ngozi Adichie (Nigeria), Tsitsi Dangarembga (Zimbabwe), and Leila Abuolela (Sudan). Though these five writers may be considered too few to represent the female writers who have been actively writing for forty years, Zulfiqar seems to have taken liberties to select the five and cover the geographical scope as well as the religio-political realities of Africa. Apart from these five writers, she makes regular references to other female writers (Flora Nwapa, Ama Ata Aidoo, Grace Ogot, Nawal El Saadawi, and Akachi Adimora-Ezeigbo), as well as African male writers (Chinua Achebe, Leopold Senghor, Ngugi wa Thiong'o, Camara Laye, Wole Soyinka, Ken Saro-Wiwa and Hamidou Kane) as a way of interrogating and challenging the usual rhetoric that female writings, themes, motifs, and so on are both frivolous and inferior to those by men.

Zulfiqar also provides copious descriptions of Western feminist theories, and juxtaposes them with the African theories/concepts. She notes feminism as a movement that is Western-oriented, and which caters only for the needs and aspirations of white women. In a bid to protect the interests of women of colour in the diaspora, Alice Walker evolved Womanism, which did not make provisions for the issues that affect black women from the continent. In consequence, African women got involved in the politics of feminism and sought to define the implications of feminism on the typical African woman. While few prominent female writers took positions that revealed their apparent apprehension about being labelled feminist, some others made clear statements and advanced concepts that can serve black African women. Thus, African alternatives to feminism include Womanism (Chikwenye Okonjo Ogunyemi), Stiwanism – Social Transformation Including Women in Africa (Molara Ogundipe-Leslie), Motherism (Catherine Acholonu) and Negofeminism (Obioma Nnaemeka). Special note is made to distinguish Chikwenye Okonjo Ogunyemi's Womanism from Alice Walker's. The former deals with specific issues that are germane to African women from their diverse backgrounds – poverty, problems of the extended family structure, the dynamics of the oppression of younger women by older women who may be older co-wives, the complexities of polygyny and wife abuse, religious fundamentalism, the male-child syndrome, and so on. Ogunyemi's Womanism does not provide for lesbianism, a notion that seems to underlie Walker's Womanism. These theories have served as suitable parameters for the criticism of African women's writings, and also save critics from the temptation of applying foreign canons to writings by African women.

There are specific issues that dominate this book in varying degrees of intensity. They are portrayed directly, and they sometimes interface with each other, thus the subject matters seem to be interrelated. The issues include women in marriage, women as mothers, women in war time, the girl-child and the socio-economic challenges in the family and society, female solidarity as well as women in Islam. Confronted by the fact that the male writers hardly capture these realities properly in their works, the female writers have felt duty-bound to tell their stories with the detailed nuance of those who actually have the experiences. Zulfiqar has done a meticulous appraisal of how these subject matters are depicted in the select texts.

Considering the detestable marriage conditions of Nnu Ego and Nnaife in Buchi Emecheta's *The Joys of Motherhood*, Zulfiqar argues that Nnu Ego's travails are exacerbated by imperialism – Nnaife washes Mrs Meers' undergarments, and he is trapped by the master/mistress–servant liaison because he is not empowered to contemplate anything different from what he has, or to aspire to a better life. Staying in the emergent urban environment of Lagos, Nnu Ego loses the warmth, conviviality, and male prowess that are prevalent values in Ibuza, yet Lagos fails to offer her what she deserves. Furthermore, she denies herself a lot of luxuries, and sacrifices everything to her loveless marriage that authorizes Nnaife to have sex with her on the urine-stained and stinking mats of the bug-ridden bed. But the more ambitious Adaku, Nnaife's younger wife, whom he inherited from his deceased brother, rebels against a marriage from which she gains nothing, and which has no future for her two daughters. Conscious that she has no male child, and is neither educated nor economically empowered, Adaku plans to go into prostitution to build up a financial base that will ensure credible education for her two daughters.

From Emecheta's *The Joys of Motherhood*, Zulfiqar demonstrates that motherhood and the loss of selfhood are mutually exclusive. She also stresses that contemporary women, including Adaku, do not wish to live miserably in marriages that hold no future for them because they do not bear sons in the family. That Adaku walks away with her daughters sharply contrasts with Nnu Ego who is hopeless and dies a lonely mother of many sons and daughters.

Also, in Emecheta's *The Bride Price*, Akunna rebels and marries Chike against her parents' consent, so that even though Akunna dies in childbirth, she successfully makes the point that rebellion is possible. In Emecheta's *Double Yoke*, Ete Kamba is obliquely condemned as he makes love desperately with Nko, as a means of establishing her chastity. His neurosis for Nko's virginity is his undoing on the one hand, and a source of empowerment and liberation for Nko on the other hand, for Nko gains voice to talk back at him, and musters the courage to walk out of the relationship.

The male child syndrome, which Emecheta depicts in *The Joys of Motherhood*, is also prominent in Tsitsi Dangaremgba's *Nervous Conditions* as Tambu's deep desire for formal education makes her not grieve over the death of her brother. Her parents had made her stay back (because she is a girl) while her brother went to school. Indeed, the colonial policies aggravate the gender disparity and further entrench female marginalization in all spheres of life in Rhodesia: only five per cent enrolment is allotted to female candidates in the colonial school.

Within the perspective of war, Zulfiqar provides a detailed background to the Nigerian Civil War, the different activities and events that led to it, the major stakeholders, as well as the literary responses to it. She analyses the important roles that women perform, the abuses they suffer, the risks they take unavoidably, the dangers they are exposed to, and the losses they incur. She notes that women must face difficulties because the army signifies patriarchal Nigerian society, so the woman must battle hard to survive. This is the bane of women in the time of war. However, in spite of all that women go through, including especially rape, they are undaunted, because their participation in the war energises the very fibre of their motherhood and or womanhood. The tenuous atmosphere of the war makes the women more suspicious, yet more resilient, courageous, assiduous and adventurous. Both Emecheta's *Destination Biafra* and Adichie's *Half of a Yellow Sun* portray Debbie and Olanna and Kainene respectively relating with their men on equal bases, or nearly superior to the men as in the case of Kainene and Richard Churchill. They are independent women who have surmounted the socio-political hurdles that encumber womanhood, and transcended all hindrances that manacle women in their efforts at actualizing self.

The issue of polygyny has engaged several African female writers, and their characters respond differently to it. Sadia Zulfiqar argues that the woman's reaction to polygyny is often a result of how the man handles the same issue. For instance, Aissatou in Mariama Ba's *So Long a Letter* divorces Mawdo Ba and leaves with their two sons because Mawdo Ba's mother has pressurized him to marry young Nabou, who is from the royal lineage. But Ramatoulaye, on the other hand, stays on in her marriage to Modou Fall in spite of his marrying Binetou, who is a friend and age-mate of their daughter. Yet after Modou's death, Ramatoulaye rejects both leviration as her brother-in-law, Tamsir, approaches her, and being a second wife to Daouda Dieng.

Within the background as set by Mariama Ba in her oeuvre, Zulfiqar examines Leila Aboulela's writings. Prominently, Aboulela stresses that Islam is not responsible for women's oppression and marginalization as is oftentimes claimed. She posits that Islam provides specific privileges and rights for women, but women may be prevented from enjoying those by some mundane factors which include traditions and men. Aboulela highlights that polygyny is more traditional than religious. It was in practice before the advent of Islam. She identifies other forms of marriage to include polyandry (the practice of having more than one husband or male partner), sororate (a man's marriage of his wife's sister), levirate (a man's inheritance of the wife of his deceased brother or male relative), surrogacy (marriage between two women, but not a lesbian relationship). Its motive is to get the married wife to bear children [especially sons] into the family.

Generally, Sadia Zulfiqar's *African Women Writers and the Politics of Gender* is an invaluable resource with an impressively comprehensive bibliography. However, there are few blemishes which may be checked in the course of revision in future. That the book has no index is a significant omission. The works cited, along with the in-text citation method, would have made the reading of the book less disruptive than the footnote model, which requires the reader to break the trend of reading and go to check for the details of citation. Indeed, the footnote method had become outmoded for researches in literature.

The following typographical errors should also be noted for corrections: Amadium should be 'Amadiume' on page 108 (line 2, first paragraph); Adimore should be 'Adimora' on page 45 (line 7, from bottom of page); women should be 'women's' on page 117 (line 8 after the indented quote); Gown should be 'Gowon' on page 185 (penultimate line); become should be 'becomes' on page 64 (line 10 from bottom of page); May 30, 1976 should be 'May 30, 1966' on page 79 (first line after sub-title).

Essentially, the language adopted by Zulfiqar for the book is simple and even though she makes extensive references to many sources as a way of setting the framework for her opinions, there is no ambiguity at any point. She often presents views appertaining to other scholars, then modestly, states her agreement with them or otherwise, and offers reasons. A few samples will suffice. On page 38, Zulfiqar asserts that she disagrees with Obioma Nnaemeka on her opinion that Mariama Ba displays radical and enigmatic ambivalence towards feminist tenets. She immediately explains that 'Ba is proud of her African heritage but at the same time, she refines a reformist agenda by subjecting the indigenous structures of Senegalese society to searching critique.' On page 76, Zulfiqar disagrees with Catherine Obianuju Acholonu's consideration of Adaku as Emecheta's ideal woman. She rather agrees with Julia Essien Oku's idea that Adaku's resorting to prostitution is her only means of attaining independence, and thus she escapes from limiting identity closure, only to get into the strictures of another stereotype to which she has succumbed. By this style deployed in this insightful critique, the author offers an update on specific previous interpretations of the issues that she addresses in each section of the book, and that should be one of the major motives of this book.

INIOBONG UKO
University of Uyo
Nigeria

Safiya Ismaila Yero, *Naja*

Lagos: Malthouse Press, Limited, 2019, 186 pp.
ISBN: 978-978-56575-6-9, paperback

A marked feature of Nigerian literature since its inception is its resolved inclination towards interrogating aspects of the society that strike inimically at the collective social advancement of the Nigerian people and the world at large. Nigerian literature not only mirrors but also reflects on the society revealing unbridled chains of civil oppression, class inequality and gender imbalance at all levels of human existence. Although much espoused in several works of earlier and contemporary Nigerian authors, the issue of gender oppression seems to still resonate in different parts of the country, forming the core of the socio-cultural life of such areas.

Looking at Northern Nigeria, Safiya Ismaila Yero's *Naja* reveals the struggles of women and their quest for agency in typical patriarchal African societies. It chronicles the story of a sixteen-year-old teenager, Naja' atu, who is married off to a much older man, Mallam Ilu, against her will. Tailing her fights against various shades of patriarchy in her community, Wase, the novel unfolds in episodes with each chapter x-raying and calling into account a major aspect of female subjugation in an epitomic Islamic state. These include problems of child marriage, denial of access to formal education, domestic violence, rape and maternal mortality.

As the novel begins, Naja is discontent with her forced marriage to Mallam Ilu. Defiant to the tripartite pressure of family, religion and community, she asserts her displeasure by denying Mallam Ilu consummation of their marriage. She convinces him to allow her to run an Islamic study group within their compound. This group revolutionalizes the plot of the narrative angling out forms of domestic abuse being suffered by women who remain hushed within the rusty confines of organized cultural inhibitions. Naja uses her teachings to challenge hegemonic indoctrinations that deny women agency in Wase, inspiring her students to speak out against such conventions.

The intimating texture of Safiya's narrative voice would, doubtlessly, compel any reader into realizing that she, perhaps, must have been a victim of this oppressive system, and accounts for the desperate precision and palpable realism with which she details the events of the novel. This ardent social commitment and seeming intolerance for needless flowery description nearly jeopardizes the craft of the work for she ends up leaving the reader with a little more than a creative memoir.

The tragedy of *Naja* is largely external to the work itself. For although our main character, Naja' atu, is triumphant in the novel, her story personifies only a small minority of the suffering of women across patriarchal cultures. The sociological import of the work, however, is embedded in the fact that this minority is being called out of relative obscurity and comfort to a place of pragmatic social engagement. 'She encouraged women to always speak up against any form of injustice' (186). Through *Naja*, Safiya summons liberated women to reach out and liberate others.

Is *Naja* a feminist novel? I'd argue a work of fictional realism instead. For although it mirrors struggle through the lens of the female folk, it echoes struggle after all, and that is a common trajectory of human historical progression, especially when cast against the canvas of the sheer conspiracy between civil and religious institutions to keep the oppressed perpetually down. So, who should read *Naja*? The oppressed, and anyone who stands against civil oppression.

UCHECHUKWU AGBO
English Department
University of Michigan-Flint

Ada Uzoamaka Azodo (ed.), *African Feminisms in the Global Arena: Novel Perspectives on Gender, Class, Ethnicity, and Race*

Glassboro, New Jersey: Goldline and Jacobs Publishing, 2019, 270 pp.
ISBN: 978-1-938598-32-6, paperback

African feminism in recent times has taken a backseat in the global discourse of feminisms. The feminist spirit has always dwelled in Africa as history is replete with stories of African women and female groups from precolonial and colonial to contemporary times embodying and enacting protest and resistance to patriarchal and colonial hegemonies. The Aba women's riot of 1929, the Niger Delta women's protest against ecological degradation in the Delta and oil industrialists, Wangari Maathai's Green Belt Movement, and the political activism of Fumilayo Ransome Kuti in the 1950s are just a few examples that ground the struggle against female oppression as core to the African spirit, thereby negating the notion that feminism is a co-opted concept from the

West, alien to Africa. African feminism, as can be gleaned from these examples, grows from the ground up, building upon African cultural impetus, realities and worldview. The essays in this collection not only trace the genealogy of feminist movement and thought in the continent, but also foreground feminist ideals of equity and resistance to diverse forms of domination as being indigenous to Africa.

African Feminisms in the Global Arena is a collection of twelve essays divided into three sections: 'Indigenous Feminisms', 'Hierarchies, Patriarchies and Power', and 'Feminisms and Race'. The four essays of the first section postulate feminist frameworks that take cognizance of Africa's cultural past even as African women navigate the patriarchal present. Unique feminist perspectives are offered through di-feminism, snail-sense feminism, focu-feminism and negro-feminism. These theories decolonize feminist knowledge and establish that any feminist approach removed from African cultural and indigenous knowledge is inadequate to fit the heterogenous demands of African women within the peculiarities of African society. By putting these theories in conversation with each other, African feminisms offer a vibrant expansion of the global feminist horizon on issues of marginalization.

In the section titled 'Hierarchies, Patriarchies and Power', the authors grapple with asymmetrical power relations through the critical analysis of cultural texts such as plays, an autobiography, novels, and case studies from Africa. Of significance is the interrogation of inter-female hostility, an idea that is often neglected in some feminist discourse. In line with this, Irene Salami-Agunloye notes that 'in many African societies, women act as oppressive agents to other women especially as co-wives, mother in-law, daughter-in-law, older women, step-mothers, etc' (128). The complicity of women in patriarchal violence must be acknowledged and criticized in the fight for equality. This notion becomes urgent when we recognize that domestic power politics reflects power dynamics in the public sphere.

In the last section, titled 'Feminisms and Race', African feminist theorization is taken up as a counter discourse that urges an inclusive field of feminist engagement devoid of its hegemonic status as Western knowledge with Western epistemologies. Obioma Nnaemeka calls for a decolonization of feminisms, and according to the theorist, 'the process of decolonization/ "detoxification" must entail the re-examination of the academy as site of hegemonies, particularly on epistemological grounds (in terms of knowledge construction and dissemination)' ... and the privileging of certain knowledge and marginalization of others (186). Nnaemeka places the bulk of this burden on African intellectuals as researchers and pedagogues, urging them to counter Western hegemonic structures so as to undo asymmetrical power relations in knowledge production and circulation. The author calls out a recent publication from Routledge on local and global perspectives on feminist theories that included only two essays from African scholars in a fifty-four chaptered book (188). *African Feminisms in the Global Arena* can therefore be read as a praxis of feminist decolonization.

Across each essay, the authors establish African women as knowledge producers and objects for knowledge production. By centering African women and culture, emphasis is placed on African oral narratives, stories, songs, and proverbs as theoretical sites upon which Africans must continue to draw from in theorizing differently. Drawing upon indigenous forms of protest through women-led groups and women-only groups reveals the relation between theory and praxis. Emphasis on the genealogy of African feminist movements and its foundation on African culture is a laudable decolonization move. Although a valuable addition to the global discourse on feminisms, *African Feminisms in the Global Arena* could have presented a more robust discussion with a wider set of contributors. A powerful offering nonetheless, voices from other regions of Africa would make for a more diversified conversation on African feminisms.

The contributors for *African Feminisms in the Global Arena* are seasoned feminist scholars that continue to offer important readings on African indigenous feminisms as relevant in the global arena. By challenging knowledge hegemony, *African Feminisms in the Global Arena* has blazed an important trail for a crucial discourse. The collection of essays is a recommended read for scholars and researchers of African literature, African feminisms, indigenous feminisms, intersectional feminisms, global feminisms, gender and politics, and critical race theory.

KUFRE USANGA
University of Alberta
Canada